Modernism Is the Literature of Celebrity

Literary Modernism Series
Thomas F. Staley, Editor

JONATHAN GOLDMAN

Modernism Is the Literature of Celebrity

University of Texas Press *Austin*

An earlier version of chapter 2 was published as "Joyce the Propheteer" in *Novel: A Forum on Fiction* 38(1) 84–102.

Copyright © 2011 by the University of Texas Press
All rights reserved
Printed in the United States of America
First edition, 2011

Requests for permission to reproduce material from this work should be sent to:
   Permissions
   University of Texas Press
   P.O. Box 7819
   Austin, TX 78713-7819
   www.utexas.edu/utpress/about/bpermission.html

∞ The paper used in this book meets the minimum requirements of ANSI/NISO Z39.48-1992 (R1997) (Permanence of Paper).

LIBRARY OF CONGRESS CATALOGING-IN-PUBLICATION DATA

Goldman, Jonathan (Jonathan E.)
Modernism is the literature of celebrity / Jonathan Goldman.
       p.   cm. — (Literary modernism series)
Includes bibliographical references and index.
ISBN 978-0-292-74404-2
   1. American literature—20th century—History and criticism. 2. Modernism (Literature)—United States. 3. English literature—20th century—History and criticism. 4. Modernism (Literature)—Great Britain. 5. Celebrities—History—20th century. 6. Fame—History—20th century. 7. Popular culture—History—20th century. I. Title.
PS228.M63G63   2011
820.9′00912—dc22
                                                          2010035091

First Paperback Printing, 2012

To Joe Schleifer: *nachas*.

Contents

Acknowledgments   ix

Introduction: **Modernism Is the Literature of Celebrity**   1

    Critical Problem Solving: Modernism and Popular Culture   2
    The Field of Modernism and the Culture of Celebrity   5
    Considering Celebrity   8
    Why Modernism Is the Literature of Celebrity   10

Chapter 1. **Oscar Wilde, Fashioning Fame**   19

    Copying Oneself   21
    Judging by Appearances in *Dorian Gray*   33
    The Tragic Commodity   39
    Deep Thoughts: Embodying the Subject in *De Profundis*   44

Chapter 2. **James Joyce and Modernist Exceptionalism**   55

    Styling the Author   57
    "Peeping and prying into greenroom gossip of the day"   64
    "Famous Son of a Famous Father": Author, Character, Holy Ghost   69
    The Dream of Immateriality   74
    E.T.: The Extra-Textual   75
    The Ghost of the Author   79

Chapter 3. **Gertrude Stein, Everybody's Celebrity**   81

    Elite by Association   86
    Unstable Values   90
    The Trademark of Time   98
    Name of Constant Value   102
    A Democracy of One   108

Chapter 4. **Charlie Chaplin, Author of Modernist Celebrity**   111

    Happy Endings   112
    An Author Is Born   116

Sign of the Times   123
The Object of Celebrity   128

CHAPTER 5. **Rhys, the Obscure:**
The Literature of Celebrity at the Margins   132

That Obscure Abject of Desire   134
Bildung in the Dark   141
The Hidden Rhys   145
Wide Sargasso City   148
Posthuman Beings   152
Celebrity on the Margins   157
Sighting Rhys   159

EPILOGUE. *"Everybody who was anybody was there":*
After Modernism, After Celebrity, John Dos Passos   160

The Camera, I   161
The In Crowd   164
Stein and They, Hemingway   167
U.S.A. and Hem   169

NOTES   175

WORKS CITED   187

INDEX   197

Acknowledgments

Primary acknowledgment is due to Rita Barnard and Tamar Katz, and especially Nancy Armstrong, all of whom encouraged and shaped this book from its beginning. Digging deeper, John Bishop and Robert Scholes fostered my interest in modernist literature and culture. More recent but no less emphatic gratitude goes to the University of Texas Press, where Jim Burr found merit in the project, enthusiastically pushed it onward, and patiently answered naïve queries; where Faye Hammill (reviewing anonymously) and Thomas Staley supported its publication and provided insightful advice; and where Sebastian Langdell skillfully edited for precision. The staff at the Press has demonstrated its expertise and consideration every step of the way.

Over the years numerous colleagues and friends have read and shredded to pieces sections of this project. They include: Jeffrey Dillon Brown, Amy Feinstein, Alisa Hartz, Aaron Jaffe, Pearl James, Sean Latham, and Jacob Leland. Other instances of intense and productive critique occurred at conferences of the Modernist Studies Association, the International James Joyce Symposium, and the Modern Language Association, and at a 2005 meeting of the modernism group at the University of Pennsylvania.

Support in the form of time, grant money, and research assistance was provided by the English departments, administrations, and libraries of Brown University, Florida Atlantic University, and the New York Institute of Technology, where grants and course releases hastened this book's completion. David Smith, Jay Barksdale, and the Wertheim Study at the New York Public Library offered me a classy and quiet work oasis within New York City. Carrie Johnson and Jane Mikkelson contributed editorial help at crucial moments.

Remaining unnamed here but always in my thoughts are many other friends, students, faculty, and family members who have been along for the ride and helped with every kind of encouragement imaginable.

I can never show Carolyn, Kathi, and Larry Goldman the gratitude they deserve.

Versions of sections of this book appear elsewhere in print and are printed here with permission. An earlier version of Chapter 2 was published as "Joyce, the Propheteer" in *Novel: A Forum on Fiction* 38 (1) 84–102. Parallel to this volume, I am publishing an essay titled "Modernism is the Age of Chaplin" in *Modernist Star Maps: Celebrity, Modernity,*

Culture, edited by Jonathan Goldman and Aaron Jaffe, forthcoming in 2010 from Ashgate Publications. It enlists some of the ideas and language of this book's Chapter 4. A much briefer and more tentative version of that chapter's argument appears in my essay "Double Exposure: Charlie Chaplin as Author and Celebrity" in the online journal *M/C Journal* 7 (5).

Modernism Is the Literature of Celebrity

> *Bart: What's it like being famous, Dad?*
> *Homer: People know your name, but you don't know theirs. It's great.*
>
> THE SIMPSONS, "HOMERPALOOZA," 1996

> *A man should control his life. Mine is controlling me. I don't like it.*
>
> RUDOLPH VALENTINO, 1924

INTRODUCTION

Modernism Is the Literature of Celebrity

Like modernism, celebrity is not all fun and games. My epigraphs above, respectively comic and tragic, illustrate two persistent aspects of twentieth-century celebrity discourse, both of which find a correspondence in modernist literature. The exchange between Simpson père and Simpson fils imagines celebrity as a glorious way of rising above the masses and transcending the anonymity that settles on ordinary citizens of society. However, the consequence of such exceptionalism, as the über-famous Valentino lamented just two years before his death at the age of thirty-one, may be that celebrity makes the self contingent; identity depends on an audience for its continued existence, turning the individual into a stereotype, condemned to perform itself until death. This process, we might say, turns the psychological subject into an object, something that lacks agency over itself. So if celebrity offers a transcendent version of personality, what Roland Barthes, in his essay about Greta Garbo, describes as "a sort of Platonic Idea of the human creature" (*Mythologies* 56), then the celebrated person may become subject to that ideal, something actually less than an individual.

This contradiction between extraordinary self-production and the object that is produced pervades both the popular culture of celebrity that Valentino experienced and helped shape, and that other early twentieth-century system of self-production, the beast known as modernist literature, a category that includes, strikingly enough, many of the texts and authors—James Joyce, Gertrude Stein, T. S. Eliot, Virginia Woolf, Marcel Proust—that have been used to define high culture in our society from then until now. For a half-century after the modernist moment, readers were trained to think of such authors as free from any influence of the popular marketplace, the sphere that would include celebrity. This book, though, contributes to a current that tacks in quite the opposite direction. Here, I investigate the histories of literary high modernism and early twentieth-century celebrity precisely in order to demonstrate that these two supposedly separate aspects of culture are, in truth, mutually constitutive, two sides of the same cultural coin. I will be arguing that the canonical writings of Anglo-American modernism, situated within a newly mechanized society saturated with reproducible images, participate in the phenomenon of celebrity. Modernism generates a figure of the author as a unique, larger-than-life personality, a choreographer of disparate discourses and repository of encoded meaning, though one that can only be read as such after it has been turned into a kind of object. The texts that have come to define elite culture, I will argue, make this idea of the exceptional personality available to popular culture, thus sharing in the re-shaping of celebrity discourse over the final years of the nineteenth century and the early decades of the twentieth. Through readings of figures from both sides of the Atlantic and both sides of the so-called great divide of high and low culture—Oscar Wilde, James Joyce, Gertrude Stein, Charlie Chaplin, Jean Rhys, and John Dos Passos—I will show how the signature styles of modernism and celebrity produce similar forms of cultural value and together strive to reaffirm the centrality of the individual within mass society.

Critical Problem Solving: Modernism and Popular Culture

By showing that modernism and celebrity perform similar cultural work on the notion of the exceptional individual, I am proposing celebrity as a sort of missing link between two domains that our culture has spent the last century categorizing, respectively, as high and low. For example, in that they share what we might call the cultural logic of celebrity, modernist literature and popular cinema—whose star system of the 1920s constitutes the most visible manifestation of the period's celebrity culture—address the same set of historical concerns, even if they generate different audiences. Once we view modernism's model of the author alongside the production of popular celebrity, we can, I propose, conceptualize the relationship between these supposedly divergent spheres of culture as more of a collaboration than a parting of the ways of cultural production. I will be arguing, that is, against the very division that literary modernism helped create.

Over the last two decades, major studies of modernist literature have demonstrated how its authors attempt to set themselves apart from early twentieth-century popular entertainment by appropriating and subverting certain of its discourses. In the 1990s, such influential writers as Lawrence Rainey, Michael North, and the coterie of critics contributing to the *Marketing Modernisms* volume persuasively argued that modernism, far from being indifferent to popular culture and the production associated with it, defines itself in relation to that culture, and usually establishes itself as the antithesis of the most commercially successful products. Andreas Huyssen may be considered the ghost in all this critical machinery in that his game-changing *After the Great Divide* (1986) alerts readers to the idea that "modernism constituted itself through a conscious strategy of exclusion, an anxiety of contamination by its other: an increasingly consuming and engulfing mass culture" (vii). Huyssen, by now an obligatory reference in introductions to critical works in the new modernisms/materialist modernisms vein,[1] illuminates how previous critical movements, for example the American New Criticism that helped institutionalize modernism, buy into the modernists' own myth, engaging in a critical approach that one might think of as tautological criticism. In other words, to treat literature as if it disengaged from popular culture one hundred years ago is to treat it in exactly the way modernist writings seem to promote and modernist writers seem to desire. Marshall Berman notes, "Modernism . . . appeared as a great attempt to free modern artists from the impurities, vulgarities of modern life. . . . art and literary critics—have been grateful to this modernism for establishing the autonomy and dignity of their vocations" (30). The critics to whom Berman refers, imagining a modernism untainted by the real world and tailoring their criticism to the same fantasy, tacitly support what Huyssen calls "the great divide" between high and low culture. But Huyssen's argument and the work created in his wake have forced scholars to step out of the shadow of the modernist ideal of cultural autonomy and reassess modernism as partaking of the texts and logic of mass culture.

The material modernisms criticism has rewritten the rules of modernist studies, foregrounding modernism's implication in its manifold material cultures. But it has not been entirely successful in one of its implicit goals: re-evaluating the modernist writings to imagine a great divide that is porous rather than solid. Critics have, to be sure, enlisted the history of the society out of which modernism emerged to reveal new connections between canonical works and mass culture. Rereading modernism within the culture of the commodities marketplace has proved especially rewarding. For instance, in *The Public Face of Modernism*, Mark Morrisson explains that the moment associated with high modernism, the 1920s, "was the decade in which twentieth-century consumer culture, and the publication and advertising institutions that shaped it, consolidated and became firmly established in their modern forms in both Britain and America" (203–204). Morrisson is primarily concerned with how modernists mobilized consumer culture to promote their writings and their selves: "Many modernists found the energies of promotional culture too attractive to ignore, especially when it came to advertising and publication techniques" (6). While this approach demythologizes the modernists by revealing their engagement with the practical aspects of their profession, Morrisson stops short of extending his critique to the aesthetics of canonical works. In what may be seen as characteristic of much work in this vein, Morrisson does not view the modernists' formal characteristics as a corresponding manifestation of their involvement with the market. He demonstrates that the modernists were quite cognizant of the workings of consumerism, but does not consider how their writings register and readdress the incursions of market culture. Other scholars do parse the most formally dense modernist writings and discover them partly or greatly composed of popular discourses, among them advertising, detective literature, pulp fiction, popular music and jazz, comedy, comic strips, the structures of cinema, radio, vaudeville, and cocktails—not to mention racial and gender others. They tend to treat such findings as evidence that Joyce, Stein, Woolf, and company have incorporated such material into their aesthetic projects and converted it into component parts of individuated differential systems. They focus, that is, on the literature's capacity to "contain, suppress, stratify, and transform" cultural discourses.[2]

In other words, many of those approaches that reveal the modernists' use of marketplace culture remain beholden to older formulations. Douglas Mao and Rebecca Walkowitz notice this, writing that "even the most surprising elucidations of modernism's promotional strategies . . . can be said to be under the sway of the anti-commodification paradigm inasmuch as they keep its terms in the foreground instead of asking what other questions it has tended to overshadow" (745). In so doing, such criticism subtly, probably unwittingly, reinforces the high art/mass culture bifurcation it sets out to destabilize. It depicts a modernism that reaches over the great divide for popular material, but makes such appropriations visible in a way that reaffirms its distance from popular texts.

The Field of Modernism and the Culture of Celebrity

If the heyday of the marketing modernisms movement constitutes the last identifiable quantum leap in modernist studies, the next leap forward is springing out of celebrity, a cultural phenomenon that the critics discussed above engage with, although they rarely make it their central focus. Rainey, in his *Institutions of Modernism*, writes that "the theme of authorial self-construction has been crucial to a great deal of recent scholarship," including his own, which focuses on "new strategies for reputation building—involving theatricality, spectacle, publicity, and novel modes of cultural marketing and media manipulation" (4). His use of the term "new strategies" clearly alludes to the celebrity culture emerging alongside modernism, but he does not push this logic to consider the aesthetic of the literary text itself as a product of and a participant in the larger cultural imperative to produce celebrity. Even more germane here, Jennifer Wicke argues that "the social sea change which sweeps in celebrity in its wake is registered and even embraced by the particularities of *Ulysses* as a text" ("Enchantment" 129), but leaves analysis of those particularities from this perspective to the next critical wave.

Indeed, the scholarship represented by Rainey and Wicke invites an investigation of modernism through the lens of celebrity culture, as testified to by recent critical works. I wish to highlight three such works that influence my study beyond the degree to which they are actually cited in these pages. Aaron Jaffe's *Modernism and the Culture of Celebrity* offers up the instrumental idea of the "imprimatur"—the stylistic signature of the author as brand name. Jaffe particularly paves the way with his argument that "the same way modernists and modernism's literary economists fetishize authorship, celebrities and their publicists fetishize the production of self" (34). This fetishizing produces a new version of authorship, one that undergirds Faye Hammill's *Women, Celebrity, and Literary Culture Between the Wars*. Hammill examines the "celebrity author [who] is magnified, elevated above ordinary mortals" (1) in order to understand the way public recognition of her figures of study inflects their writings and their reception, often relegating them to second-tier, middlebrow status. Hammill spurs on my focus on modernist technique by noting that "attention to style is connected in various ways to literary celebrity" (209). Mining a similar vein, Loren Glass's *Authors Inc.: Literary Celebrity in the United States, 1880–1980* argues for a specifically twentieth-century (the long twentieth century) version of celebrity; he traces the American history of authors whose self-creation matches their celebrification, arguing that "the modern consciousness of the literary genius emerges in tandem with the public subjectivity of the mass cultural celebrity" (23). These works jointly illuminate the correlation between celebrity and modernist authorial self-fashioning.

They are supported by or engage in tacit dialogue with a host of other twenty-first-century publications, including Karen Leick's *Gertrude Stein and the Making of an American Celebrity*, Lorraine York's *Literary Celebrity in Canada*, David Haven Blake's *Walt Whitman and the Culture of American Celebrity*, Joe Moran's *Star Authors: Literary Celebrity in America*, Michael Garval's *'A Dream of Stone': Fame, Vision, and Monumentality in Nineteenth-Century French Literary Culture*, Tom Mole's *Byron's Romantic Celebrity*, and, more briefly but just as influentially, John Frow and James F. English's essay "Literary Authorship and Celebrity Culture." Aside from Leick's thorough materialist chronicle of Stein's fame, these texts, evidence of a genuine scholarly movement toward celebrity-literature studies, investigate iterations of fame that differ crucially from the version that concerns my work, a version which, as I will show, is specifically grounded in the modernist period.

Where Jaffe, Hammill, and Glass leave off, I pick up, wedding their various notions of the author's imprimatur to my readings of modernist technique. What makes modernism modernism is style; thus this book's ultimate goal is to read formal characteristics anew, to forge an argument about why the way the modernists wrote is what we think of when we think of modernism. There are many modernisms, of course, and not all of them announce themselves as engaging in the making new of narrative and linguistic techniques. But it is style that created the sense of a literary moment, that led to the institutionalizing of the high modernists, and that is their most obvious legacy.[3] Modernist writings promote technique, the use of "formal density, textual dissonance, and the rejection of the realist codes" (Latham 120) as a doctrine by which the text should be understood. Georg Lukács writes of Joyce: "the stream-of-consciousness technique is no mere stylistic device; it is itself the formative principle governing the narrative pattern. . . . Technique is here something absolute, it is part and parcel of the aesthetic ambition informing *Ulysses*" (18). Lukács summarizes a modernist ethos that not only elevates form, but also weaves that elevation into the reading experience. But my own view parts ways with Lukács; making technique the text's governing principle, I contend, does not make it absolute. Modernism makes style its basis for objectifying the inimitable individual, the modernist author as exception to the norm. In so doing it claims to disavow its relation to its cultural-historical context, while implicitly acknowledging it. As Raymond Williams puts it:

> The particular achievements of Joyce and Virginia Woolf are as historical, in every real sense, as the achievements of Dickens and George Eliot . . . the question of good prose, of what is called style, can be abstracted from the whole experience of these years in which a land and a people have been transformed. (117–118)

Williams argues for a treatment of style that thinks beyond the achievements of the author to perceive that aesthetic projects originate in culture. This tactic has proved difficult for even revisionist modernist critics, in part, I would argue, because such an approach necessarily undermines values that have underwritten much of the scholarship—such principles as the individual agency and cultural authority of the author.

This book proposes that celebrity can help us surmount this problem. In a sense, I am pointing out that style is not the way modernists went about writing about things, but rather that style constitutes the thing they were writing about most: the creation of the new style of individual—or rather, that the individual is simply the thing they were writing, period. While English and Frow find that "what the text is 'about' is the story it tells, not the storyteller" (52), I argue that the discourse of celebrity tells us otherwise. A text such as *Ulysses* constitutes the idealization of the author through an idiosyncratic aesthetic that draws on the celebrity of such figures as Wilde and Chaplin. In order to see what modernism shares with popular celebrity, we need to understand how modernist style constitutes an entirely new kind of author—as not only the art object par excellence, but also the master choreographer of the culture that contains him as such an object. We need to understand modernist technique, I am suggesting, not merely as a difficult way of encoding popular material for a specialized domain of art—the implication of previous criticism—but as an expression of the same need for the subject to become an object that drives popular culture. This view of modernism brings it in close proximity to celebrity, allowing us to historicize modernist style as a means of self-production within the text that accompanies, and in fact supercedes, the self-production of marketing and promotional activities. It is through style, and the attendant productions of irreproducibility and difficulty, that high modernism defines itself and achieves at once its convergence with and separation from mass culture.

Considering Celebrity

The period of literary modernism, which I identify roughly with the beginning of the twentieth century through 1940, witnessed the development of a new kind of celebrity that flourished especially during the years between World Wars I and II. Richard Schickel hyperbolically claims that "there was no such thing as celebrity prior to the beginning of the twentieth century" (*Intimate Strangers* 31). Where fame had once been "the by-product of concrete, commonly agreed upon, perhaps even measurable achievement" (31), Schickel sees the new celebrity as tossing aside longstanding hierarchies of achievement. The many sociologists and cultural historians who share this view—and they are indeed legion—often consider celebrity to be the "democratizing" of fame.[4] Critics who align fame with tradition and celebrity with novelty are often reproducing the thematic of social researcher Leo Lowenthal. In 1943, Lowenthal surveyed biographies published in the United States since the beginning of the twentieth century and identified a dramatic change in the subjects represented, which he cast as a "considerable decrease of people from the serious and important professions and a corresponding increase of entertainers" (111). Along with this development, he claims, the form and structure of biographical texts undergo a comparable stylistic transformation, visible even in the biographies categorized as "serious and important."[5] His bias against entertainers aside, Lowenthal's study reveals an important change in the figures on whom the public would lavish attention, and a transformation in the narrative conventions governing them.

Scholars have found two visual media central to this celebrity makeover: photography and cinema. Leo Braudy writes, "The photograph, with its exaltation of a momentary state of physical being, and the motion picture, which further emphasized its subject's immersion in a passing time, helped create the more uneasy relation we now share with those in the spotlight"—in contrast with earlier, pre-photographic versions of fame (554). If, as he claims, this new celebrity depended to some degree on photographic reproduction, then it did not arrive fully formed in the year 1900, but rather evolved over the second half of the nineteenth century. Writing of technological advances over the last decades of the 1800s, John F. Kasson notes, "The passion for studio portraits, awakened with the rise of photography, not only seized people of all classes but helped to make possible a new celebrity culture" (18). According to Nancy Armstrong, even by the 1860s photographic portraits "were no longer reserved for people of birth, wealth, or prominence" (*Fiction* 129), and thus could contribute to the elevation to celebrity status of figures of less traditional categories.

As photographic images spread, mass-produced images were consumed, and their subjects recognized, throughout the Western world. We might think of how the widespread celebrity of a figure such as Harry Houdini seems impossible before his heyday in the early years of the 1900s, or of the differences between the international fame of stage legend Sarah Bernhardt in the late 1800s through the turn of the century and that of Charlie Chaplin almost immediately afterward. According to recent writings about celebrity by such cultural critics as Richard Dyer and P. David Marshall, the proliferation of images made it possible for a modernized, mechanized, capitalist society to maintain and promote itself through an individual:

> As Dyer states, the star is universally individualized, for the star is representative of the potential of the individual. From the time of the Enlightenment, Western thought has concentrated on affirming the concept of the individual. Despite evidence to the contrary—the disintegration of individual power through the establishment of mass society—the individual continues to represent the ideological center of capitalist culture. (Marshall 17)

Marshall explains how the celebrity that depends on fame generated by film and television serves to reaffirm the individual in a society that seems bent on rendering people anonymous through the very same media.

While the critical consensus holds that celebrity is dependent on the reproducible image, the image in question has to be an intertextual sign, invoking multiple forms of cultural production. One influential study of celebrity, Miriam Hansen's *Babel and Babylon*, considers the discourse of the Valentino cult during the 1920s, including cartoons, fan letters, etc., to read his films. Charles Eckert's essay "Shirley Temple and the House of Rockefeller" takes a similar approach to argue that the star's value as commodity is written into the cinematic experience. These treatments of celebrity suggest a strategy that can revise both verbal and visual texts by acknowledging that celebrity discourse—the production of a subject who purportedly exists outside of the text—is an essential dynamic of the text itself. I will be drawing on such studies of celebrity in visual media to think about the verbal counterpart. Part of this project entails looking beyond treatments of the individual celebrity and how its specific audience reads its image, and considering the celebrity sign in relation to other signs in a manner that parallels the production of relational value of commodities in the marketplace.

It is this kinship to the commodity, the idea that celebrity can, "like gas engines or soda crackers or other consumer goods, be mass manufactured" (Leff xiii)—as opposed to an idealized, organic form of renown—that inspires the view of celebrity as little more than the symptom of a debased culture.[6] We have a signature example in Daniel Boorstin's internally corrosive tautology that *"the celebrity is a person who is known for his well-knownness"* (57), a formulation that tradition has reworded into the catchier sound bite that celebrities are famous for being famous. With this in mind, the critical impulse might be to argue that modernism sought to correct this supposed imbalance of achievement and renown by reclaiming celebrity for an artistic elite. And yet, I would argue, modernism, in order to produce the individual, relies on a logic of displacement and the formation of a system of relational value that is similar to Marx's definition of the commodity. As Jaffe explains, both celebrity and modernism "presume a notion of production that cannot be confined to a single productive source but that instead measures production in terms of both the circulation and the relative valuation of its commodities" (34). It is this similarity that forces us to understand the modernist text as a component of early twentieth-century culture rather than as the "autonomous, self-regarding artifact" (Eagleton 140) it wants to be.

Why Modernism Is the Literature of Celebrity

That early twentieth-century literature is fascinated by the explosion of celebrity all around it is clear from the period's proliferation of narratives about celebrities or characters who take on attributes of celebrity culture. A short survey of such works might include Max Beerbohm's *Zuleika Dobson* (1911), which portrays a calamitous conflict between a hack-magician-cum-celebrity-diva—the title character—and an institution of British aristocratic traditions, Oxford University. (Oxford loses.) It might take account of some standards of the U.S. literary canon, such as Theodore Dreiser's *Sister Carrie* (1900) for its title character's ascent from working class to lithograph; Edith Wharton's *The Age of Innocence* (1920) for its portrayal of Fanny Ring, a figure of societal transition; F. Scott Fitzgerald's *The Great Gatsby* (1924) for its depiction of the self-fashioned American of the Jazz Age (Gatsby loses); and Nathaniel West's *The Day of the Locust* (1937) for its riotous finale depicting Hollywood celebrity culture gone wrong (everybody loses). Arguments will be made for the inclusion of Woolf, W. B. Yeats, Evelyn Waugh, P. G. Wodehouse, and a wonderment of others. Furthermore, the modernists' obsession goes beyond fictional ponderings. Writers such as Stein, Yeats, Fitzgerald, Lytton Strachey, Wyndham Lewis, Janet Flanner, and James Agee devoted pages to theorizing celebrity and/or individual celebrities. The Paris avant-garde swooned for Chaplin and Josephine Baker as post–World War II intellectuals would swoon for Marilyn Monroe and Madonna; Ernest Hemingway wrote the introduction to the memoirs of Montparnasse icon Kiki (a volume banned by U.S. customs, putting it in the company of *Ulysses* and D. H. Lawrence's *Lady Chatterley's Lover*). These texts suggest the inevitability that modernist aesthetics would incorporate the logic of how celebrity works and what celebrity is. Such is my concern, rather than with the writings that fictionally represent celebrity, and rather than with celebrity authorship as actual fame—with the degree to which the modernists achieved renown in their time, and their strategies for doing so. (Otherwise Hemingway, who pops up occasionally here, would be a more prominent topic.)

Celebrity and its logic suffused modernism via style more discreetly than in its fictional portrayals of fame. Notoriously suspicious of mass-reproducible images, modernist technique conceives of the author as an idealized, incorporeal entity, a self that carries on a perplexed relation to the body and to any picture of that body. This dynamic is thematized, in one example, by Proust's treatment of the writer Bergotte:

> in Bergotte's case, my preconceived idea of him from his name troubled me far less than my familiarity with his work, to which I was obliged to attach, as to the cord of a balloon, the man with the goatee beard, without knowing whether it would still have the strength to raise him from the ground. (418)

The narrator experiences discomfort as he attempts to reconcile Bergotte's writing with the unseemly person before him. The moment illustrates high modernism's resistance to locating the subject in materiality, which is subject to the laws of nature, alluded to here by the gravity that would keep Bergotte's body from sailing upward with the balloon.

Instead, modernist style, an objectified version of Jaffe's authorial imprimatur, serves to identify the authorial subject with the text. By situating the subject within writing, modernism, we might say, fantasizes that it can insulate the subject from material culture. Modernism thus advances the idea of the author, and therefore the celebrity, as a paradigmatic subjectivity, all the while replicating the process by which one turns the self into an object. As this subjectivity is located within writing and not the body, it might be said to in fact constitute the text, which therefore emerges as a variation on the celebrity sign. Thus modernist style comes to serve as a modified version of the trademark, as I will be showing in the chapters that follow.

I have organized those chapters as a roughly chronological—there remain overlap and analepses—series of readings. For illustrative purposes, each examines particular figures—in the case of Joyce's *Ulysses* and Dos Passos's *U.S.A.*, mostly one particular work—for what they reveal about the ongoing interrelation of the cultural phenomena of modernism and celebrity. The study begins at the end of the Victorian era, a transitional and yet formative moment for both literary and celebrity discourses. My first chapter finds foundations of both systems in the syncretism underpinning Wilde's life and work. I argue that Wilde not only inaugurates modern celebrity by reducing his identity to a set of visual emblems, but also, late in his career, prefigures celebrity's influence on modernism by rejecting the image as a bearer of the subject.

On his 1882 lecture tour of America, Wilde was confronted with bourgeois notions of the individual—particularly the model of the subject that supposes that a true identity exists within the body's interior. In response, he invoked aristocratic traditions of identity, decking himself out as an object on display. Wilde's signature long hair, flamboyant clothing, and eccentric accouterments fashioned him into a distinct and instantly identifiable image that functioned like a commodity, a sign whose value accrues in relation to other signs and other individuals as it circulates on the market. Wilde would spend the rest of his life and literary career reckoning with this gesture. In *The Picture of Dorian Gray* he collapses the division between body and subject by producing an image, the portrait, which supernaturally embodies Dorian's subjectivity. While the portrait remains sequestered, Dorian's body circulates and spreads corruption, suggesting that to keep the subject out of circulation empties the individual of value. Having set in motion the traits of modern celebrity, Wilde eventually fell victim to the very phenomenon he had defined, enduring a celebrity trial and going to prison for making public what society wanted hidden. Written from jail, his *De Profundis* recognizes that by turning himself into an object, Wilde has relinquished control of his meaning. His body confined and no longer able to circulate, Wilde replaces the image with writing: *De Profundis* will fashion him as a complete subject. As I will show, modernism adopts this strategy. Thus Wilde consequently raises the question of how much the modernist notion of the imprimatur owes to the version of celebrity that Wilde develops on his U.S. tour. Indeed, one underlying theme of this book is its portrayal of modernism as a distinctly transatlantic phenomenon; the figures focused on are in varying degrees all products of cross-fertilization between Europe and North America.[7]

Wilde's turn away from the visual component of celebrity presages high modernism's suspicion of images and anxiety about containing meaning within a system of signs that is governed by one authorized consciousness. Much of what we recognize as modernist style emerges from these concerns, as I argue in the second and third chapters. In Chapter 2, I read *Ulysses* to show that Joyce follows Wilde's example by locating the subject within the text. Joyce's distinctive collage of narrative styles produces the author by activating meaning that, unrelated to the diegesis—the events and characters that compose the narrative—invokes the author's virtuosity, and thus his inimitability. Style therefore functions as a trademark of Joyce's originality, the hypervisual text taking the place of the image. Indeed, one might propose that with *Ulysses*, one need not read the novel at all, as at a glance trained readers can recognize Joyce's writing and thus derive the text's ultimate meaning: the author as exception. That the final word of high modernism, which, everyone knows, is supposed to be ingested slowly, carefully, and reverently, can actually be gulped down by simply flipping through its pages, digested quickly and easily like popular entertainment, is not the intended suggestion of my study. But it is perhaps the most provocative.

As *Ulysses*'s formal machinations are only legible in terms of the exceptional author, the novel literalizes Barthes's and Michel Foucault's poststructuralist notions of the author as a discourse that restricts signification and interpretation. It also, however, contravenes these approaches by foregrounding the apparatus that creates the author, renouncing all reference to an author anterior to the novel and located in a physical body. Raising Wilde's stakes, Joyce imagines himself as origin and referent of the text, subjugating all possible readings of the novel to the author. Among other implications I explore here, I consider how through Joyce we can see modernist style taking over the role played in the nineteenth century by the *Bildungsroman*; authorial self-fashioning supplants the coming-of-age character as fiction's chief way of understanding the creation of the individual. By establishing the author as both a function of the text and the means of decoding it, Joyce enacts the fantasy of a complete, bounded subjectivity, uncontaminated by culture. There is no longer a need for the *Bildungsroman* genre and its narrative of the subject who acclimates to society and vice versa.

Joyce makes an inevitable site of inquiry for this project, not only because of the machinations of his texts, but also because of the immense body of criticism that they have spawned, much of which may be said to enact the cult of the author that I see as a manifestation of celebrity. While Joyce may be peerless in both of these regards, Stein probably comes close. In Chapter 3, I argue that Stein, like Joyce, uses the idiosyncrasies of style to produce herself as an author. She does so, however, only while challenging the notion that value inheres in the celebrity in isolation from other figures, other objects of self-production. Indeed, Stein's work takes a step beyond Joyce in its revision of popular celebrity value. Stein establishes the importance of linking celebrities within a closed circuit to produce a network of individuals who, in relation to one another, enter into a mutually defining association of individuals who exist above the ordinary. Considered another way, Stein enlists the tradition of the artistic coterie and updates it for the age of celebrity.

Stein's writings produce this relational system through name-dropping. Implicitly debunking the value of the celebrity image, Stein puts similar stress on the celebrity name. Stein proposes that even a celebrated name accrues value only by assuming a place within a system of signifiers composed of other names. *The Autobiography of Alice B. Toklas* makes it clear that Stein is not only the centerpiece of this system but also its composer. Here, Stein's name-dropping consigns celebrities to domestic narratives and equates them with her acquaintances, including her cars and dogs. She turns her Paris home into a salon, art gallery, and tourist attraction, transforming interior space into a collection of people and objects that produce her as cultural authority. Only these relationships, she makes clear, generate significance—not the object in isolation. Like her re-inscription of domestic life, such characteristic techniques as her penchant for repetition and accumulation insist that meaning, like any form of value, resides only in the accretion of individual signs that circulate around her exceptional personality.

Just when early celebrity culture was peaking during the 1920s, the appeal of the image as the repository of a unique subjectivity declined for the high modernists, and also for one figure of mass popularity: Chaplin. My fourth chapter examines how Chaplin manages to combine modernism's production of the author, founded on a distrust of images, with the logic of visuality that idealizes Chaplin himself as an author responsible for producing the visual traces of his body. Chaplin's author-production, unlike that found in Wilde, Joyce, and Stein, functions while the image remains visible. Yet Chaplin, drawing on the traditions of slapstick, which first created his fame, resists investing the image with subjectivity. Paradoxically, Chaplin's films invoke the familiarity of the Tramp, Chaplin's signature character, in order to indicate that the author is located elsewhere. Rather than wholly rejecting the image, though, Chaplin transforms it into a signifier of his audience. *Modern Times* recoups the image as a sign of Chaplin's popularity and his historical moment, enlisting recognition of the Tramp to foreground the act of identification that unites Chaplin's mass audience. Chaplin stages the modernist desire to situate subjectivity in the ontology of the text instead of in an image of the embodied subject; this impulse to separate the subject from visuality expands the role of the icon and authorizes celebrity images to crystallize our culture. In this way, modernism, having rejected the celebrity image but absorbed much of its logic, may be said to indirectly usher in a culture in which celebrity images constitute the telling of history.

Viewed together, Chaplin's shaping of the celebrity icon and the modernist authorial self-production enact the creation of an idealized embodiment of the self that demonstrates mastery over the culture—precisely because of his or her disconnect from that culture. It is with this in mind that I turn in my fifth chapter to the strange career of Rhys, whose life and work, like that of Wilde, proceed along parallel lines. In the 1920s, Rhys followed a familiar modernist script, forging a distinctive written style and a bohemian expatriate existence. But Rhys did not mirror her contemporaries' self-fashioning either in or out of her writing. Rhys's protagonists in her short works and such novels as *Good Morning, Midnight*, since closely identified with her own life experiences, almost exclusively constitute the abject figure in the realm of her fiction; they are exceptional by virtue of being below, rather than above the mass. Yet it is the materials of celebrity that position these women: they are on display, objects of the gaze of the plebeian and pedestrian, and, however they try to fit in with the crowd, unique. Rhys, on the other hand, was to drop out of sight. For almost the entirety of the 1940s she lived in obscurity, having been actually presumed dead. Her fortunes swung finally after the appearance of *Wide Sargasso Sea*, a novel about Bertha Rochester, the most famously hidden character in English literary history. My readings of these texts and of Rhys's biography argue that celebrity underwrites her work. As Rhys is central to the inception and development of the scholarly discipline of postcolonial studies, I suggest that the discourse of celebrity emerges as an organizing principle of that field. Celebrity, I conclude, provides great explanatory power for texts beyond the modernist moment, enabling a new understanding of the way critical fields are imagined.

That explanatory power extends to modernist writers whose reputations are as ambiguously constructed as that of Rhys. So, in a (somewhat idiosyncratic) epilogue, I address another modernist rarely thought of as an embodiment of celebrity authorship: Dos Passos. I use a brief reading of Dos Passos's *U.S.A.* to frame my backward glance at some of the implications of my study. Dos Passos's trilogy, I argue, in fact signals a critical consideration of the modernism and celebrity intersection, long before this book, or Huyssen, or the new modernisms. *U.S.A.* serves as an appropriate final object of study because it revisits several dimensions of my argument, including the idea of a visually distinct literary style (as in Joyce), the identification of celebrity with a historical moment (as in Chaplin) and the idea of celebrity networking (as in Stein). Most dramatic, though, is Dos Passos's reappraisal of modernist authorial self-fashioning, which he portrays as generating an insidious ideological model of the individual. His primary strategy for this, I demonstrate, lies in *U.S.A.*'s characterization of form in its "Camera Eye" sections. These passages depict modernist style's emphatic production of subjectivity as corollary to a disengagement from culture and politics. To launch his critique, Dos Passos invokes Stein, and more clearly Hemingway, his friend and obverse, in a rhetorical gesture that warns against modernist exceptionalism even as it partakes of this new version of the individual, therefore signaling the cultural ubiquity of celebrity discourse.

Celebrity culture provided modernists with the methods of commodification and objectification that enabled them to generate this new form of subjectivity. As my readings imply, however, the creation of the self that Wilde, Joyce, Stein, Rhys, Dos Passos, and Chaplin perform leads to their entrapment within their own textual strategies. By producing the self as an object valued in circulation and through its relation to other objects, these figures rely on the recognition of the audience for their identity; this dependence opens the door to the dislocation of the self and the lack of agency that Valentino bemoans. It begins, of course, with Wilde, whose self-stereotyping brings about his self-destruction. Braudy writes, "It is in Wilde's own life, where painter, sitter, and canvas become one, that we see the coming shadow of twentieth-century show business self-destruction written plain in his active agitation for the trial and publicity that lead to his death" (581). My later sites of inquiry may be said to have followed suit, though with less tragic consequences. In varying ways, they all enact the pattern of having the object exert control over the self. In the case of Joyce, the need to control textual meaning and produce an audience of authorized readers leads him to disseminate the guides that both explain his novel and reduce it to a schematic. Stein, by locating value in the links between proximate celebrity signs, undermines both the text's capacity to establish stable value at all and, certainly, her pretense at a democratized form of celebrity. With Chaplin the creation of the image, even as a sign of a disembodied subjectivity, most clearly controls identity. Chaplin becomes subject to the Tramp image to the extent that, first of all, he can hardly appear publicly without it making an appearance, and secondly, his films can only be read through the prism of his celebrity. Rhys spends years republishing the same script; then she lives it. Dos Passos repudiates an aesthetic as he reaffirms its cultural ascendancy. Ultimately, these resonances among my readings portray the relationship of modernism to celebrity as not only that of twin cultural phenomena with shared origins and systems, but also as manifestations of the same impulse. In the pages to follow I intend to show that modernism can be read as an offshoot of celebrity culture, and that modernist literature should very much be read as the literature of celebrity.

CHAPTER 1

Oscar Wilde, Fashioning Fame

elebrities are more than brand names; they are irreproducible characters, imprimaturs, trademarked styles. The world's first legal trademarked image, trademark number one of Britain's Trade Mark Registration Act of 1875, is the red triangle logo that is found, still, on bottles of Bass Ale. This triangle filters into modernism through, as we will see, Edouard Manet and Joyce, and also makes appearances in works by Pablo Picasso and Juan Gris. The image was filed as intellectual property on January 1, 1876.[1] Eight years later, in 1884, photographs became copyrightable property, following a legal battle that was focused on the use of a picture of Oscar Wilde in a cigar advertisement—although Wilde did not himself own the rights to the image, as Michael North points out ("Picture" 185-187). That Wilde's image should be at the center of a somewhat paradoxical legal battle during the early years of copyright is appropriate: for two years Wilde had been making discursive use of trademarking, creating a distinct persona showing the characteristics of a trademarked image.

If twentieth-century celebrity has an originary moment, it occurred on January 3, 1882, when Wilde arrived at United States customs and announced, "I have nothing to declare except my genius."[2] This quip summarizes the major tropes of Wilde's celebrity, which in turn establish a pattern for the cultural phenomenon that follows. Wilde invokes the idea of genius, usually thought of as an intangible quality residing inside a person, and represents it as an object, which he carries like luggage; it accompanies the body but is not necessarily housed within it. Wilde enters his exceptionalism into the public record; by declaring his genius, Wilde announces it as having such value that he cannot cross borders without drawing attention to it. Lastly, Wilde performs a trademark of both his writing and his public persona; his play with the meaning of the word "declare," his forming an epigram out of the institutional language of the customs office, demonstrates his ability to subvert conventional speech. Thus Wilde's prototypal remark turns something supposedly interior, genius, into something exterior, and makes it a public matter that can function as both currency and an insignia of his persona. This moment effectively foretells much of the way Wilde's lifelong brush with fame would paint his adult years and color his entire oeuvre.

In this chapter I will read Wilde to show that, in his life and his writings, in his model of the individual and his treatment of literary form, he grappled with the implications of his self-creation as a celebrity, as an object on display whose value depends on its relation to others. While Wilde's critics have engaged with the ways that his public image and self-promotion reflect the composition and reception of his writings, they have stopped short of examining the model of celebrity Wilde was offering up, or how his writings would continue to rework its categories. Here I provide a reading of how the machinations of celebrity wormed their way to the core of Wilde's aesthetic, specifically in his lone novel, *The Picture of Dorian Gray*, and his last long work, *De Profundis*. Ultimately I argue that Wilde's negotiations with celebrity produced a version of the subject that presages the construction of the author in literary modernism.

The story begins with that arrival in the United States. It was on his 1882 lecture tour of America that Wilde encountered the logic of late Victorian celebrity, which treated images of the body as though they referred to an individual's hidden, true, and natural identity. He set out to revise that logic. Wilde conceived of a new kind of individual, one whose distinguishing attributes—trademarks—are worn on the body, rather than concealed within it. Wilde disdained the division of exterior and interior, preferring—in a gesture foreshadowing much of twentieth-century celebrity—to view the individual as a public image that circulates on the market. By turning his insides out and wearing his subjectivity on his lapel, as it were, Wilde turned himself into a commodity. His subsequent life and work become intelligible within this system, which Wilde would retrace over and over. In *Dorian Gray* he invokes his reconception of celebrity, turning Dorian's subjectivity into an image. The novel explores the consequences of keeping this image screened from the public while circulating the body, proposing that this separation turns the subject into an object. A few tragic years later, Wilde himself was withheld from circulation, imprisoned from 1895 to 1897. While in confinement Wilde composed *De Profundis*, which casts his image as debased, rejecting it as a location of the subject. Wilde instead imagines the author as a fully bounded subject, situated within the text of *De Profundis*, an object that will circulate even as he himself will not. Wilde ultimately supplants the celebrity image with writing itself. This final revision of celebrity presages a modernist conception of an idealized author whose writing is the sign of its subjectivity, an ideal that, as my later chapters will show, was retraced by Joyce, Stein, and their contemporaries. Through Wilde, celebrity emerges as a link between turn-of-the-century mass culture's conception of the individual and the production of the author that characterizes modernism and permeates much of twentieth-century culture.

Copying Oneself

By the time he embarked on his tour, Wilde had already experienced a kind of fame, having evolved from a figure familiar among Oxford and London coteries to one well-known to the British public. "He became a celebrity" by 1881, claims Frank Harris, writing in 1916 (49). Wilde's reputation rested not on his lone published volume, *Poems* (1881), but rather on Wilde the social phenomenon: his playful personification of the aesthetic movement, and his wit. Joseph Bristow writes:

> At a comparatively young age Wilde made an impact seldom matched by his literary contemporaries. In the late 1870s and early 1880s, Wilde's rising status as the outlandish doyen of aestheticism roused the press to a frenzy . . . his quick-witted conversation, together with his dazzling couture, transformed the recent Oxford graduate into a national celebrity. . . . It was in the years 1880 and 1881 that Wilde first caught the public's notice on a large scale. (10–11)

Bristow's claim that Wilde was very much in the British public eye by 1881 is supported by Wilde's appearance in mass-reproduced illustrations. If

Barthes is right to suppose that appearing in cartoons is the "sign that [one] has become a legend" (*Mythologies* 69), then Wilde was legendary indeed as he sailed for America. Sketches and caricatures of Wilde had begun to proliferate two years before. Bristow writes, "The visual ridicule dates roughly from 1880, when, aged twenty-five, he promoted himself as a fashionable young gentleman moving among the cultural elite of London." In other words, Wilde garnered fame by circulating publicly and comporting himself as an aesthete, even as there was little evidence that he would one day gain stature as a writer. This state of affairs continued when he arrived in New York. Reporters found newsworthy his long green fur-trimmed coat, his jewelry, his significant height and girth, his broad face, and his voice (Ellmann, *Oscar Wilde* 150–151). It was at roughly this point that Wilde's "face, his body, and his clothing all became distinctive stylistic hallmarks that were instantly attributable to him," as Lisa Hamilton puts it ("Importance" 4). Visual tokens constituted nearly the entirety of his celebrity.

The plan was to stay four months; the tour was successful enough financially, and enjoyable enough to Wilde, to last nearly a year. As Wilde crisscrossed the continent, he found that the United States of the late nineteenth century was fertile grounds for frankly re-creating oneself in public. After all, the country was obsessed with confidence men, the subject of Herman Melville's novel of that name as well as of Edgar Allan Poe's story celebrating swindlers, "Diddling Considered as One of the Exact Sciences." It was inhabited by professional con men writ large such as P. T. Barnum, by bunko-men such as Soapy Smith, and by shameless self-promoters such as Thomas Edison. The United States as a nation could be easily gripped by infatuation with individuals arising from unofficial social spheres; when Wilde woke up in San Francisco on April 4, 1882, he could read newspaper accounts of the martyring of no less a cultural icon than Jesse James, and upon arriving in St. Louis two weeks later he had to compete for public attention with the story of the outlaw's hanging.[3] The United States was also transforming literary figures into a kind of celebrity; Wilde's meeting with his idol, Walt Whitman, famous for his poetry and his persona, merited a lengthy article in the *Philadelphia Press*.[4] Indeed, not long after Wilde's tour, as Loren Glass has written, Mark Twain was busy producing a new form of literary identity, claiming legal authority over his name (and, implicitly, his style). Glass writes that Twain remade "the authorial name or signature as a metaphorical form of trade mark" that "explicitly acknowledges a cultural relation of recognition between the public and the text" (26). From Glass, we see that Wilde's self-branding would not be out of place in this America. What Wilde added to the mix, as I will soon explain, was the distillation of the self into the reproducible celebrity image.

Wilde chroniclers share a tradition of emphasizing that the tour was a high point of the lifelong pursuit of fame that Wilde willfully, indefatigably, and gleefully engaged in, telling his peers to do the same. Wilde advised Harris "to seize every opportunity of advertising yourself" (Harris 72),[5] and reputedly encouraged Yeats to "invent his own myth."[6] Wilde is depicted as publicly embracing and enhancing his fame from an early age—and at least partly for economic reasons. Commentators such as Gagnier have astutely read Wilde's self-promotion as motivated by simple finances. In this spirit, the lecture tour has popularly been understood as Wilde's strategy to amplify, and cash in on, his burgeoning celebrity.[7]

Backstage details of the tour complicate matters. Wilde's lectures—the first about the aesthetic movement, a later one about interior decoration—were more the pretext than the purpose for his trip. In truth Wilde was working to promote Gilbert and Sullivan's operetta *Patience*, which tells the story of an aesthete named Bunthorne, widely understood as based on Wilde. Wilde's tour was arranged by Gilbert and Sullivan's promoter, Richard D'Oyly Carte, who aimed to increase the opera's box office by selling Wilde to American audiences.[8] On the surface, then, the tour presented the original (Wilde) in the wake of the copy (Bunthorne), an inversion that would echo throughout Wilde's aesthetics. Wilde was compensated for lecturing on aestheticism and for publicly appearing in garb that would be recognized as suitably "aesthetic."[9] Though veiled in loftier intentions, the tour appears to have been an exercise in celebrity from the start—the production of an individual to embody a set of ideas, and to promote a commercial venture. It is not for nothing that Wilde was derided as a "sham" in New York and as "the $-sthete" by Harvard University students (Lewis and Smith 421, 127). It was a formative moment in modern celebrity: on tour, Wilde was in effect playing himself, not as a person, but as a personification of aesthetic style come to life.

This aspect of Wilde's celebrity, along with the fact that his reputation rested little on traditional markers of accomplishment, diverges from earlier attempts to sell individuals to the public. The contrast is pointed up by the rethinking of the notion of "genius" as Wilde is credited with employing it at the tour's outset. A literary generation before Wilde, Carlyle, on his own lecture tour, intones the word "genius" to describe one of the qualities of the heroic literary figure. In *On Heroes, Hero-Worship, and the Heroic in History* (1841), he states: "the Hero as Man of Letters ... is uttering forth, in such way as he has, the inspired soul of him; all that a man, in any case, can do. I say *inspired*; for what we call 'originality,' 'sincerity,' 'genius,' the heroic quality we have no good name for, signifies that" (155). Carlyle imagines that his Man of Letters contains genius within the body, and emits it in the direction of the rest of us. That this genius moves from inside to outside the body is reinforced by his description of the Man of Letters "discharging his function." Forty years before Wilde, Romantic "genius" manifests itself in inspired writings that spontaneously arise in and overflow the body housing it.

In contrast, Wilde's tour entails no concept of interiority. Rather, he seems to employ "genius" to indicate the persona composed of his dress, his accouterments, and his wit.[10] Clothing and accouterments are found on the outside of the body; to wit I will return. Genius, on Wilde's tour, is not situated within the body but worn on the surface. It manifests itself as that body circulates in public replete with its famous tokens, acquiring instant recognition. Years after the implications of Wilde's life and work would set in, Irving Babbitt would note, "A man may advertise his genius and originality by departing from the accepted modes of costume" (59). By thus using his body as a means of setting himself visibly apart, Wilde advertised his version of genius (and *Patience*) via the exterior of his body. Crucial to Wilde's invention of celebrity is this relocation of self-creation from inside the body to its surface.

In another important contrast to Wilde, Carlyle's Man of Letters is characterized by "originality." The pre-Wilde notion of originality permeates another lecture tour that contrasts Wilde's—the tour undertaken some fifteen years earlier by Charles Dickens. Dickens's second U.S. tour, as Ivan Kreilkamp has explained, constitutes an attempt to establish the author as the original site of literary production. Dickens exploits celebrity to authorize the relationship between himself and the production of a set of ideas or language; the celebrity status of the author, his public readings and appearances, affirm his body as the source of the literary work. To Kreilkamp, Dickens's "participat[ion] in the invention of the role of an international celebrity author" asserts "that to read him properly required seeing and hearing him as well" (90). Dickens's tour, in other words, establishes the body as the site of original writings; it posits that one has to be in his presence to receive his work properly.

By casting its protagonist as the originary point for a set of ideas—the superior sartorial taste, the "aesthetic" philosophy of Bunthorne—Wilde's tour reverberates strangely with Dickens, reasserting the concept of originality. But Wilde, as I have been suggesting, undermines the concept. Unlike the previous generation of lecturers, Wilde was not establishing his body as the original place from which writings emanate. And of course, as the tour claims Wilde as the original of Bunthorne, those claims are repudiated by the fact that aestheticism was a well-established, in fact voguish, school of thought before Wilde came along.[11] Further subverting the prior notions of originality, Wilde was, it turns out, contractually required to attire himself in a fashion recognizably Bunthornesque. The contract suggests, in fact, that Wilde performed a stereotype of himself: his outfits, patterned after a stereotype patterned after Wilde, who was following a fashion, undermine the version of originality conceived by Dickens and Carlyle.

Even Wilde's famous witticisms, though a variety of literary production,[12] destabilize Carlyle and Dickens's notions of originality, genius, and celebrity. Wilde's wit mainly manifests in epigrams; Regenia Gagnier calls it a "polished technique of epigrams and paradoxes subverting the tropes and truisms of Victorian life" (176). In other words, Wilde's quips are so strikingly unforgettable because they invoke commonplace language and introduce a surprising, often irrational, substitution or reversal of the phrase. "Divorces are made in heaven," says Algernon in *The Importance of Being Earnest*.[13] The simple substitution of "divorces" for "marriage" subverts the axiom and thus the bourgeois ideal of nuptial divinity. It delights in divorce by foregrounding the manipulation of popular speech. Gagnier therefore likens Wilde's wit to a "technique of ironic reference: the use of popular symbology by its critics in order to be both commercially competitive and critical" (8). The epigrams, that is, take up decidedly *un*original ideas. Seen in this manner, Wilde's particular gift of gab constitutes a perverted mimicry of public speech, which, though unique in its way, surely deviates from the models of originality conceived of by Carlyle and Dickens. In this way, the epigrams function like Wilde's costumes. Of course, wit is by definition funny, if not what we might call laugh-out-loud funny, and humor is fairly foreign to those authors' concepts of the literary author's originality.

The subverted idiom of the epigram nonetheless constitutes a trademark for Wilde, his formula, an immediately recognizable verbal tic. It operates for Wilde in a manner similar to how a famous scientific formula, "$E=mc^2$," does for Albert Einstein. According to Barthes, "Through the mythology of Einstein, the world blissfully regained the image of knowledge reduced to a formula" (*Mythologies* 69). That is, Einstein's "$E=mc^2$" instantly represents the way one man uniquely understood the world for an audience unable to fathom that understanding, or what the formula does to quantum mechanics, or the genius of the person who produced it. Einstein's formula allows the public to comprehend just how hard it is to understand Einstein; it provides a shorthand for conveying the idea of the exceptional mind. Wilde's epigrams, similarly, constitute a formula that encapsulates his wit—his relation to the dominant culture, his mastery of and distance from it—to an audience that could only think in terms of that culture. As in the case of Einstein, the ordinary person's inability to keep up with the celebrity's brain is part of the shorthand; one grasps the code without having to wrestle with its meaning. Bristow notes that one 1910 reviewer of Wilde's *Collected Works* calls the trademark epigrammatic technique "a machine-made verbal jingle" (7). The idea of wit as "machine-made," as automatic and uncreative, insinuates that the cultural material that goes into Wilde's brain comes out processed as a uniformly, instantly recognizable product of Wilde. It makes Wilde both into a model of someone with a critical relation to his culture, and into a parrot, one who regurgitates available language rather than inventing his own.

But neither Wilde's wit nor his identification with European aestheticism would have worked to create his celebrity were it not for his image. Hamilton writes, "one of the less discussed attributes of celebrity after Wilde is its component of immediate physical recognizability. His face, his body, and his clothing all became distinctive stylistic hallmarks that were instantly attributable to him" ("Importance" 4). Wilde's celebrity, she explains, gives rise to the idea that the celebrity image can be a universally identifiable representation of the person. Again, it was Wilde's wardrobe, and hair, and such other accessories as buttonhole flowers and jewelry that Wilde forged into components of his celebrity image. Harris writes, "He began to go abroad in the evening in knee breeches and silk stockings wearing strange flowers in his coat—green cornflowers and gilded lilies. . . . Very soon his name came into everyone's mouth" (49). When Wilde's tour arrived in New Orleans, the *Sunday States* derided his "huge shock of mahogany-colored hair, his daring velvet dress coat, his knee-breeches and all that." Wilde's clothes and accouterments set him apart by encoding his mastery of the materials available for adorning oneself within an image. Fortunately for us, we can see this image distilled into the iconic photographs Napoleon Sarony took of Wilde just days after his New York landing. In some of these Wilde wears a cape, but in several, including that reproduced here, he wears his adored green fur-trimmed coat. On display is his shoulder-length hair. For accouterments there are his cane, a pinky ring, and the gloves grasped in his hand. Once one has digested the outfit, one might notice that Wilde's index finger points to his temple, as if to announce that fashion is replacing intellect in this figure.

As the Sarony photographs show, Wilde's sartorial choices incorporate material taste into his persona. Pierre Bourdieu calls taste "the propensity and capacity to appropriate (materially or symbolically) a given class of classified, classifying objects or practices" (173). That is, taste comprises

FIGURE 1.1. Oscar Wilde, January 1882. Photograph by Napoleon Sarony.

the objects a person selects from the market, and what those choices communicate to an audience. Thus Wilde's outfits can be seen as a technique for culling objects from the culture and reassembling them, according to a recognizable formula that came to be associated with him—as his epigrams indicate his ability to manipulate popular language. Wilde contrived to make his signature appearance one that could be reproduced anywhere. That he was successful in achieving this is proven by the fact that Sarony's pictures were used, illegally, in postcard advertisements selling cigars and hats.[14]

The success is also reflected in the caricatures, appearing before and during the tour, that invoke Wilde with just a few features of physiognomy and dress. The caricatures highlight the nuanced manipulation of gender stereotypes that go into Wilde's image, though his own audience did not regard such features as coded indications of Wilde's hidden sexuality. In his own day his appearance was popularly associated with effeminacy; for instance, George du Maurier's caricatures for *Punch* portray Wilde adorned with lilies and flowing locks. These exemplify how the caricatures, in Hamilton's words, "emphasize an imagined femininity of his waist and hips, and exaggerate his lips, eyelashes, and long curling hair, while placing him in the midst of flowers (especially lilies and sunflowers), china, and drawing-room culture" ("Wilde" 239). Such depictions recognize and exaggerate the way Wilde wielded signifiers of femininity. They do not, however, conceive of Wilde's gender machinations as signs of homosexuality. During Wilde's time, Alan Sinfield has pointed out, "effeminacy and homosexuality did not correlate in the way they have done subsequently" (4).[15] In other words, Wilde's flamboyant dress was not necessarily, if at all, associated with his sexual preference.

On the contrary, to many, Wilde's image represents a threatening signal of potent, or at least potential, heterosexuality. Max Nordau, who of course had his own axe to grind, anxiously speculates that Wilde's clothes will appeal to women, writing, "The adornment of the exterior has its origin in the strong desire to be admired by others—primarily by the opposite sex" (318). Nordau attributes Wilde's appearance to a heterosexual drive. In *Patience*, moreover, Bunthorne has a gaggle of female admirers. Such evidence that Victorian notions of effeminacy do not correlate with homosexuality can easily be missed by readers one hundred years later. As Hamilton puts it, "the tendency has been to over-read effeminacy as a stable signifier of homosexuality in the works of the nineteenth century" ("Oscar Wilde" 231). Such over-reading performs a de-historicization that distorts our understanding of Wilde's play with his appearance, usually in favor of turning Wilde into a reflection of more recent, turn-of-the-millennium attitudes toward categories of sexuality. Wilde's image does not, as I have argued, signify something concealed within the body, whether genius, originality, or sexual desire. Wilde's celebrity fashioning had no hidden agenda. He was not interested in having clothes and appearance become subservient signifiers of his interiority. Rather, Wilde's version of celebrity overturns any such hierarchy of inside to outside.

To apply bourgeois notions of sexuality to Wilde's appearance is to overlook the sartorial traditions Wilde invokes, and the sheer spirit of fun with which he mobilizes them. Wilde's dress, in fact, constitutes a response to the specific male attire that had evolved by the Victorian era: the gentleman's dark suit and short hair. Kaja Silverman notes that from the end of the eighteenth century onward, male clothing had conformed to that standard. She writes, "Whereas in earlier centuries dominant male dress gave a certain play to fancy, it has subsequently settled into sobriety and rectitude. Since the sartorial revolution, male dress has also given a very small margin for variation" (147). Wilde's clothing, then, demonstrates his irreverent disregard for traditional categories of gender. It stands out against the 1882 backdrop, marking him as less sober and erect. It also evokes a bygone age of sumptuary laws, when only a select few could attire themselves so flamboyantly. Before Silverman's sartorial revolution, "ornate dress was primarily a class rather than a gender prerogative during the fifteenth, sixteenth, and seventeenth centuries, a prerogative that was protected by law... sartorial extravagance was a mark of aristocratic power and privilege" (139). Wilde's ornate dress draws on a tradition in which class, not gender, designated who qualified to adorn themselves for public display. He was, in a sense, asserting himself as an aristocrat, albeit one distinguished by matters of taste rather than economics, one whose superior choices are what make him the object of the plebeian gaze. The aristocratic tradition enters a web of signification—along with the styles associated with the aesthetic movement, and the indicators of dandyism and pre-Raphaelitism—to compose Wilde's look.[16] Wilde's dress, operating in the register of class rather than of sexuality, illuminates his manipulation of the image to fashion the exceptional individual who would stand out against other members of society—the celebrity.

The celebrity is thus created as a surface display of attributes of the subject. In this way Wilde's concept of celebrity implies a new understanding of what a self is, what constitutes an individual. As Jerome H. Buckley writes of Wilde, "If the self as a separate entity seemed elusive and amorphous, or if, perhaps, it did not exist at all, it must be invented, dressed up, and projected" (2). In other words, the self is given a physical existence by Wilde's clothing. Wilde wears his markers of subjectivity on his body as features of the visible object that circulates in the marketplace of images.

In this way Wilde turns the celebrity into something like a commodity. Critics often refer to Wilde's self-commodification, enlisting the language of the marketplace, writing that Wilde sold or advertised himself. Celebrities in general have often been considered in the same way, without a clear investigation of the implications therein. But likening a human being to a commodity constitutes a drastic cultural intervention on Wilde's part. In many respects, the undertaking echoes Marx's understanding of the commodity fetish. About the commodity, Marx writes, "in it the social character of men's labour appears as an objective character stamped upon the product of that labour . . . the existence of things *quâ* commodities, and the value-relation between the products of labour which stamps them as commodities, have absolutely no connexion with their physical properties and with the material relations arising therefrom" (72). For Marx, in capitalist consumer culture, it is the act of exchange that imposes a value on the commodity that has only an arbitrary relationship to the material conditions producing the object. That is, value derives from circulation, not from something in the object, much less from the subjects who produce it. Indeed, in Marx's analysis, the relationship between subjects and objects breaks down, becomes displaced by mediating images that convert "every product into a social hieroglyph" (74). This hieroglyph then serves as the key to some meaning that must be interpreted, or, in his words: "later on, we try to decipher the hieroglyphic, to get behind the secret of our own social products." But the gesture of "deciphering" the hieroglyph to discover its "secret" is based on the misrecognition of value as an "objective character" of the product. In other words, the hieroglyph will only refer outward toward the commodity's value in a system of exchange, rather than point to any essential value of the object. In fact, by this process, Marx is saying, we no longer encounter the object, but only the commodity, an image that signifies a relationally determined value.

Wilde's celebrity operates within a system similar to Marx's. Indeed, Wilde refuses any determination of the body as having inherent value. The body's value is located in an image that takes the place of the body in a system of social signs. The celebrity becomes a hieroglyph, on which all that can be read is its value in relationship to other images, of political figures, or of ordinary people—what might be called "normal people." In this system the subject itself has no constant meaning; identity is strictly relational, who you are by virtue of not being other people. Wilde would spend the rest of his life, and his literary career, reckoning with this gesture.

I have been arguing that Wilde, on his tour, was in the throes of creating a new kind of celebrity, but I do not mean to imply that the work was executed in isolation. I have already mentioned Barnum and Twain, whose machinations bear some resemblance to Wilde's. More directly implicated in the Wilde phenomenon are the caricatures that enlist, enforce, and revise Wilde's celebrity production, and that materialize the reaction of Wilde's audience to his performance. Caricature, writes Diderot, is "the representation . . . of a subject, in which truth and exact resemblance are altered by an excess of ridiculousness."[17] Caricatures of Wilde, for example, manipulate "truth and exact resemblance" by taking up the hallmarks that Wilde offers—his clothes, hair, and accouterments. They exaggerate those trademarks to signify one aspect of the individual, as if in a synecdochic manner. For example, the lily, a signature adornment of the aesthete, becomes omnipresent in these works. A *Punch* caricature by Beerbohm called "Days With Celebrities" satirizes Wilde's aestheticism by depicting Wilde eating a lily for breakfast. The irony is predicated on the absurd idea that the aesthete is so beyond the normal needs of the body that he subsists on these idealized ornaments of the self.[18] The "ridiculousness" that Diderot describes sometimes results from the contrast between Wilde's iconic tokens and features Wilde does not possess. A lithograph from 1882 makes Wilde a cartoonish "Chinese" character, bearing a Fu Manchu mustache and a ponytail that reaches his ankles, grasping a sunflower, and that lily again. Here it is clear that as long as tokens (such as the flowers) are included to ensure identification of the celebrity body, anything else (the ponytail and mustache) might be attached to it. Thus, we might say that the caricatures expand the circulation of Wilde's image, trading in on and increasing its recognizability.

Caricatures like the one that makes Wilde "Chinese" claim to reveal a hidden truth that Wilde's actual performance masks. This is a different logic from that which governs most of Victorian society, what Nancy Armstrong describes as the "basic principle that a natural and necessary bond connect[s] objects to their images" ("Modernism's Iconophobia" 48). In other words, these images are not photographs claiming to perfectly render reality. Rather, the caricatures enlist visual distortion, exaggerating the trademark aspects of Wilde's appearance or supplementing them with other features. The grotesqueries mean to illuminate his corruption, whether pictured in terms of race, sexuality, corpulence, or madness. Walter Benjamin quotes Edouard Drumont's claim that caricatures are able to extract "the latent self" from the person pictured (*Arcades Project* b1, 1, 740). Clearly, then, caricatures do not share Wilde's locating attributes of the subject on the exterior of the body. Instead, they suggest that the body houses invisible aspects of the subject, which caricature can reveal. It may, of course, be seen as a quixotic gesture to caricaturize someone who is already enacting a stereotype. That's just it, though: by creating his

FIGURE 1.2. Lithograph of Oscar Wilde. Unidentified clipping, William Andrews Clark Library, UCLA.

trademark image, meant as a stamp of distinction, Wilde makes that icon public property, and allows the caricatures to stake their claim to greater insight into the subject.

Wilde affected to ignore the caricatures, writing in a June 1882 letter, "I regard all caricature and satire as absolutely beneath notice" (*Complete Letters* 174). But he noticed. Wilde's literary path retraces much of the same ground of the lecture tour I have been outlining, including the struggle for authority over one's public image. While his public persona creates a version of celebrity that commodifies the individual by locating the subject in the circulating image, his *Dorian Gray* re-examines that concept, along with the idea that attributes of the subject are visible on the body, and, furthermore, whether it is desirable to conceive of the subject in relation to the body at all.

Judging by Appearances in Dorian Gray

When Lois Cucullu notes that *Dorian Gray* revolves around the idea that "an image can be the source of intelligibility for subjects no less than for objects" (20), she encapsulates the effect of Wilde's celebrity while also showing how Wilde's self-fashioning helps us understand the novel. Viewed alongside Wilde's lecture tour, *Dorian Gray* constitutes a treatise on celebrity—not in the way that, say, the narrative of his *An Ideal Husband* (1893) actually revolves around a character's public reputation, but rather in the way the novel draws heavily on the negotiations between subject, body, and image that characterize Wilde's own celebrity. *Dorian Gray* enlists and reassesses the two models of the subject's relationship to the body implied by Wilde's American tour. To mediate between them, the narrative focuses on the body of Dorian, which circulates throughout society, and the supernatural portrait he leaves behind. Dorian's experience leaves its marks on the surface of the painting, which seems to represent attributes of the subject, but, on closer inspection, provides only an exaggerated reflection of Dorian's subjectivity. Ultimately, as I will show, the novel refuses to fully locate the subject in relation either to the body or to the image. Instead, Wilde uses these shifts in celebrity logic to propose that an individual has no constant or inherent value—that identity is relative to society. In other words, the questions of where to locate the subject emerge as subordinate to Wilde's use of that cultural material to reconceive of identity as having a relational value with the public. As part of the novel's work, *Dorian Gray* invokes generic aspects of the *Bildungsroman* genre to critique a society that relies on a meretricious association of inside and out.

Wilde situates the narrative of *Dorian Gray* within a culture unified by the conviction that people are coherent subjects, housed within bodies, made legible by the bodies' exteriors. This belief is the novel's binding social paradigm. For example, when characters learn that Dorian's unblemished face is actually masking his misdeeds, rather than proving his virtue, they are systematically removed. Basil Hallward and Alan Campbell see the evidence of the corrupted portrait; James Vane learns Dorian's secret from the ruined woman outside the opium den. All—and eventually Dorian himself—are killed off. That is, those who are exposed to the duplicity of Dorian's appearance, who learn the fact that his appearance is not a natural manifestation of the subject, are elements that must be expelled in order for society to continue functioning; most simply do not survive the novel.

Other characters are otherwise expunged from the social order, such as the woman in the opium den Dorian visits. She says, "They say he has sold himself to the devil for a pretty face." Having granted her this insight, Wilde proceeds to describe her in insubstantial terms such as "shadowy," and last mentions her having "vanished" from sight and knowledge (204). The opium den itself, where other patrons demonstrate some knowledge of Dorian and his habits, allegorically sits at the border of the British Empire, in a marginalized position, as Marez points out (28). Indeed, when he encounters Adrian Singleton in the opium den, Dorian says, "I thought you had left England," as if to liken being in the opium den to being expunged from the nation (199). Thus, those who come to understand the contradiction between appearance and self are eliminated from society or relegated to its margins. Conversely, in mainstream social circles, Dorian's transgressions are kept as the subject of rumor and speculation (163). When the Duke of Berwick apparently suspects that Dorian is not all he seems, he registers distaste by leaving the room when Dorian enters; his belief that Dorian's unblemished looks mask foul acts precludes his participation in a society that embraces Dorian for his appearance's testimony of goodness. By removing those characters who have reason to question the correlation between Dorian's exterior and his behavior, Wilde creates a salon culture whose members are bound together by the belief, or at least the pretense, that there is no contradiction between the image and the interior.

This principle further circumscribes the novel's society when characters repeatedly assert the belief that appearances, specifically bodies and faces, signify the ostensibly intangible and invisible attributes of the subject. Both upper and lower class characters (representing this novel's fantasy of only two classes) voice this idea. Basil Hallward states, "Sin is a thing that writes itself across a man's face" (162). He treats literally the idea that bodies are legible. Dorian's exchange with the "village girl" Hetty Morton echoes Basil's thought: "He had told her once that he was wicked, and she had laughed at him and answered that wicked people were always very old and very ugly" (231). These moments illustrate a common morality. They posit a formulation of the subject, like Carlyle's, which imagines the body as a container for the subject. They also reflect the kind of thinking, germane to caricature, that postulates that this interior subjectivity can be read on the body. Obviously, both utterances are undermined and satirized by the fact that they are addressed to Dorian, whose perpetually youthful appearance precludes the principles they espouse, as it thwarts the possibility of reading his behavior on the body.

Basil and Hetty's remarks echo like commonplaces, and thus contrast with Wilde's trademark of turning such platitudes into epigrams. Set quite apart from such mouthing of received wisdom is the speech of Lord Henry, which not only occasionally takes the form of Wildean epigrams, but also demonstrates attitudes that recall Wilde's work locating attributes of the subject on the outside of the body. For example, Henry says, "It is only shallow people who do not judge by appearances" (39). This statement, celebrating the idea that one need not look below the surface of a person, might seem to agree with the view held by the novel's other characters. However, Henry's epigram actually takes the idea that one can read people by their exteriors and radicalizes it. As commonplace thought would have it, shallow people are those not "deep" enough to see past appearances, to a person's interior. According to Henry, shallowness, paradoxically, entails trying to see deeper than the exterior. Henry insinuates that people should be judged by their exteriors, but not because exteriors correspond to an interior truth. Rather, he proposes that appearances, where one displays taste and class, tell more about a person than any imagined interiority. Therefore people who are not shallow, himself included, disdain all this peering into a person's interior. Henry's statement castigates those who would look past the signs of the surface. It thus reinforces the idea of a society united by a belief in the legibility of the body while providing a different way to judge by appearances.

Significantly, Henry does not imply that the exterior is a manifestation of the subject housed within the body. Therefore, he emerges as one who stands slightly apart from the society of the novel. Of course, there is a traditional critical opinion that Henry is "peculiarly Wilde's mouthpiece," which dates back as far as Harris (82). This treatment doubtlessly stems from the fact that Henry consistently demonstrates a Wildean wit. It therefore does not seem overly deterministic to say that Henry's posture parallels Wilde's celebrity self-fashioning. His view of the surface as legible does not make the exterior a signifier of the subject. Rather, Henry locates real meaning on the body. Between Henry's formulation of how the subject can be read on the body and that represented by commonplace thought, the novel invokes the two versions of the subject's relationship to the body found in the discourse of Wilde's American tour.

The early sections of *Dorian Gray* set Basil and Henry in opposition, propounding contrary ways of reading the body. Wilde introduces Dorian, and eventually the portrait, to test out these two ways of thinking. Before Dorian's initial appearance in the novel, Wilde sets his stage by having both Basil and Henry theorize about the relationship between appearances and the self, both in regard to Dorian. Basil describes his first glimpse of Dorian, actually across a crowded room, thus: "I turned halfway round and saw Dorian Gray for the first time. When our eyes met, I knew that I had come face to face with someone whose mere personality was so fascinating that, if I allowed it to do so, it would absorb my whole nature" (24). Basil, upon seeing Dorian's surface, his face, perceives what he calls "personality," which seems to exist beyond Dorian's appearance. He imagines that this personality contains dimension sufficient to engulf his own "nature"—his self. The sentence falls on the words "face to face," with a "personality," as if to indicate the cultural logic that allows Basil to move from the visible surface to the abstract interior. Basil suggests that faces are legible images by which one can read the subject within, but the novel seems to be pointing out the leap of faith this thinking requires.[19] The novel's vocabulary of interiority, furthermore, becomes unstable. The words "nature" and "personality" will be soon joined by "conscience," "soul," and "places within," in an extensive language that this society uses to imagine the interior, which, Wilde suggests, should not be imagined.

Henry's first sight of Dorian is preceded and mediated by the as yet unfinished portrait. Even so, Henry too is moved to ruminate about appearances. While Basil's formulation insinuates a relationship between seeing and knowing that assumes a degree of depth, "beneath" the surface but making an imprint upon it, Henry sees only the surface.

> But beauty, real beauty, ends where an intellectual expression begins. Intellect itself is a mode of exaggeration, and destroys the harmony of any face. The moment one sits down to think, one becomes all nose, or all forehead, or something horrid. . . . Your mysterious young friend, whose name you have never told me, but whose picture really fascinates me, never thinks. I feel quite sure of that. He is some brainless beautiful creature. (21)

Henry claims that any intrusion of thought onto the body, while legible on that body, would basically alter its appearance, transform it into something else. Again, Henry does not claim that Dorian's body represents his interior. Rather, he speculates that if Dorian were to think, it would exaggerate aspects of the body—he would *become* "all nose" (not "look like" all nose). To Henry, thought, commonly considered an intangible component of the subject, manifests itself by exaggerating an aspect of the body. In other words, Henry takes an element of the interior and relocates it on the exterior, thereby collapsing the opposition of inside and out.

While Henry conflates Dorian's interior and exterior, he also conflates Dorian and the painting of Dorian that Basil is creating. Henry moves effortlessly from thinking about the painting to thinking about Dorian's personality, but refuses to question whether, though he may be reading the painting correctly, the painting represents its subject. The omission allows the novel to link the question of whether the body makes the subject legible with the question of whether an image can make the subject legible. By connecting these two problems, the novel leaves open various interpretations of the portrait. For one, the picture of Dorian might be seen as functioning similarly to Wilde's own celebrity persona, literalizing the idea of an image that substitutes for a binary relationship between subject and object. In that case, society's failure to recognize the collapsed binary, the ongoing assumption of Dorian's inner value, produces the tragedies of the plot. On the other hand, Dorian refers to the portrait as his "conscience" and, more often, his "soul." Thus the novel associates the painting with the bourgeois notions of invisible and intangible attributes of the subject. In this sense, the novel would suggest that, indeed, the body can be a signifier of the interior, but that in the case of Dorian, the supernatural picture has usurped the body's role. The gothic horrors of the plot follow as a result.

To reconcile these two models, it is useful to investigate what kind of cultural material goes into the picture of Dorian Gray. The picture merges elements from, first of all, the literary trope of the portrait possessing a supernatural link to its sitter, and secondly, a popular tradition: caricature. The depiction of a portrait with an unexplained, metaphysical relationship to its subject is a common literary conceit, probably familiar to Victorian literary audiences from Edgar Allan Poe's "The Oval Portrait" (1842) and Henry James's "The Liar" (1889). Poe's story, for example, depicts an artist who obsessively paints a portrait of his wife. But he refuses to notice that "the tints which he spread on the canvas were drawn from the cheeks of her who sate beside him," that is, that the portrait has, in its "life-likeness," expropriated something essential from its source (383–384). The painting's existence, furthermore, comes at the expense of the subject's life; the story concludes with the artist proclaiming the painting to be "*Life* itself," as the conterminous wife dies. This final moment suggests the impossibility that copy and original can coexist; Poe preserves the copy, as if to show that art is more alive than life.

James's story, published nearly simultaneously with *Dorian Gray*, provides another version of this trope. "The Liar" depicts Oliver Lyons painting his subject, Colonel Capadose, in a way that reveals his invisible "nature," characterized by his compulsive lying that goes publicly unacknowledged (352). Lyons accomplishes his task so well, though, that the enraged colonel plunges a knife into his facsimile to destroy it. James compares the action to a murder, describing how Capadose takes up the knife and "dashe[s] it again several times into the face of the likeness, exactly as if he were stabbing a human victim: it had the oddest effect—that of a sort of figurative suicide" (362). The moment mirrors the finale of *Dorian*, which features Dorian taking up a knife and stabbing his "soul-life," his portrait, thereby committing actual suicide (167). In James's account, however, the human subject suffers no physical effects; in "The Liar," art reveals what life does not, and thus the copy is deemed too threatening to continue to exist. These stories indicate that the picture of Dorian and its role at the novel's conclusion would be recognizable to Victorian readers, and would align *Dorian Gray* with products of high literary culture.

Wilde overlays this literary tradition with the logic of caricature. Two aspects of the picture recall the logic of caricature. First of all, the painting is unidirectional: Dorian notices that the portrait's gradual transformation reflects his debased acts but not his attempts to redeem himself. Finding that the portrait does not acknowledge his "sparing" of Hetty Morton, he calls it "an unjust mirror" (234). The injustice he perceives is the picture's failure to register what Dorian imagines as a moment of good behavior. As caricatures would satirize only one aspect of Wilde, the painting records only one aspect of Dorian: "The portrait was to bear the burden of his shame: that was all" (120).

Dorian's initial resentment of what he regards as an "unjust" representation later succumbs to acceptance. Upon discovering the portrait's initial changes, he resolves to resist all temptation (107), but eventually, seeing that he cannot reverse the direction of the portrait's deterioration, he becomes resigned to his dissipation. He decides he has no choice but to live a life of "infinite passion, pleasures subtle and secret, wild joys and wilder sins" (120). These avowals are made in the presence of the picture, as if under its influence. In this sense, the portrait again enacts the logic of celebrity articulated by Wilde's tour. In the United States, Wilde performs a stereotype of himself in following Bunthorne, a copy of Wilde. In the novel, the copy (the painting) dictates the behavior of the original (Dorian). In both cases the image begins to control the individual who supposedly originates it. The unidirectional representation of the portrait leads the subject to act more unidirectionally. This reduction of personality to one characteristic, first illustrated by the portrait, then enacted by Dorian, most overtly links the portrait to the idea of caricature.

The second way the portrait obeys the logic of caricature is by adding features not of Dorian's body, similar to the way that one caricature of Wilde makes him "Chinese" by giving him a mustache. Like caricature, this imitation deviates from its source in order to more accurately figure the "truth" of the person. Specifically, the novel paints the portrait with blood. Dorian wonders, "What was that loathsome red dew that gleamed, wet and glistening, on one of the hands, as though the canvas had sweated blood?" (185). Like caricatures that take liberties with Wilde's features, the portrait affixes blood to signify Dorian's culpability for Basil's death. To Dorian it appears as though the blood has emerged from within the portrait, moved from inside to outside. Dorian's understanding of the portrait literalizes the idea of an image that displays interior things on the exterior. Certainly, it must be mentioned that to leak blood is to become a holy incarnate; Wilde here plays with the idea that Dorian, were his body experiencing this stigmata of sorts, would be turning into a religious icon, sacrificing the body in order to follow his hedonistic lifestyle. In a more literal reading of the narrative, though, the blood is Basil's. It appears in response to Basil's death, and indicates that Dorian has Basil's blood on his hands. These two resemblances to caricature are reinforced by Basil's speculation that the painting is "some foul parody, some infamous ignoble satire" of his original work (168), as he assumes that the distorted and exaggerated image before him must be an imitation of his original, challenging the relationship between the painting and its source.

The Tragic Commodity

While caricature functions via mass reproduction and circulation, Dorian's portrait, like the portraits in Poe's and James's stories, remains hidden and off the market.[20] Dorian guards the picture from "the shallow prying eyes" (28) of the world, keeping it literally screened from view in the room that was once his schoolroom, located in his attic, like the proverbial madwoman. Moments in the plot hinge on the picture remaining unseen. For example, Basil plans to make the portrait the highlight of an exhibition; Dorian dissuades him (126). The novel ensures that the picture stays away from both the marketplace and the market—at least within the narrative. Of course, it is depicted in a novel that is first published in *Lippincott's Monthly Magazine*—an American publication which had been known only a few years earlier as *Lippincott's Magazine of Popular Literature and Science*—and then in its own volume. Both versions are mass-reproduced, both gain wide readership. Within the narrative, though, the picture remains irreproducible, stationary, and sequestered from the world. As it is never put in exchange, it never develops exchange value.

Instead, the picture enables Dorian to circulate in society; if the portrait were not masking his misdeeds, Dorian would clearly not maintain his secure social position and his ability to penetrate social circles at will. As Dorian circulates, though, he wreaks serious ramifications for both himself and the society through which he moves. The problems he causes stem from the fact that Dorian's interiority seems to be an object, permeable and subject to outside forces as he circulates. Ultimately, Dorian takes on attributes of a commodity, the object read by virtue of its relation to others. For example, at the outset of the novel Dorian's interior life is produced by Basil's creation of the portrait and dependent on Henry's discoursing on influence. While Dorian sits for the portrait, Henry says, "to influence a person is to give him one's own soul. He does not think his natural thoughts, or burn with his natural passions. . . . He becomes an echo of someone else's music, an actor of a part that has not been written for him" (34-35). Henry's words reverberate with the change in Dorian and on his surface. Basil notices "that a look had come into the lad's face that he had never seen there before" (35). Here, the change in appearance constitutes evidence that a transformation occurs within Dorian, generating a new kind of subject. The novel uses free indirect discourse to show Dorian thinking that "entirely fresh influences were at work within him" (36). These influences are clearly Basil's painting the picture and Henry's injecting "poisonous theories" (107) into Dorian's mind. When Dorian gets his first look at the finished portrait, it is "as if he had recognised himself for the first time" (33). In this moment, Dorian "begins to develop a sense of self-consciousness" (Felski 97). The novel creates a subject within Dorian's body specifically in response to these external influences, implying that Dorian's subjectivity is not a purely spiritual entity, untouchable by the world.

Dorian's interior is altered by contact with others as he circulates. The novel Henry lends Dorian provides a model for this transformation. Calling it a "poisonous book," Wilde casts it as an extension of Henry's "poisonous" influence, and indicates that this influence crossing the boundary of the body, moves from outside to inside. This characterization suggests the porous definition of Dorian's interior. In the novel's waning moments, Dorian gains the insight that what society considers intangible and private, for him has become an object. He tells Henry, "The soul is a terrible reality. It can be bought, and sold, and bartered away. It can be poisoned, or made perfect" (227). The passive voice in this speech heightens the sense of the subject as something acted upon and changed, an object. The language of the marketplace—the words "bought," "sold," "bartered"— hammer home that the portrait has been kept private, off the market, while Dorian's subjectivity has been substituted for it, circulating promiscuously in public.

The most pervasive consequences of Dorian's circulation are visited upon others. As he circulates through society he spreads his poison, reproducing his diseased interior within others. Basil says, "One has a right to judge a man by the effect he has over his friends. Yours seem to lose all sense of honour, of goodness, of purity. . . . You have filled them with a madness of pleasure. They have gone down into the depths" (164).[21] Honor, goodness, purity, depths: Basil employs words that nominally assign value to one's interior—and tops it off by equating immorality with a model of the person whose depths are a place of horror. Contact with Dorian contaminates the interior, spreading the corruption throughout society. The invisible corruption his body bears spreads throughout the social body as a consequence for its naïve assumption that Dorian's appearance signals his virtue.

The corruption of others is practically all that the novel portrays of Dorian's acts. Despite the reported accusations by and apparent effect on others, Dorian's exact activities with his consorts are generally left to hearsay and rumor. We know that, upon realizing his magical relationship to his portrait, Dorian begins to desire: "Eternal youth, infinite passion, pleasures subtle and secret, wild joys and wilder sins—he was to have all these things" (120). Yet the scene soon shifts to some eighteen years later. Wilde provides only a summary depiction of the events in between, comprising Dorian's hobbies and imperialist-exotic collecting, not the social interactions that produce the effects on others to which Basil refers. To be sure, at this later stage of the novel, the older Dorian visits the opium den and murders Basil, but these things transpire after years of supposed sinfulness and simply draw attention to the mystery of what else he has been doing. Basil, in fact, confronts Dorian with a series of questions: "Why is it, Dorian, that a man like the Duke of Berwick leaves the room of a club when you enter it? Why is it that so many gentlemen in London will neither go to your house nor invite you to theirs? . . . Why is your friendship so fatal to young men? . . . What about your country house, and the life that is led there?" (117). The novel teases readers; the sins of Dorian are hinted at, never articulated. Wilde was asked about his treatment of Dorian's sins during his first trial, and he responded by quoting Walter Pater's comment that a "veil of mystery" hangs over the narrative (Holland, *The Real Trial* 219). There is a hole in the novel where Dorian's actions might be.

In lieu of Dorian's social activities, Wilde portrays the effects of those actions on the people Dorian contaminates, and on the portrait, because this effect is what matters most in the novel. Basil is correct to "judge a man by the effect he has," because these effects are all the novel makes available. That is to say, Wilde does not condemn Dorian's hedonistic actions. On the contrary, a stilted neutrality lies behind such descriptions as, "He had mad hungers that grew more ravenous as he fed them" (143). The portrait, it may be said, does not reveal an evil that inheres in Dorian himself. Rather it changes in response to the results of Dorian's actions. The disfiguration represents the consequences of external influences on the social body as a whole.

In other words, those invisible attributes of subjectivity remain invisible, as will the exact nature of Dorian's actions. After all, when Basil looks behind the curtain at the fantastically altered painting, he sees only a caricature, and even for that he is killed. Thus, in one final way, the novel echoes the logic of celebrity. It values Dorian in relation to others. That valuation, we can say, is analogous to the relational value of the commodity that marks Wilde's production of celebrity. As Dorian is a circulating object, the effect he has on society constitutes a gauge of his relational value.

Wilde's omitting a full account of Dorian's social actions, the rushed passage of time, is one part of his generic play in *Dorian Gray*. Wilde toys with characteristics of not only the novel generally, but also the sub-genre of *Bildungsroman*, which was integral to bourgeois nineteenth-century culture. *Dorian Gray* negates the middle-class segment of the population. It offers an ellipsis at the center of the narrative instead of a depiction of the subject's development, acquisition of domestic security, and incorporation into society that mark the *Bildungsroman*. These gestures reveal Wilde as enlisting a bourgeois genre and revamping it for aristocratic aims, similar to how he forms epigrams from middle-class platitudes. The gestures also illuminate Wilde's use of the tradition of the literary representation of the portrait; the trope incorporates a high-art object, the painting, which situates the novel within a high-art tradition. It thus draws attention away from Wilde's use of mass culture: his enlisting of caricature and his creation of a mass-reproducible object that itself initially appeared in a mass-produced magazine.

Wilde's play with generic conventions is most pronounced in the novel's treatment of the trope of marriage. Nineteenth-century novels, everyone knows, are supposed to end in marriage (as Wilde's stage comedies do, fulfilling that genre's conventions), and with the promise that the genetic line will continue. *Dorian Gray*, however, depicts Dorian as the sole heir of his family; this precludes the possibility of the conventional conclusion. Indeed, Wilde directly links the generic disappointment to bourgeois interiority. Dorian's flirtation with marriage to Sybil Vane is thwarted when she shocks him by developing a stable subjectivity. Prior to this, Dorian has celebrated the flexible nature of Sybil's identity. He describes her in terms of her exterior changes, but rhetorically treats her as if those changes alter the person as well. He says, "One evening she is Rosalind. And the next she is Imogen" (67). Kerry Powell explains that Dorian's fascination with this multiplicity relates to his own lack of an interior identity, writing, "Dorian can locate no single, fixed identity behind the revolving wheel of selves" (187). After her betrothal to Dorian, however, a singular identity takes shape. Sybil says:

> Before I knew you acting was the one reality of my life. It was only in the theatre that I lived. I thought it was all true.... You came... and you freed my soul from prison. You taught me what reality really is. To-night, for the first time in my life, I saw through the hollowness, the sham.... You had brought me something higher, something of which all art is but a reflection. You had made me understand what love really is.... I might mimic a passion that I do not feel, but I cannot mimic one that burns me like fire. (101–102)

From one extreme to another: Sybil develops a stable, interior subjectivity, which leads, first of all, to the idea that art is a subordinate "reflection" of life, and, secondly, to the corresponding belief that her acting is less "real" than her new desires. To add insult to injury, she attributes the change to meeting Dorian. "For this," Gagnier writes, "Wilde kills her." Dorian's horror at Sybil's speech prompts his rejection of her, her suicide, and the ensuing change to the portrait. By interweaving the portrait's supernatural function with the Sybil episode, Wilde implicates Dorian's own lack of a stable subjectivity in his failure to wed and biologically reproduce.

Dorian Gray ends in Dorian's death, and the servants' discovery of the unrecognizable corpse lying before the portrait. This moment further invokes the novelistic trope of marriage. "It was not till they had examined the rings that they recognized who it was" (235). The detail of the rings invites comparison to a happy ending that would feature wedding bands, and highlights that Dorian's death is the death of his hereditary line.[22] The only marriage here is one of Dorian's body and the biological ravages of time. Now, the portrait represents Dorian as he was last seen, "in all the wonder of his exquisite youth and beauty," but his body is "wrinkled, withered, and loathsome of visage." This loss of youth and beauty, the turning of Dorian into a loathsome object, is punishment itself coming from Wilde.

The critique here operates in both directions, of course. Wilde not only satirizes the *Bildungsroman* genre's middle-class values, but also turns Dorian into a tragic commodity. In death, Dorian becomes a caricature of himself, his body (the original), appropriating its appearance from the copy (the painting), and only recognizable by its accouterments (the rings) that recall the death of his hereditary line. Dorian has become a problem for this novel. So he gets eradicated. Here we come upon Wilde's last laugh at the expense of this society he has created. It seems the "wild joys and wilder sins"—who could miss the allusion to the author's name?—are too much for this society. This commingling of joy and sin indicates that what this society loses without Dorian is more a range of experience than an unequivocal poison. Yet, his influence threatens the social fabric of that society. The ambivalences *Dorian Gray* registers concerning the repositioning of the subject in relation to the body and the image are shown to be subordinate to the final relational value of the person, which, as it is determined in relation to society, is subject to the language, categories, and laws of that society's system. Thus, another tragic commodity is the novel itself, which, in its portrait of a soulless hedonist, was taken by many readers as a direct representation of the degenerate nature of its author—an exterior that reveals its author's interior. Indeed, passages of the novel were read at Wilde's trial, and conceived of as evidence of his subversive influence, with grave consequences. Wilde's loss of control over the meaning of his image and his writing portended the turn that his career—and the modernist literary celebrity—would take.

Deep Thoughts: Embodying the Subject in De Profundis

De Profundis, whose title announces an emergence from the depths, concludes Wilde's project of locating the subject in relation to the body by inverting the model of celebrity he developed on his American tour.[23]

Writing while imprisoned for "gross indecency," fifteen years after the tour, Wilde explores what happens when the body is unable to bear the celebrity image. In *De Profundis*, a long confessional treatise on life and art masquerading as a letter to his longtime lover Lord Alfred Douglas, Wilde depicts himself as either displayed publicly as a debased object or incarcerated. He remedies this by imagining an immaterial subjectivity, closed to external influence, represented by creative agency and imagination. This production of the subject, resting on the fact that the body is no longer an aristocratic object of the plebeian gaze, suggests that it is only when the celebrity image does not circulate publicly that an intangible, invisible self comes into being. The intangible subject is only conceivable when the body is off the market, a situation incommensurate with the idea that value only exists in circulation. To retain the public self that can circulate, Wilde locates the subject in the lone remaining circulating object, the text of *De Profundis*. Text replaces image as bearer of the subject.

Setting up the terms by which Wilde ultimately produces his identity as something textual, *De Profundis* poses a generic problem.[24] Wilde oscillates between emphasizing the work's resemblance to private correspondence and its qualities as a narrative, theoretical essay, one intended for a wider readership. He addresses the letter "Dear Bosie" and writes in the first person, casting *De Profundis* as a private letter. Private letters, whatever their eventual use, make an initial claim to being for the eyes of one person only. Derrida, analyzing Lacan's approach to another famous letter, writes that "since it can be diverted, [a letter] must have a course which is proper to it" (59). The proper course of *De Profundis*, ostensibly from Wilde to Bosie, gets diverted. Wilde never actually thought of the work as private, according to Richard Ellmann.[25] Gagnier argues that, "Wilde used Douglas to fill the place of the absent audience, writing a self-serving biography in order to write an autobiography that explained Wilde to the world" (180). To Gagnier, Bosie acts as substitute for the audience; the proper course is from Wilde to the reading public. Supporting this view, the text repeatedly complicates the idea of private communication from one single person to another. *De Profundis* signals its wider audience by repeatedly depicting letters that circulate beyond one addressee.

> I wrote at once to Robbie . . . and desired that the words I had written of you should be copied out carefully and sent to you. . . . My letter seems to have arrived not a moment too soon. It fell on you, as far as I can judge, like a thunderbolt. You describe yourself, in your answer to Robbie, as being "deprived of all power of thought and expression." (907–908)

Wilde's letter to Robbie intends Bosie as audience, and Bosie responds, not to Wilde, but to Robbie, who, presumably, forwards the response to Wilde. These letters travel beyond their named audiences to other multiple readers, though they remain within a select group. In another instance, Wilde refers to *De Profundis* reflexively, telling Bosie, "I strongly advise you to let her [Bosie's mother] see this letter" (942). The exhortation calls attention to the material quality of the letter, reminding us that it is an object that can reach multiple destinations. In such moments *De Profundis* not only disputes its own status as private correspondence by showing that such a thing might not exist, but also shows that a letter's proper course may include multiple readers.

This gesture widens in implication as *De Profundis* portrays the problem of letters that go beyond the intended coterie audience. Wilde excoriates Bosie: "Look at the history of that letter! It passes from you into the hands of a loathsome companion." The word "loathsome" is a loaded epithet coming from Wilde, appearing as it does in descriptions of both Dorian's portrait and Dorian's face at the end of *De Profundis*. Here it refers to Bosie's "companion" but infects the letter itself as well. That is to say, as the letter travels further from the safety of friends and proper nouns, it becomes degraded. This problem becomes more drastic as Wilde mentions that the publication of this particular letter becomes damaging legal evidence: "Ultimately [the letter] forms part of a criminal charge.... I go to prison for it at last" (889–890). *De Profundis* emphasizes that when texts circulate beyond their prescribed boundary, the authors lose control over their readership, with dire results. The need to keep private correspondence from going public arises early in Wilde's work: it is seen in Wilde's *An Ideal Husband,* whose plot hinges on possession of a letter that would compromise a character's public reputation. Both texts, then, demonstrate anxiety over a letter as something private that, when not contained within the author's circuit of control, ruins a public image.

These texts, of course, echo in Wilde's biography. Indeed, Wilde's trials are littered with accounts of letters—for example the one that I have cited from *De Profundis*—which reach the wrong hands.[26] Many of these are allegedly blackmail letters; in fact, Wilde's solicitor Edward Clarke foolishly entered one such letter as evidence, assuming the prosecution knew of it in advance.[27] That instance of private correspondence becoming public ends disastrously for Wilde's case. Of course, Wilde's trial and punishment resulted from his own accusation of libel against the Marquess of Queensberry, Bosie's father, which was spurred by a card Queensberry had left at his club, on which was scrawled, "For Oscar Wilde, posing somdomite [*sic*]." Wilde's troubles began here, with correspondence that Wilde considered too public to stomach, even though it was likely seen by fewer than three pairs of eyes.[28] In this instance, a text that straddles public and private, not originating with Wilde but referring to him, constitutes a crisis. During his trials, some letters used as evidence contained names that were not read aloud during the proceedings, in order not to implicate in scandal those mentioned. So Wilde would have witnessed the inconsistent, unpredictable way these letters circulate and visit their consequences.

The extent that Wilde, while composing *De Profundis*, thematizes letters that go public under conscious influence of the trials, we of course will never know (and might not care). These moments at the trials, however, are significant because the trials were a hugely publicized event, the ins and outs of which were public currency. Any contemporary readers would likely recognize that material from Wilde's celebrity had made its way into the text and become a major problem there. That is to say, the anxiety of circulating letters makes its imprint on the generic ambiguity of the text, which exhibits elements of being both private correspondence for Bosie and a public missive for a wide readership. The shiftiness of genre in *De Profundis*, then, is inextricably bound with questions of whether this is a text that circulates—and registers a deep ambivalence over whether it should be one. The disasters incurred by the circulation of the letters, in turn, set up the text's concern with the circulation of the body. Wilde suggests that, just as when a text circulates its author loses control over destination and effect, when a body is made into a public object, the subject likewise risks losing control. Indeed, the individual might lose the ability to produce itself as a subject. For example, Wilde depicts himself at trial listening to the charges against him, and suddenly thinking *"How splendid it would be if I was saying all this about myself"* (947). Here, Wilde desires not to change the terms of his public identity, but to proclaim them himself.

De Profundis's simultaneous investigations into genre and subjectivity are made significant by the fact that circulation, as I have shown, plays a major role in Wilde's notion of celebrity. In Wilde's model of celebrity enacted on his U.S. tour, the subject is located on the body, as a celebrity image whose value depends on its relation to other objects in the market. In *De Profundis*, the body is generally cast as an image subject to the gaze of others, but this is a bad thing, because the body, poorly-clothed and sickly, is debased, a source of shame. As such, it creates a disparity between the image and the celebrity. For example, Wilde recounts an episode in which he flees his hotel room while ill and attired in sleeping clothes. He cites Bosie's note (another one) that reads, *"It was an ugly moment for you."* Wilde agrees: "Ah! I felt it but too well" (887). Being a disfavored spectacle for others begets regret that the body is visible. At another moment, Wilde's body is displayed while being transferred between prisons:

> I had to stand on a centre platform of Clapham Junction in convict dress, and handcuffed, for the world to look at. I had been taken out of the Hospital Ward without a moment's notice being given to me. Of all possible objects I was the most grotesque. When people saw me they laughed.... That was, of course, before they knew who I was. As soon as they had been informed they laughed still more. For a half an hour I stood there in the grey November rain surrounded by a jeering mob. (937)

The passage emphasizes Wilde's to-be-looked-at-ness with the language of visuality, making him an object on public display. He is debased by his drab general-issue clothing, and by the bland, conformist hue of the rain. Weather, of course, is something no one can control; we are all equal in the eyes of a rainstorm. In these moments he has lost control over his public appearance—a situation contrasting with Wilde's carefully cultivated image while on his lecture tour. Indeed, during Wilde's prison term his brother sold off his beloved fur-trimmed coat, as if to symbolize the metamorphosis (Holland, *The Wilde Album* 68.)

In the same section of *De Profundis*, Wilde imagines an alternative to the model of celebrity that he had produced through his image. The debased image reveals a subject housed within the body. "Our very dress makes us grotesques. We are the zanies of sorrow. We are clowns whose hearts are broken" (937). This passage commences with passive voice; it is the clothing that makes Wilde into this object, rather than Wilde making himself into something. It progresses to a description of Wilde as grotesque object, and finally describes the inside of his body, his breaking heart. That is to say, the passage moves from the inability to control one's image to the inability to control one's interior. In fact, throughout *De Profundis* Wilde repeatedly insinuates that his debased image entails a relocating of attributes of the subject. He writes, "There is not a single degradation of the body which I must not try and make into a spiritualizing of the soul" (915). This avowal indicates that the spiritualized soul, the intangible subject, will have no connection to the body. Wilde sacrifices the body to perform himself as a subject.

The kind of subject that Wilde imagines, the nature of the kind of individual he fashions for himself after his disgrace, incorporates both the degraded image and the signifier of an extraordinary relationship to culture. Wilde's self-fashioning in *De Profundis* is perhaps best understood through Wilde's comparison of himself to Christ.[29] As Buckley puts it,

Wilde "refashions [Christ] quite arbitrarily in his own image as the 'artist in sympathy,' the arch-individualist, the determined Romantic, and the determined anti-Philistine" (3). What Buckley understates in this description is how visual display associates Christ with Wilde. *De Profundis* depicts Christ as a celebrity whose image has been debased as it is displayed. Wilde writes of "the crucifixion of the Innocent One before the eyes of his mother and the disciple whom he loved: the soldiers gambling and throwing dice for his clothes ... the terrible death by which he gave the world its most eternal symbol" (924). This passage links Wilde and Christ as two who suffer the same kinds of ignominy: the public display of their degenerated bodies, the scandal of their clothes. Wilde calls Christ a "symbol," further transforming him into a celebrity hieroglyph, though here it is a debased image that takes on the role of icon. This moment, moreover, echoes Wilde's claim to stand "in symbolic relations to the art and culture of [his] age" (912).[30] He shares with Christ the status of icon and degraded image.

De Profundis alters the kind of celebrity of Wilde's tour by introducing the idea of the celebrity as artist. Christ's "place is with the poets"; he "ranks with the poets" (923–924). Wilde claims Christ for the artists, and categorizes himself among them as well—fifteen years and many editions sold after the lecture tour. He writes, "I devoted myself to the Art" (883). Significantly, Christ's artistry is one of "imagination." Wilde claims, "The very basis of his nature was the same as that of the nature of the artist, an intense and flamelike imagination" (923). Here, Christ possesses a stable essence, an intangible aspect of the subject, demarcated by his imagination. His relations with people are marked by "imaginative sympathy." Indeed, imagination imbues every facet of his life. In fact, Christ is not just any artist or poet, but the "true precursor of the romantic movement in life" (923).

That the idea of imagination represents another departure from Wilde's earlier model of celebrity becomes clear when *De Profundis* suggests that imagination enables Christ to create an intangible subjectivity, one not specifically located in relation to the body. The imagination, then, is a very different kind of attribute of the subject than, say, taste, or a contract stipulating that Wilde wear certain outfits. To be sure, when Wilde refers to Christ's trade, writing, "Out of the carpenter's shop at Nazareth had come a personality," he suggests a physical construction, built with tools and wood (922). These tools, however, are subsequently turned back into intangibles: "Out of His own imagination entirely did Jesus of Nazareth create Himself" (929).[31] Indeed, the portrait of Christ in *De Profundis* is a surprisingly non-corporeal one. Arata points out that Wilde eschews much traditional and contemporary language of Christ's body, writing that Wilde's "Jesus is an oddly disembodied figure ... Wilde seldom avails himself of the vocabularies of decadence, eroticism, or even of physical beauty when he writes of Christ" (261). Avoiding language about Christ's corpus illuminates Wilde's new treatment of the subject, one that de-emphasizes the body.

Wilde writes, "Jesus of Nazareth create[s] Himself." Like Wilde's earlier model of celebrity, part of Christ's appeal is his self-creation. "Christ was not merely the supreme individualist, but he was the first individualist in history" (926). This individualism contrasts with Wilde's earlier revisions of nineteenth-century originality. Again, on Wilde's lecture tour, originality entails a capacity to incorporate and reconfigure cultural material. Similarly, Wilde's writings prior to *De Profundis* generally eschew the concept that originality is defined by a mind producing unique ideas. For example, Paul K. Saint-Amour reads Wilde's "The Portrait of Mr. W. H." to argue that Wilde refuses to privilege the popular version of originality. He considers the story "a parable of literary property," in which "ideas ... circulate like physical property" (96). In this conception, ideas can be transferred throughout culture, attached to different people, without losing value. The idea of original thought does not define the subject.

But in *De Profundis* individualism indicates a fixed quality, a stability that depends on restricting the influence of society. Wilde writes, "one only realizes one's soul by getting rid of ... all acquired culture, and all external possessions be they good or evil" (925). So while, like in *Dorian Gray*, external forces can gain access and wield influence over the subject, in this text Wilde imagines a boundary around that subject that would keep it uncontaminated. For example, *De Profundis* continually depicts Wilde's struggle to act as he wants to, or as he knows he should, usually regarding ridding himself of Bosie. The presence of another person impedes Wilde's desire to act in a way consistent with his true self. The text's wish for a fixed, bounded subject emerges in Wilde's repeated statements to the effect that his "ruin came, not from too great individualism of life, but from too little" (937). In other words, he blames his misfortune on his failure to cordon off his subjectivity. In this context, when Wilde writes that "most people are other people" (926), he implicates himself as one of "most people." He suggests that people absorb too much of others' personalities, and thus lose their own respective essences. Finally, he claims, he has surmounted this difficulty, writing that he achieved happiness as he "reached [his] soul in its ultimate essence" (926). (To think that for a similar statement he sentenced Sybil Vane to death!)

In this way Wilde portrays himself as ultimately establishing a stable foundation for his own subjectivity. In light of Wilde's earlier negotiations between the subject and the body, it makes sense to wonder where this subject resides. Thus we come to the inescapable fact that Wilde narrates *De Profundis* from jail. His body is taken out of the equation; it remains behind walls, obscured from public view except for brief exposures as a debased, pitiable object. So Wilde's claim to have produced himself as a true, circumscribed subject is only made when the body has ceased to circulate or be on display. Throughout *De Profundis* Wilde thrusts aside the need for a body. He states, "the thing that I have to do . . . is to absorb into my nature all that has been done to me, to make it a part of me . . ." (915–916). Here the substantial word "absorb" might hint that Wilde is re-inscribing the subject within the body, following a model akin to Carlyle or Dickens. However, he is thinking of the world's effects on the subject in the past—that is, in the present perfect (passive), as in the phrase, "has been done." There are no current effects. The body is sheltered. Indeed, at another moment Wilde belittles the idea of a relationship between the body and time. "The past, the present, and the future are but one moment in the sight of God. . . . The Imagination can transcend them" (956). Clearly, the body here functions as a subordinate to the imagination. If it were circulating in public, though, it would impede this version of the subject, its presence thwarting the ability to imagine oneself transcending time. After all, normally one is not in prison, one does circulate in society, and so one is reminded of one's corporeality. Thus the genre of the prison letter undermines Wilde's project of reconceiving the subject. In the end, *De Profundis* conveys its resignation to the impossibility of producing oneself as a subject that could be attached to a body that circulates publicly.

Instead, the text places its hope in that which does circulate: the text. As simple private correspondence, *De Profundis* would likely have a restricted circle of movement. However, as a text dressed as private correspondence, but really intended for many readers, which sounds here like a critical-biographical sketch, there like a treatise on aesthetic and cultural theory, now like a diary, then like a lovers' quarrel, which has a celebrity author's name attached to it, and which, according to Small, might have been intended as the basis of a later work, it becomes an object that circulates in the market. It is a commodity, on the market, accruing readers even now.

Of his eventual release from jail, Wilde writes, "Still, in the very fact that people will recognize me wherever I go, and know all about my life, as far as its follies go, I can discern something good for me. It will force on me the necessity of again asserting myself as an artist, and as soon as I possibly can" (917). The retreat from public visibility into a space of the subject explicitly means a retreat into an aesthetic realm. So, in several ways, *De Profundis* is an ideal location for Wilde's version of the subject. It is not a body, and so not subject to the degradations he and Christ experience in the text. Like the imagination, it can "transcend" the past, present, and future, always existing in its own unfolding of narrative time. It "contains" Wilde's treasured aesthetic musings, and even includes his trademark epigrammatic wit: "All bad art is the result of good intentions" (941). Both its movements and its content can be, and are, influenced by others, of course. Partly this results from Wilde's premature death and the text's posthumous publication, partly from Wilde's trusting Robbie Ross to execute his estate faithfully, and partly because "personal" content was edited out in every edition before 1962 (Small 88). Even so, it could be perhaps hoped that, with Wilde's celebrity name attached, fidelity to the author's written intentions would win out eventually.

Most significantly, this text, despite its pretense of being private, is mass reproducible, and so can circulate indefinitely. This is crucial to Wilde. Even imprisoned, Wilde never fails to assign value to the individual based on whether his or her subjectivity is put in relation to that of others. For example, he proclaims that the significance of Christ's imagination rests in its enabling his compassion toward people, asserting, "He realised in the entire sphere of human relations that imaginative sympathy which in the sphere of Art is the sole secret of creation" (923). One can only create art if one can imagine the situation of others, he says. Extended logically, this suggests that one must compose art with the audience in mind. Wilde writes, "while Christ did not say to men 'Live for others,' he pointed out that there was no difference at all between the lives of others and one's own life" (926). Here engagement with the world is hardly avoidable. People circulate, says Christ; and as we know, for Wilde value is determined relationally. As we have seen, in *De Profundis* the idea of an intangible and impermeable subjectivity is only shown as possible when the body is taken out of the equation, debased and/or squirreled away. Since there must be circulation for there to be meaning, however, *De Profundis* suggests that the text, instead, embodies the subject. The text can convey the subject into the market where it will contact others.

Thus the text inherits the role played by the iconic image of Wilde on tour. Once, asked about the audience of *The Ballad of Reading Gaol* (1896), Wilde quipped that it should be published in a journal called *Reynolds's*, explaining, "It circulates widely among the criminal classes . . . so I shall be read by my peers" (*Letters* 581). Wilde's witty play on "peers," which refers to those at one's level either social, intellectual, or, here, legal, implies that, in fact, he values his writing, and thus, his subjectivity, precisely because of its relationship to others, as that is how its value is generated.

Wilde's conceiving of a subject that resides within the mass-circulating text supports the idea of a Wilde whose art is not supposed to exist on a separate plane from the world. This repudiates certain tenets Wilde has been supposed to represent for over a century. For example, far from supporting the idea in the "Preface to *Dorian Gray*" that "No artist has ethical sympathies," the approach to society that emerges from Wilde's celebrity negotiations insists on engaging with the world—an ethical position by itself.[32] So whereas Wilde might have appreciated being associated with the aesthetic catchphrase "art for art's sake," we misread Wilde when we read that statement to indicate that the object of art is to be created without regard for its audience. In fact Wilde values both art and the artist for their public status. Really, one might say that art is merely a single component of Wilde's idea of celebrity, which is based on the idea of an object—be it image or text—circulating in public.

By arguing that *De Profundis* suggests the idea of a text as a bounded entity that conveys the subject, it may sound as if I am nudging Wilde in the direction of high modernism, which is, to generalize, notoriously suspicious of the body and concerned with establishing a kind of disembodied authorship. I am. Wilde's final retreat from public visibility into a textual model of subjectivity implies a retreat into an aesthetic realm. This version of interiority matches what Nancy Armstrong describes as the "unseen interiorities [that] novelists Woolf, Joyce, Lawrence and others, equated with aesthetic space itself" (48). Furthermore, critics point to the 1895 Wilde trials as a turning point for sexuality, the moment when the English world begins to categorize individuals according to sexual preference, and thus also a moment when homosexuality becomes more covert.[33] I see Wilde's trials and their subsequent developments—including the tragedy of Wilde's imprisonment and his resulting, quickly subsequent death—as helping bring about a modernist model of having the subject participate in the market without the inconvenience of sending a body out there. Thus, Wilde's texts, in their desire to construct an identity that is neither visible nor reproducible, foreshadow the high modernists to come, and may have even warned of the necessity of developing that unseen interiority. For the modernists, Peter Gay writes, Wilde is "a wry kind of model" (68). But when he writes of Wilde's fate that "neither the autonomy of art nor the sovereignty of the artist was much advanced by it," he approaches the problem too literally. Modernism followed Wilde's example insofar as its writings do create a textually based idea of the exceptional personality that resides above and beyond the text, on a different, disembodied plane; the subject participates in the market through the artifact while the author retreats into the mysterious life of the coterie. From the perspective of *De Profundis,* modernism emerges as an inversion of the form of celebrity that Wilde fashions on tour, performing a stereotype of himself. His embodied model of a signature style becomes simply displaced from the image of the individual to the text, which can circulate without impeaching its sources. Modernism's production of the author, its cult of the author, may in this way be said to emanate from Wilde's sufferings of the slings and arrows of celebrity and his negotiations in response.

CHAPTER 2

James Joyce and Modernist Exceptionalism

This chapter arrives at the heart of the matter of this book, exploring celebrity's mutually enabling relationship with high modernism via the works of James Joyce. Joyce, I will show, picked up where Wilde left off, in the sense that he followed Wilde's model of self-fashioning in ways that appropriate, mimic, and revise celebrity discourse. Of course, Joyce never reached Wilde's particular pinnacle of fame, though it might now seem like Joyce has always been a celebrity author. In our time, his image appears on T-shirts, rock album covers, tote bags, bookstore chain mugs, Irish postal stamps, and an episode of *The Simpsons*. But in his day, Joyce's fame, like his readership, was not particularly widespread. True, Joyce was the subject of a 1934 *Time* cover story, but during his lifetime and for a period after his death in 1941 there was scant information about his private life available to the public.[1] It is the fact that his writings turn him into an irreproducible figure of the modernist author par excellence, the zenith of modernist exceptionalism—rather than the celebrity status he achieved in life—that makes Joyce the perfect nexus of the intertwining histories of modernist literature and celebrity culture that this book explores. Indeed, as Fritz Senn notes, "Joyce has been selected a prototype" for modern authorship by critics (70). We can think of Joyce's relationship to high modernism now, seventy years after his death, as an echo of Wilde's complex relationship to aestheticism at the time he set off for America over a century ago. In each case, issues of originality—the degree to which the figure generates the movement in question—become irrelevant as the writer performs and realizes his personification of a cultural movement.

In this chapter, I examine Joyce's use of the logic of celebrity to constitute his identity as author of, and in, *Ulysses*, the work that guaranteed this reputation. Rather than showing that *Ulysses* is "about" celebrity in the way of Beerbohm's *Zuleika Dobson*, I am primarily examining the ways that the explosion of celebrity as a popular phenomenon informs the novel. My analysis of celebrity in *Ulysses* revises the way we look at Joyce's manipulation of the autobiographical figure Stephen Dedalus; at the schema, the chapter-by-chapter guides for reading *Ulysses* that Joyce disseminated and that have actually been overlooked as objects of critical study themselves; and, most of all and most central to this volume, at Joyce's legendary technical mastery—his stylistic variations.

Between Wilde's death and *Ulysses*'s publication, and specifically during the years 1914 to 1922 when Joyce was writing the novel, popular culture—the cinema especially—was churning out a historically unprecedented version of celebrity. Critics consense upon this moment as when traditional achievement constituted the basis of celebrity. "In this period," writes Schickel, "the public ceased to insist that there be an obvious correlation between achievement and fame" ("His Picture in the Papers" 125). That is, in Braudy's terminology, fame, which was dependent on traditional hierarchies of class, was transforming into celebrity, dependent on the mass reproduction of images. In particular, the variety of celebrity most visible and most documented—the Hollywood variety—was based on the notion that each image of a star refers to an "identity that is constituted elsewhere, in the discourses 'outside' the [text]" (deCordova 19). In other words, cinematic images of actors such as Valentino or Mary Pickford were meant to combine with advertising and promotion to evoke an individual who lives outside of the film, in the real world. The Hollywood star system made this possible with its own aesthetics and its marketing strategies. That this new version of celebrity became as widespread as it did at the moment of high modernism—Joyce's moment—is, of course, no coincidence.

Joyce, I will argue, manipulates this version of celebrity in his self-production as author, supplanting the celebrity image with the written text. Distrusting the idea of "discourses 'outside'" the text, Joyce turns *Ulysses* into an object that simultaneously embodies and refers not to the celebrity but to the author—an idealized, non-corporeal entity. The author serves both as origin and referent of *Ulysses,* and moreover, as a discourse that controls textual meaning. By establishing the author as both a function of the writing and the means of decoding it, Joyce enacts a fantasy of a complete and bounded subjectivity, uncontaminated by and impermeable to the outside world.

This effect is, in fact, summarized by a caricature: César Abin's 1932 image, published in *transition,* turns Joyce into a question mark, an embodiment of enigma and inscrutability resting amid the clouds over the globe. In this caricature Joyce becomes a sign whose only interpretation is its uninterpretability as it hovers above the rest of us. His authorial identity is distilled into a formula meant to be both recognizable and indecipherable: the same logic of celebrity identified by Barthes's discussion of Einstein and embodied by Wilde. In that Joyce was the first to use the celebrity logic to transform the author in such a grandiose and overt way, I consider his production of the author the best demonstration of how modernism enabled the popular celebrity to serve as Barthes's "Platonic Idea." The modernist author, and, by extension, the celebrity, emerge from the text and context of *Ulysses* as parallel productions of a singular individual, above and apart from mass culture: this is what I am calling the modernist exception.

Styling the Author

In the introduction to this book I mention that Huyssen portrays modernism as an art striving to set itself apart from what it saw as a degraded popular culture, an art that challenges that "kind of discourse which insists on the categorical distinction between high art and mass culture" (viii). But I also discuss how his intervention has in some respects had a constrictive influence. In their very efforts to bridge the "great divide," many critics following in Huyssen's wake reproduce precisely the binary between highbrow modernism and lowbrow mass culture that his work interrogates. The field of Joyce studies exemplifies this circuit. Lawrence Rainey, Paul Delaney, and Joyce Wexler, for example, all compare the material production and marketing practices of *Ulysses* with the material production and advertising of popular commodities, but they stop short of exploring the parallel representational techniques of these high and low objects. Another well-known example is the *Marketing Modernisms* essay

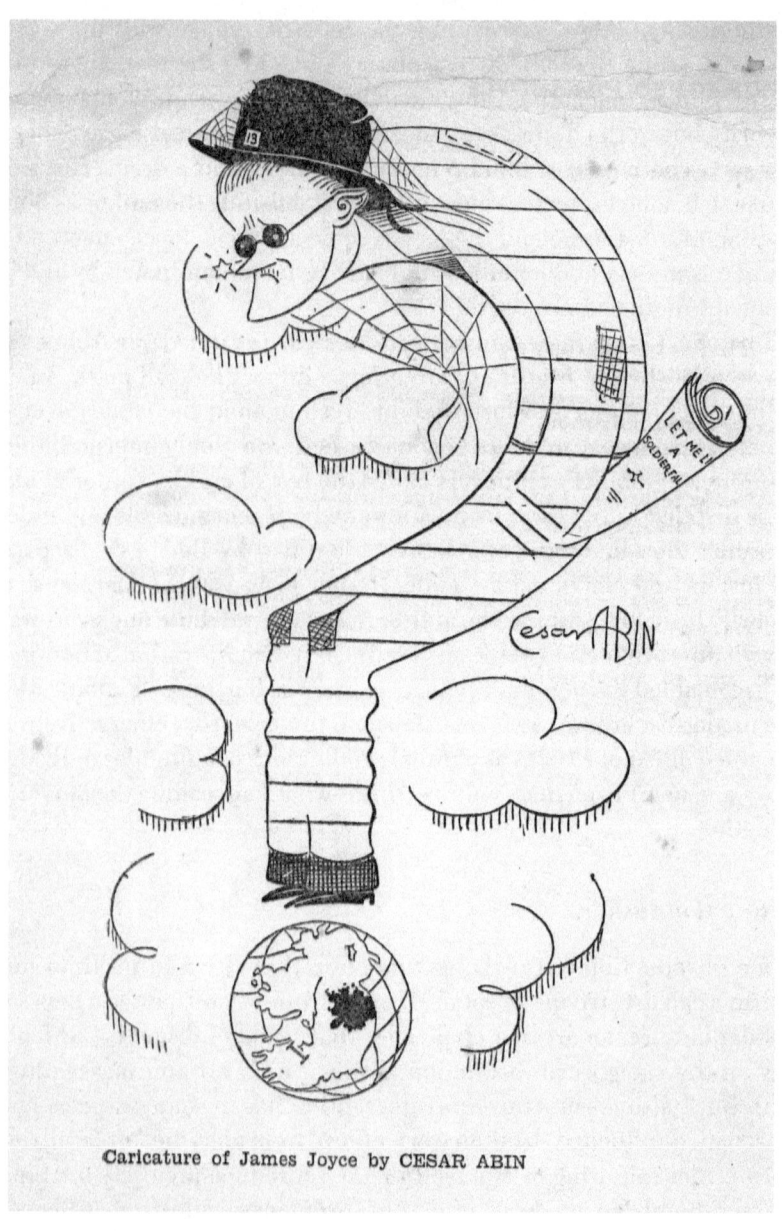

FIGURE 2.1. Caricature of James Joyce by César Abin, originally published in *transition*, March 1932.

co-authored by Maurizia Boscagli and Enda Duffy, "Joyce's Face," which analyzes the photographs of Joyce in the *Time* piece, and examines Joyce's author-production using contextual materials, rather than his writing's stylistic characteristics. Such critical projects pave the way for my project; they address the way Joyce represents himself as author without identifying how his writing participates in this process.

Joyce constitutes a rich vein for materialist modernism, and has been used to rewrite the history of modernism by examining its revision of cultural value. For example, Jaffe points out that Joyce's name was appropriately famous to be enlisted to advertise the work of T. S. Eliot. He writes:

> Owning the book and reading it, as publicists know, is only a temporary stopover in the greater circulation of the author's name. The reach of the name *James Joyce* during this period may best illustrate this point. Because of the troubled publication history of Joyce's work, there was an inescapable imbalance between those who knew of Joyce and those who knew Joyce's texts first hand. In the October 1922 *Dial*, the issue preceding the *Waste Land* number, the editors puff Eliot's coming attraction with a comparison to *Ulysses*, which comes out of this context: "It is not improbable that the appearance of *The Waste Land* will rank with that of *Ulysses* in the degree of interest it will call forth." Why was this judged to be effective publicity? After all, who at this time in the United States or England was reading a complete copy of Joyce's *Ulysses*? (*Modernism* 73)

It seems that in 1922 the name Joyce, along with that of his novel *Ulysses*, fell familiarly on enough ears to make it an advertising instrument for readers of *The Dial*. This, as Jaffe points out, belies how difficult it was to actually obtain Joyce's books in Anglophone countries in 1922. One wonders with Jaffe: why was *Ulysses* used in the Eliot "puff"?

Part of Jaffe's answer lies in his argument that an "ideology of scarcity" underwrites modernism, that delimited textual circulation becomes part of the authorial signature (*Modernism* 65). This we can modify by considering the wider circulation of Joyce's name and its attached discourse of cultural recognizability. The *Dial* audience was large by "little magazine" standards.[2] Its readers were the literati, in a wide—if not the widest possible—definition. For them, the brand name Joyce would conjure up a mixture of modernist difficulty, virtuosity, and elusiveness. We see this combination of elements summarized in an invocation to Joyce in the classic movie *The Third Man* (1949), released a quarter century after the *Dial* reference and eight years after Joyce's death. In Carol Reed's film, Holly Martins (Joseph Cotton), a writer of cowboy novels, is briefly mistaken for a figure of high culture. Consequently, the British cultural council invites him to address a literary gathering. There, a steely-eyed Austrian with a *Mitteleuropa* accent asks Martins his opinion of "stream of consciousness." Martins is unfamiliar with that term. The inquisitor follows that with the question, "Mr. James Joyce, where would you put him?" distinctly intoning the syllables of the author's name as if it communicates secret meaning. Martins stares at him blankly. The man persists, demanding, "Where would you put Mr. James Joyce? In what category?" Before Martins can yet again fail to reply, one of the movie's villains arrives to menace Martins and the thriller plot resumes.

Here, the name Joyce and his famous formula for representing interiority, spoken with a specifically elite-culture pronunciation, become a test of specialized knowledge that separates the intelligentsia from the pedestrian. Indeed, the host has introduced Martins to the audience as being from "the other side." This phrase ostensibly refers to the other side of the Atlantic, but the film also repeatedly suggests that as a pulp novelist Martins is from the other side—the wrong side—of the great divide.[3] This elitism of readership corresponds, of course, to the elitism insinuated by reference to the author and his work. As Ellmann writes, "To have read *Ulysses*, or parts of it, became [in the years following its publication] the mark of the knowledgeable expatriate" (*James Joyce* 527). Rod Rosenquist puts it that the work was "a cultural monument long before it had a substantial readership" (5). Joyce's easy identification with elite culture and high modernist technique became a badge for his enthusiasts.

To explain how this particular reputation of author and work is created, I supplement the contextual studies of Joyce by focusing on the textual Joyce—the author in, rather than of, *Ulysses*, the idealized author generated by the writing, rather than the biographical entity of the material world. Foucault invites such an approach when he writes, "We are used to thinking that the author is so different from all other men, and so transcendent with regard to all languages, that, as soon as he speaks, meaning begins to proliferate . . . indefinitely. The truth is quite the contrary . . . the author does not precede the works" (221). Foucault points out that the author does not simply create a text; rather the text itself generates the author as discourse, a special class of being to serve as the source of complex, polysemic language. Describing this discourse as a "series of specific and complex operations" (216), Foucault indicates the kind of author that Joyce produces via the idiosyncratic blend of literary styles that narrates *Ulysses*.

Style, to Joyce scholars, usually means the overt, opaque aspect of narrative, that which Derek Attridge calls "the use of formal features that . . .

draw attention to themselves in some way" (152). In *Ulysses*, the styles that "draw attention to themselves" tend to draw readerly attention *away* from the diegesis, to borrow a narratological term common in cinema studies. That is, the formal characteristics of *Ulysses* draw attention away from the novel's world of fictional people, places, and things, and toward an extra-diegetic (or non-diegetic) space, toward aspects of the text that do not represent that fictional realm, or exist within it. The idea of the diegesis, in film, may be best understood by cinema music. The music to which John Travolta dances in a *Saturday Night Fever* nightclub is part of the story; the character Tony Manero hears it: diegetic. The music played on the *Rocky* soundtrack during the montages of Sylvester Stallone training for his next fight is not part of the story; Rocky does not hear it: extradiegetic. Translated to written narratives, we might think about how fictional characters "hear" spoken dialogue (diegetic) but do not "hear" the descriptions of the narrative (extradiegetic); they know what other characters say to them but do not know how their surroundings are described. (Obviously, this breaks down somewhat in first-person narratives or variations of internal monologue, free indirect discourse, etc.) Specifically in terms of *Ulysses*, we might think about how Leopold Bloom "knows" about 1904 Dublin (diegetic) but does not "know" he is cast as a modern Odysseus (extradiegetic).

These distinctions are significant because Joyce's style becomes legible only when one considers the rationale justifying the formal changes made in each episode. Often these rationales refer to Homer, the perfect example of extradiegesis. The "Cyclops" chapter, for example, is the novel's only example of first-person narration. This is a joke, an extended pun; the narrating "I" playfully refers to the one "eye" of Homer's Cyclops. The sudden switch into first person thus gestures beyond the fictional events of *Ulysses* (diegesis) and calls attention to Joyce's witticism (extradiegesis). The joke's punchline is ultimately the author; the pun on "I" shifts the basis of textual meaning onto the methods by which the author turns that narrative into elite literature. Similar examples abound. The boldfaced, capitalized headline-esque subtitles that appear interspersed throughout the "Aeolus" chapter befit, readers may think, a scene in a newspaper office.[4] Although it is tempting to imagine Stephen or Bloom thinking up these interjections, they cannot be attributed to any one character's thought, as no single character remains present for the chapter's duration. The device of the subtitles, again, points toward the author's decision to justify a stylistic change in reference to non-diegetic material.

The stylistic changes in *Ulysses*, by continually asking readers to guess Joyce's extradiegetic rationale for that change, create the idea of the author. Franco Moretti writes, "In Joyce, when one episode is presented in two or three or fifty different styles, the procedure is not based on any codified literary motivation" (*Signs Taken for Wonders* 206). To Moretti, the changes in narrative mode never become legible in terms of character psychology, unlike, say, the stylistic shifts of modernists such as Woolf or Faulkner, which invoke varying interiorities. Although the "Nausikaa" and "Eumaeus" chapters might seem to contradict this, Moretti's main point—namely, that *Ulysses*'s styles fulfill a different purpose than those of a novel like Faulkner's *The Sound and the Fury*—holds true. Rather than refer to the vicissitudes and vagaries of consciousness, Joyce's stylistic changes shift the text onto a register of meaning that signifies what lies beyond the narrative.[5]

These stylistic fluctuations thus invoke Joyce's virtuosity, his mastery over multiple forms of language. This becomes apparent in the first half of "Nausikaa," which comprises clichés of Irish femininity drawn from Victorian-era fiction and advertising:

> The waxen pallor of her face was almost spiritual in its ivorylike purity though her rosebud mouth was a genuine Cupid's bow, Greekly perfect. Her hands were of finely veined alabaster with tapering fingers and white as lemonjuice and queen of ointments could make them . . . (286)

Upping the ante, *Ulysses*'s next chapter, "Oxen of the Sun," delivers a series of imitations of English writers, including a section of sentimental prose in the manner of Charles Dickens:

> And as her loving eyes behold her babe she wishes only one blessing more, to have her dear Doady there with her to share her joy, to lay in his arms that mite of God's clay, the fruit of their lawful embraces. He is older now (you and I may whisper it) . . . (343)

In such passages Joyce demonstrates not only his ability to mimic other voices but also the way those voices impose a limited, ideologically oriented, interpretation of the events of the narrative. To Moretti, these styles are shown as "equally *irrelevant* as interpretations of reality" (206). As it reveals the failings of the model being imitated, Joyce's text subordinates these conventional styles to the author's mimetic capability.

Indeed, Joyce's stylistic fluctuations have generally inspired critics to exalt *Ulysses* for its brilliance without considering the implications underlying the fact that Joyce himself has led them to draw that conclusion. As Moretti puts it, "*Ulysses* has for a long time been the hunting ground of a critical trend that is satisfied with recognizing and cataloging its stylistic procedures, and which, in so doing, becomes inebriated, and in its euphoria extols the novel's 'wealth', and reads and describes it as an unorthodox but magnificent summary of the history of literature and of rhetoric" (204). Moretti implies that *Ulysses*'s stylistic virtuosity is responsible for a critical school that continues in Joyce's author-production by making Joyce the culmination and bedrock of all analysis. In such a system the author functions as not only the origin of the novel but also the last critical word on its meaning. This manipulation of the reading process makes style the trademark of the author and validates Joyce's claim to originality by serving notice that one exceptional individual produced the book.

The visual component of Joyce's narrative shifts both reinforces this logic and demonstrates its kinship with the popular logic of celebrity. The frequent changes in narrative mode from the "Sirens" chapter (XI) onward are announced by changes in the visual surface of the text itself. Other examples include the "Aeolus" headlines, the overture that commences "Sirens," the script format in "Circe," the questions and responses that make up the catechistic style of "Eumaeus," and the nearly unbroken block of continuous text that comprises the forty-odd pages of "Penelope." These visual characteristics make *Ulysses* recognizable at a glance as Joyce's work. Joyce himself is reported to have compared the visual, instantly recognizable aspects of *Finnegans Wake* to the illuminations in *The Book of Kells*, saying "I would like it to be possible to pick up any page of my book and know at once what book it is" (Ellmann, *James Joyce* 545). Joyce uses visual style, typographical variation, to fashion his text into an object of the gaze, therefore fashioning himself in relation to that object, as "transcendent in regard to languages," in Foucault's words (221). In this respect, what Frederic Jameson describes as "the high modernist ideology of style—what is as unique and unmistakable as your own fingerprints" (17), like Jaffe's imprimatur of the author, operates much like the celebrity image. It elevates the author of *Ulysses* above the ordinary and anonymous language user—even with a quick glance at the page—much the same way that Wilde's particular style of dress sets him apart.

That Joyce's hypervisual formal play operates as a trademark is underlined, even, by the appearance of the Bass Ale bottle in "Oxen," the chapter that includes Joyce's most ostentatious demonstration of technique. There, Leopold Bloom becomes transfixed by the "scarlet label" (340). Although Bloom's fascination suggests his deficient sense of Irish nationalism, Bass being a British product, the text emphasizes that the image represents a distinct, instantly identifiable object: "he had been staring hard at a certain amount of number one Bass bottled by Messrs Bass and Co at Burton-on-Trent which happened to be situated among a lot of others right opposite to where he was." Joyce is sure to depict the way the visual trademark elevates one object above the anonymous rest, drawing attention to his own stylistic visual apparatus.

The parallel to Wilde—namely, the use of a unique and immediately identifiable visual style—recasts one of the most noticeable and discussed features of Joyce's writing: the difficulty it poses for readers. Sean Latham writes that *Ulysses* "carves out a place for itself in the complexly structured space of culture by being difficult, trading on a form of cultural capital that will secure Joyce's status as a professional author who differs qualitatively from the middlebrow hack" (120). Jaffe notes that obscurity pays modernist dividends: "It is inaccessibility that gains wider notice" (*Modernism* 14). As I have suggested, however, it is also possible to view the instantly recognizable qualities of a text like *Ulysses* as instantly accessible. Once one recognizes Joyce's formula—the "$E=mc^2$" of Joyce—then one does not need to read the text. One already grasps the code of exceptionalism. The visual surface of the text serves, at a glance, to refer to the final word—Joyce's exceptionalism.

"Peeping and prying into greenroom gossip of the day"

This consideration of the textually generated presence of the author suggests that we re-read the character of Stephen Dedalus, that we reconsider the fact that *Ulysses* features a character invested with biographical traces of Joyce. Indeed, the novel's initial chapters, which are focused on Stephen, duped early readers into thinking of *Ulysses* as a sequel to the earlier chronicle of Stephen, the *Kunstlerroman* for which Joyce earned prior accolades; *A Portrait of the Artist as a Young Man* is a work that many readers understood and many continue to understand as autobiography, thus leading readers such as Ezra Pound to expect more of the same from *Ulysses*.[6] In this section I will argue that, perhaps counterintuitively, Joyce's manipulation of the trope of the autobiographical figure makes it impossible to locate the author of *Ulysses* within a character, within a diegetic body. Stephen Dedalus makes it impossible, then, for readers to embody the author, to locate the author as subject within a physiological object. In gesturing toward an exceptional personality outside, above, and in charge of the narrative, *Ulysses* does not point toward the historical Joyce who actually penned the novel. Far from it. The style of *Ulysses* idealizes an author outside of time and unconstrained by material conditions, a figure who therefore exists in marked contrast to Stephen. My examination of the "Scylla and Charibdis" chapter of *Ulysses* will show how the novel uses Stephen and his theory of *Hamlet* to imagine an incorporeal author who is necessarily outside the narrative, but not anterior to the text; this author is created simultaneously with the text. This disembodied conception of the author provides Joyce with a means of placing himself within the text and putting himself in command of its meaning while imagining himself apart from earthly concerns.

"Scylla and Charibdis" depicts a discussion of *Hamlet* that leads to Stephen's debate with Dublin literati over whether an author's life unlocks the meaning of a work of literature. Stephen's interlocutors propose that literary texts articulate the author's Platonic "essence" rather than his tangible existence. Stephen maintains that the reader can and should grasp the writer's material and psychological life from the writing. He bases his argument on what John P. McCombe describes as "the notion that a narrative of William Shakespeare's life could be reconstituted through a careful interpretation of his art" (717).[7] Stephen invokes accepted facts of Shakespeare's biography in order to speculate that Shakespeare's wife was unfaithful with his brother, and that this infidelity spurred Shakespeare to create Hamlet's father, the betrayed and murdered King of Denmark, as an autobiographical character.

Since the biographical approach to reading is advocated by Stephen, Joyce seems to make it available as a legitimate way of reading *Ulysses* as well. The chapter's quantity of factual, historical, and autobiographical detail might agree; "Scylla and Charibdis" relies on more characters and events drawn from 1904 Ireland than do most other chapters of *Ulysses*. The chapter situates Stephen among historical Dublin personages who go by their non-fictional names (whereas many characters in *Ulysses* are pseudonymed but historically identifiable, including the poet George Russell (A. E.) and the critic John Eglinton). The doings of other historical figures, including Yeats, Lady Gregory and John Millington Synge, are discussed as if all are acquainted. Such details, added to Stephen's biographical reading of Shakespeare, invite readers to exploit Joyce's material life for exegetical purposes.

Not so fast: *Ulysses* proceeds to offer resistance to Stephen's treatment of *Hamlet* and its underlying argument that literature can be read as a window into the author's biography. For example, Stephen's approach rankles Russell, who calls investigations into Shakespeare's life "the speculation of schoolboys for schoolboys," thereby deriding the impulse to read writers' lives into their work as an unrefined and (literally and figuratively) academic form of analysis (152). He fulminates against "this prying into the family life of a great man." The exercise is: "Interesting only to the parish clerk. I mean we have the plays. I mean when we read the poetry of *King Lear* what is it to us how the poet lived?" (155). Russell believes that the author's private life and physical existence should play no part in the analysis of literature. Naturally, readers might reflexively see Stephen's voice as trumping others when it comes to aesthetic theory. However, Russell's stance receives tacit support from Stephen's vexed attitude toward his own argument. Stephen's ambivalences emerge first as he reminds himself that he is fudging dates (173), and then as he ultimately disavows his biographical reading (175).[8] Russell's disdain and Stephen's waffling combine to destabilize the interpretive authority of an author's biography.

By denouncing all the "peeping and prying into greenroom gossip of the day," Russell denounces public interest in the publicly visible Shakespeare, invalidating any investigation into the historical person who performs as a body on stage but has a private, backstage, greenroom life that infuses his work with meaning. Where Stephen's identification of Shakespeare with the cuckolded king in *Hamlet* virtually transforms the playwright into an object of the public gaze, King Hamlet, Russell treats Shakespeare only as the playwright who labors behind the scenes. When considered against the backdrop of celebrity culture, such anxiety about public visibility is logically seen as a product of 1922, the year of *Ulysses*'s publication, rather than of 1904, the year in which the narrative is set. By 1922, celebrity, the Hollywood version in particular, was a public phenomenon. As Marshall notes, "Celebrity itself generated an entire industry by the second decade of the twentieth century, with the emergence of movie fan magazines . . . that openly celebrated movie stars and their lives, subjects far removed from nineteenth-century delineations of heroism and invention" (8–9). Investigation into the author's private life, it seems, veers too close for Joyce's comfort to a twentieth-century discourse of popular celebrity that is notoriously interested in the relationship between the visible and hidden spheres of a famous individual's life. Correspondingly, as *Ulysses* discredits the idea of biographical criticism, it draws a curtain between writer and audience. Via Russell, cultural concerns about celebrity seep into the "Scylla and Charybdis" discussion of biographical criticism.

But Russell is not given the final say in this debate. Neither does *Ulysses* quite corroborate his stance. By advocating for a notion of the author as a repository of Platonic ideas, Russell retains the idea that the author's life is the origin of the work and is therefore more important than what is immanent to the text. Russell claims, "The supreme question about a work of art is out of how deep a life does it spring. The painting of Gustave Moreau is the painting of ideas. The deepest poetry of Shelley, the words of Hamlet bring our minds into contact with the eternal wisdom, Plato's world of ideas" (152). Eglinton agrees with Russell, saying, "We know nothing [of Shakespeare] but that he lived and suffered," assuming that knowledge of Shakespeare's sufferings is universally understood from the plays (159). Such remarks argue that artistic production reveals the author's interiority specifically, which supposedly exists outside and prior to its textual expression. So where Stephen invokes the author's physical existence, his interlocutors assume the author's spiritual existence. In the end, both sides of this debate believe that a literary work arises from and refers to an author outside and prior to the text. Both therefore subordinate the work to the author, making the writings important for what they reveal about the author's experiences, whether tangible or psychological.

But *Ulysses* constructs a subtler model of authorship. It overturns this priority of author over text and makes the author the writing's antecedent. The text performs this inversion in, for example, the narrative intrusion that recurs in "Scylla and Charibdis." Throughout *Ulysses*, Stephen's presence occasions brief interruptions of the third-person narration, fleeting passages when Stephen's interior monologue suddenly appears, without narratorial introduction or comment. In "Scylla and Charibdis," such instances are often formed in the imperative, second-person voice. These phrases differ typographically and contrast syntactically with the third-person narrative that dominates the chapter. They seem to be remarks that Stephen directs toward himself (diegetic), though we might also read these as transcriptions of Joyce talking to himself while composing the novel, inserting into the text language from outside of the narrative events (extradiegetic). For example, after Stephen begins his explication of *Hamlet* by conjuring Shakespeare's initial meeting with Anne Hathaway, the novel presents this string of notations:

Local colour. Work in all you know. Make them accomplices. (154)

Is this Stephen reminding himself to employ the power of visual and historical detail in his argument—to incorporate as much factual detail as he can about Shakespeare's youth, Stratford-upon-Avon, Elizabethan England, and so on? Or is this Joyce pushing himself to do so in his novel—to exploit his factual knowledge of the people and places of 1904 Dublin? It reads as both. Stephen and Joyce's interior monologues coincide perfectly to create a doubling effect, character overlaid with author, two voices in unison. However, if we understand the second-person "you" more literally, we end up with another, somewhat more fanciful, explanation: that with these words, Joyce, outside the narrative, urges Stephen, inside the narrative, to "work in" all the "local colour" he knows. This latter interpretation turns the events of the novel into a performance that Joyce is watching and whose outcome he can influence by goading Stephen. In each of these readings, this passage links Stephen's interiority to the voice of an author who is outside the narrative.

Joyce integrates more reflexive elements into this doubling of author and character, thus further teasing readers familiar with Joyce's history with the idea that Stephen flatly represents the author. The term "local colour," for example, recalls Joyce's obsession with accurate details about the specific time and locale of his narratives and thus endows Stephen's own narration with a famously "Joycean" conceit.[9] Indeed, the second-person intrusions in "Scylla and Charibdis" often implicate Stephen as the future author of *Ulysses*. As Russell, Eglinton, and Mr. Best discuss a literary party to which Stephen is clearly not invited, the third-person narration is interrupted by the words: "See this. Remember." (158). The imperative mood, again, suggests that Stephen is enjoining himself to take note and remember this moment; again, these words can simultaneously be understood as Joyce compelling himself to "see" the events of his past as he composes the novel years later. In other words, the two voices again merge.

The reflexivity intensifies as the chapter lengthens, making the events of the chapter vaguely echo Stephen's *Hamlet* theory. Stephen considers *Hamlet* a variation of a revenge play, a work in which Shakespeare imagines asking his actual son Hamnet (known to have died before the initial production of the tragedy) to punish those who have made him a cuckold. If, indeed, the injunction "See this. Remember." is a phrase that alludes to Stephen's mental recording of the chapter's events as well as Joyce's remembering it, then the words imply a sense of insult at not meriting an invitation—an insult shared by character and writer. The insult fuels its own revenge play. *Ulysses* of course famously portrays dozens of Dublin citizens—some recognizable by name, others thinly disguised—in a not terribly flattering light.[10] That Stephen of 1904 will become the writer of the novel and thus carry out this revenge is again suggested as he leaves the building thinking to himself: "One day in the national library we had a discussion. Shakes" (176). This satirical synopsis of "Scylla and Charibdis" itself constitutes yet another moment merging character and composer.[11] It is worth noting, furthermore, that those double-voiced statements first crop up two chapters earlier, in "Aeolus." There, Stephen (it seems) has thoughts such as: "Dublin. I have much, much to learn" (119). This moment implies Stephen as a refracted figure for Joyce the writer; it reminds readers that the vignette about two nuns that Stephen is recounting to his newspapermen companions would fit in well as a *Dubliners* story, full of local color and lacking dramatic action as it is. It was in fact June of 1904 that Joyce began work on "The Sisters" (nuns are sisters)—at the behest of none other than Russell;[12] June 16, 1904, is the date on which *Ulysses* takes place. The continued doubling of Joyce and Stephen through narrative clearly means to set up Stephen as the author, in a stage prior to the writing of *Ulysses*.

But the novel prevents readers from carrying this hypothesis too far. Joyce hints Stephen will become the author of *Ulysses*, but only to create the figure of the author who dangles this possibility and then rescinds it. To conceive of Stephen as a younger incarnation of Joyce would run counter to the strategies of authorial production that "Scylla and Charibdis" pursues. Instead, Joyce collapses past and present. In the phrase "See this. Remember" Joyce puts in play the double resonance of "remember," a word that either means to recall a past moment or to memorize a present moment. We "remember" the past from the present, and "remember" the present for the future. Through the overlaying of character and writer, both meanings make syntactical sense. The word "remember" confuses the progression of the narrative in order to create two separate moments of historical time, each of which can be interpolated into the other. The novel treats June 16, 1904 and the scene of Joyce's writing as discrete instances that fold into one another, thus making them concurrent. In this way the author, rather than being established as predating the text, comes into being as a figure within the writing.

"Famous Son of a Famous Father": Author, Character, Holy Ghost

That this concept of the author is historically new becomes clear when one compares it to the version of the author that is produced by the classic nineteenth-century *Bildungsroman/Kunstlerroman*, novels that depict the growth of a person and perhaps of an artist. This passage represents the genre:

> My school-days! The silent gliding on of my existence—the unseen, unfelt progress of my life—from childhood up to youth! Let me think, as I look back upon that flowing water, now a dry channel overgrown with leaves, whether there are any marks along its course, by which I can remember how it ran. (Dickens, *David Copperfield* 251)

Dickens's representation of authorial memory emphasizes the divide between the narrator in the present and the protagonist, his past self. We can be certain here that schoolboy David and narrating David will not be sharing one interior monologue. Dickens fixes this author to an external scene of writing, portraying the author as able to "see" his past only in the dimmest terms as a place "thick with growth." His memory lacks the immediacy of that of Joyce's author, whose consciousness overlaps with Stephen's. Nor can the unnamed narrator communicate with the childhood David in the manner of Joyce's author, who appears to prod Stephen; Dickens's author functions more as a supposedly extradiegetic recorder, chronicling diegetic history in sequence. For Dickens, the distance between author and character results from a process that transpires over time. The author retrieves the past by figuratively retracing the path of memory as if time were akin to physical space, moving back and forth between the interiorities of the younger and the older self, respectively. If *David Copperfield* is typical of the *Bildungsroman/Kunstlerroman*, then that literary tradition understands experience as continual, uninterrupted, and cumulative, revisited only in memory.

In contrast, Joyce's author syntactically resides in two moments simultaneously. That is to say, *Ulysses* activates moments of the past and invests them with a consciousness we may attribute to the author at the moment of composition. Stephen spells out the dynamic in these terms: "So in the future, the sister of the past, I may see myself as I sit here now but by reflection from that which then I shall be" (160). To think of the future and past as siblings, of the same generation, is to imagine an atemporal bridge over which one time can flow into the other. *Ulysses* imagines the author in much the same terms as does Barthes, who writes of

> the modern scriptor [who] is born simultaneously with the text, is in no way equipped with a being preceding or exceeding the writing, is not the subject with the book as predicate; there is no time other than that of the enunciation and every text is eternally written *here* and *now*. ("The Death of the Author" 145)

The author of *Ulysses*, like Barthes's "scriptor," does not precede the text; he is created with it, and by it. *Ulysses* portrays its author as the product of language.

While *Ulysses* imagines an author outside of time, unbounded by the biographical material of either the past or the present, it nevertheless depends on the wealth of autobiographical facts attached to the figure of Stephen, even as the novel destabilizes the simple association of character and author. The "Scylla and Charibdis" chapter confounds models that link protagonist to author in a one-to-one relationship, as Stephen, Eglinton, and Mr. Best try (and fail) to locate Shakespeare within a specific character. Eglinton challenges Stephen: "If you want to shake my belief that Shakespeare is Hamlet you have a stern task before you" (159). After Stephen shakes his belief, Eglinton concedes, "The truth is midway ... [Shakespeare] is the ghost and the prince. He is all and all." Stephen agrees, repeating, "All in all. In Cymbeline, in Othello he is bawd and cuckold. He acts and is acted on" (174). They next identify Shakespeare with Iago and, oddly enough, José from Bizet's *Carmen*. With repetition of the itself repetitive phrase "all in all," the dialogue devolves into banalities, as if to completely disparage the project of situating the author within a diegetic body—even if in multiple characters.

Ulysses's complicated reliance on autobiographical detail to re-envision the author has generated critical debate centered on Stephen that tends to oversimplify its positions. Joyce's autobiographical investment in Stephen has created in many cases a "too easy elision of Stephen and Joyce" in Joyce criticism (Johnson 216).[13] There has been, at the same time, an opposing critical compulsion to regard Stephen as the place where Joyce mounts his most withering critiques; Robert Scholes, for example, notes a "dominant view of Stephen as the victim of his author's irony" (7). Irony, as Scholes points out in reference to *A Portrait of the Artist as a Young Man*, is one of the chief means by which New Criticism valorizes literary production as high art. Although it is suggested from the outset of *Ulysses* that its Stephen cannot be regarded in the same way we regard the protagonist of *Portrait*, discussions of the *Ulysses* Stephen also tend to fall back on irony. Hugh Kenner logs Stephen's time and money spent drinking to show how Joyce distances himself from "Stephen's shabby fate" (55–60, 111), while Sean Latham demonstrates that Joyce endows Stephen with an "alienating arrogance" in order to deride snobbishness (153). These approaches exemplify the popular view of Stephen as "the cast off image of a younger self in whom Joyce was no longer interested" (Schloss 117). When feminist, queer, race-, or labor-oriented criticism targets Stephen, the conclusion is predicated on the notion either that Joyce is using the character to renounce his former self or that Joyce himself should be excoriated for his race, class, and gender biases. Critics continue to treat Stephen as an autobiographical figure that must either contain Joyce or be condemned by him.[14] Jaffe addresses this contradiction by reading his notion of the authorial imprimatur into the critical distance between author and protagonist: "Readers who recognize Joyce's irony about Stephen as interpretive necessity pass something akin to a modernist intelligence test. . . . In effect, their readings return in the guise of the reader the impulse to authoritative narrative comment" (*Modernism* 35). In other words, this is a false opposition that, from either side, invokes the author as final word.

Stephen is indeed a component of Joyce's author-production, the autobiographical figure being the chief means of maintaining the author's exceptionalism, and of keeping the author from any form of embodiment other than *Ulysses* itself. The text contrasts Stephen's corporeality with Joyce's idealized conception of the author. "Scylla and Charibdis" portrays Stephen as if he is a performer who follows a script he has had no hand in devising. Late in the chapter, "Scylla and Charibdis" metamorphoses into the typographical format of theater. It provides character names, offset dialogue, and present-tense stage directions, rather than the novelistic conventions of dialogue and past-tense description. Here, the novel allows Stephen no interior monologue—he becomes all surface, all performance. It thereby strips him of the interiority that might make him seem capable of resisting the dominant cultural narrative. Indeed, throughout the chapter Stephen is painfully aware of the degree to which he has been reduced to role-playing. He speaks, as he says, "battling against hopelessness" (170), and rebukes himself: "What the hell are you driving at. . . . Are you condemned to do this?" Stephen indeed seems consigned to repetition: Mulligan has heard his *Hamlet* theory before (15). A subject that is contained by a physical body has no agency. To be embodied is to be condemned to play out the script of history. Stephen emerges as essential to Joyce's authorial production precisely because he is, in this respect, profoundly not the author of *Ulysses*.

Stephen, restricted by history, is not the exception. The modernist exception is the author that *Ulysses* generates. Only the complete, self-regarding text, and not one of the elements within it, can embody the author. Thus Joyce imagines himself as his progenitor as well as his progeny, the creator of the novel that in turn creates him. *Ulysses* reinforces this idea of self-generation by invoking and then rejecting the corporeal aspect of patriarchy. This occurs in moments such as when Lenehan tries to cadge a drink off Stephen's father Simon by giving him a spurious salutation from Stephen: "Greetings from the famous son of a famous father."[15] To this Simon Dedalus responds, "Who may he be?" (215). Stephen's *Hamlet* theory, indeed, takes this patrilineal dissent further. Casting about for the dramatis persona who might serve as Shakespeare's autobiographical figure, Stephen settles on the ghost of King Hamlet. To locate Shakespeare, the paradigmatic author figure, within *Hamlet*, the paradigmatic work of English literature, *Ulysses* imagines him as a ghost.

"What is a ghost?" Stephen asks, and then answers himself: "One who has faded into impalpability through death, through absence, through change of manners" (154).[16] It is noteworthy that this definition merges the historical Shakespeare with the idea of impalpability, contradicting the way Stephen depends on Shakespeare's physical existence elsewhere in "Scylla and Charibdis." It is also noteworthy that ghosts throughout *Ulysses* are both patriarchal and matriarchal figures. Stephen calls up the ghost in the Holy Trinity by silently intoning one version of the Catholic liturgy: "Formless spiritual. Father, Word, and Holy Breath" (152).[17] Here Stephen combines King Hamlet, who is both father and ghost, with two-thirds of the trinity and the moment of the world's divine creation through words.[18] Stephen's ruminations on ghosts are also textually linked to his mother, according to Jeri Johnson: "May Dedalus, mother ghost, clearly a ghost 'through death,' follows Stephen" (212). As Johnson points out, matriarchy is (if not quite equal to patriarchy) another signifier of artistic creation for Stephen, who states that Socrates learned "from his mother how to bring thoughts into the world" (156). Thus it is especially noteworthy that Joyce's version of the author absorbs both male and female; it is a "formless spiritual" being, as independent of gender as it is independent of a body.

Joyce's use of his autobiography and his attaching it to Stephen suggest a dismissal of the *Bildungsroman/Kunstlerroman* tradition as he supplants it with the text that announces the author as an entity separate from the masses. *Ulysses* rejects the form narrative that aligns personal and chronological development. (For the moment I continue to keep aside *Portrait*, a work more easily read as sympathetic to that tradition, to focus on what Joyce does to the *Kunstlerroman* in *Ulysses*.) *Ulysses* signals that in the literature of celebrity, the author, that which is only identified with the text, assumes the role, once held by characters and protagonists, of reasserting the primacy of the individual. The nineteenth-century genre exemplified by Dickens, with its less synchronic view of time, emerges as valueless in the modernist moment, unable to provide a model by which the individual resists the gravitational pull of mass culture.

Joyce was not alone in the 1920s in challenging the *Bildungsroman/Kunstlerroman*. Benjamin writes: "By integrating the social process with the development of a person, [the *Bildungsroman*] bestows the most frangible justification on the order determining it. The legitimacy it provides stands in direct opposition to reality" ("The Storyteller" 88). Here Joyce's contemporary argues that the *Bildungsroman*, by focalizing the "social process" within the formation of the subject, provides the flimsiest rationalization of capitalist society; society is good because society creates individuals who live in society. Benjamin might not have approved of the way Joyce deals with this problem, though. In *Ulysses*, society is only relevant insofar as the text creates the subject who subsumes all of society within itself. Whereas the previous epochs had characters such as Werther and Jane Eyre to understand as embodiments of the unique individual, modernist readers have the idealized author. In other words, if *Bildungsroman/Kunstlerroman* novels were a primary way through which reading audiences in the nineteenth century, and indeed all the way back to Samuel Richardson's epistolary coming-of-age novels of the mid-1700s, were taught what it means for an individual to exist, then that pedagogical role is assumed by the literature of celebrity.

The Dream of Immateriality

In removing the author from messy matters of the body, the fantasy of self-production conveniently removes Joyce from the equally messy problem of cultural visibility brought on by celebrity. In 1916, Joyce kept a journal of dreams and his interpretations of them. An entry concerning one of Nora Barnacle's dreams reveals that the interweaving of Shakespeare, authorship, and fame is troublesome for him: "The figure of Shakespeare present in Elizabethan dress is a suggestion of fame, his certainly (it is the tercentenary of his death), mine not so certainly" (Ellmann, *James Joyce* 437). Joyce surmises that his wife fears his "subsequent honours . . . may bring unrest into her life." This decoding of Barnacle's dream is clearly his way of thinking through the encroachments of public reputation. The image of Shakespeare, replete with costume, suggests that Joyce is disturbed himself at the thought of unrest in his domestic life brought on by the visibility of the body associated with twentieth-century celebrity. *Ulysses*, we might conclude, constitutes his symbolic resolution to a problem with which he was unable to deal in real life. The existence Joyce invents for himself as disembodied author allows him to imagine himself as a "different" and "transcendent" (Foucault 215) entity located strictly in writing, invulnerable to the influence of celebrity culture. By splitting the author from the biographical body and locating it within the text both as source and as the limit of interpretation, Joyce imagines himself as an absolute value, as if to ensure that the authorial subject, like *Ulysses*, will require no external standard by which to be judged.

To consider the roots and the implications of this insistence on situating the authorial subject within the text, we might compare Joyce's negotiations with celebrity to those of Wilde detailed in Chapter 1. Wilde's celebrity led straight to his public prosecution for (to euphemize) matters of the body. Incarcerated, Wilde abandoned his public production of the self and wrote *De Profundis*, a work that carries out the fantasy that he is pure subject, untainted by culture. That Joyce had Wilde on his mind while writing *Ulysses* is suggested by Wicke, who makes the case that Bloom's trial in "Circe" is a celebrity trial, patterned after Wilde's. There, Bloom is decried (in words that ring with Shakespearian slang overtones) as "a wellknown . . . bigamist, bawd, and cuckold and a public nuisance" (384). The public aspect of his sexuality, like the Marquess of Queensberry's public accusation of Wilde, lands Bloom in front of a jury. Whether Wilde's trials spurred Joyce's retreat into the textual realm is not something we can determine. What I want to emphasize is that when prosecution did come to the author of *Ulysses*, it was not the novelist but the novel that went on trial for degenerate sexuality; had it been found "guilty," Joyce's body would have suffered no punishment. Initially censored in the United States and Great Britain, the book was eventually set free to circulate legally—largely because of its stylistic play. As Wexler points out, the inscrutability of *Ulysses* legally established the book's credentials as art and not smut.[19] Joyce's personal trademark, his style, was what allowed the novel finally to elude censorship, and therefore pass into circulation. That Wilde served jail time and *Ulysses* was set free testifies to the fact that Joyce's self-creation as a disembodied subject might well have made it possible for Joyce to avoid a figurative version of Wilde's fate.

E.T.: *The Extra-Textual*

Joyce's author-production enacts much the same ontological sleight of hand that Foucault and Barthes spell out in essays proclaiming the so-called death of the author. These essays rail against a supposed readerly tendency to naturalize aspects of writing by situating the work within a psychological entity that is external to the text—the author. *Ulysses*'s use of style, which—as I have argued—effectively separates author from body (thus killing off the author as biographical entity), also directs attention to the operations by which the text creates the author. While Foucault and Barthes make sophisticated theoretical fun of readers and critics whose understandings of literature are "tyrannically centered on the author" (Barthes 143), Joyce exercises that tyranny. *Ulysses* proposes that reading and understanding the novel is not centered on the author: it *is* the author.

We might say that Joyce anticipates, and literalizes, Barthes and Foucault's shared idea that the production of the author restricts the text's meaning, that the author's presence gives writing "a final signified" (Barthes, "Death" 147), or "impedes . . . the free manipulation, the free composition, decomposition, and recomposition of fiction" (Foucault 221). These theorists attribute this limiting effect to readers' naïve assumption that the author exists outside and prior to the text. Barthes writes that "the Author, when believed in, is always conceived of as the past of his own book ... is thought to *nourish* the book" ("Death" 145). Foucault simply asserts that "the author is not an indefinite source of significations that fill a work; the author does not precede the works" (221). To counter this restrictive figure, Barthes conjures up his "scriptor [who] is born simultaneously with the text," and is supposed to have "buried the Author" (145-146). The atemporality of scriptor and text, he continues, frees the text from a "single 'theological' meaning" that traditional criticism would impose. And yet Joyce, by producing just this atemporality, indeed imposes a final meaning, making himself, his inimitability and virtuosity, the signified of *Ulysses*. Although Foucault may argue that by "setting aside biographical and psychological references one has already called back into question the absolute character and founding role of the subject" (220), Joyce idealizes an author who has no biography or psychology outside of the text—precisely in order to reaffirm the absolute character of the subject.

Joyce performs this idealization through the manipulations of style, through his revision of the *Bildungsroman*, and also through extratextual material that, echoing the fanzines and publicity of popular celebrity, insists on a specific reading of *Ulysses*. Joyce provides his readers with chapter-by-chapter guides to the novel. The schema, as he called them, have been underappreciated as sites of critical inquiry themselves (making them unique in the field of Joyce studies, which has managed to publish biographies of Joyce's wife, Nora, and daughter Lucia). Much like his ringing stylistic changes, this guide to interpretation reinforces the notion that *Ulysses*'s meaning is to be found in an author who exists apart from the narrative, yet within the proliferation of language. Specifically, the guide claims to decode *Ulysses* by explaining how each chapter corresponds to both the *Odyssey* and the time and Dublin location of its events.[20] The guide also offers more obscure clues to the novel's meaning, designating a "colour," "symbol," "sense," "organ" (of the body), "science, [or] art," and "technic" for each of the episodes. Readers are supposed to use the guide to scour each chapter for reference to its designated color and evocation of its signature organ. By establishing such extradiegetic connections between the guide and the novel, Joyce converts the process of reading *Ulysses* into a literary treasure hunt; the goal is discovering the author's design in the text and the prize is appreciating his brilliant execution of that design.

In this way the guide recalls the promotional apparatus of film celebrity. Promotion, during Joyce's lifetime, became an essential part of the production of the film star, whose identity was "essentially an intertextual one" dependent on "fan magazines and the general press" (deCordova 113).[21] The promotional materials of the film industry, writes Benjamin, are designed to compensate for the audience's estrangement from the film, the lack of the "aura" that cinemagoers supposedly feel as they consume mass-reproduced images. "The film responds to the shriveling of the aura with an artificial build-up of the 'personality' outside the studio."[22] The intertextual objects of promotion and publicity that supposedly provide such "access to the real person," in Dyer's words (*Stars* 61), redress the loss of the unmediated presence of the art object. They seemingly grant the audience familiarity with the performer as a person living in the world outside of the works.

Joyce's guide, while similarly participating in the creation of identity (the author's), was shaped in obvious contrast to these popular means of promotion. It is an intertextual object that offers estrangement in lieu of familiarity and distance instead of presence, in order to elevate the author above public reach. Pretending to provide access to the biographical author's intentions, the guide in fact defamiliarizes an already difficult text. If readers who simply may be struggling to follow the plot turn to the guides for enlightenment, they will not be helped. On the contrary, Joyce's guide imposes more labor. It suggests that any experience of the novel that fails to unearth arcane clues to Joyce's larger meaning is incomplete.[23] It overloads an already overloaded novel with more information at the command of an author who must therefore be grasped, in the words of Foucault, as "a perpetual surging of invention" (221).

The very form of the guide, its visual clarity, participates in Joyce's self-production as author. Laid out in the columns and rows of a chart, the guide offers itself as a methodical reduction of *Ulysses*. This, the guide insinuates, is what the author envisioned while he wrote the novel, a comprehensive system or paradigm; without this extra-textual help, all the reader is likely to see is an "immense panorama of futility and anarchy," in Eliot's description of the novel (177). The guide's format suggests, speciously, that it refocuses the book from wide-angle to zoom. By creating this discrepancy between the cognitive processes of the author and his readers, the guide appropriates the logic of popular celebrity in support of Joyce's author-production—his creation of himself as distinct, irreproducible subject. The guide turns landscape into portraiture.

By suggesting that a systematic paradigm undergirded Joyce's account of one day in Dublin, the guide offers itself as a blueprint for *Ulysses*, as if to say that the guide preceded the novel. Eliot picks up on this early, claiming of Joyce's use of Homer, "No one else has built a novel upon such a foundation before: it has never been a necessity." In buying into the illusion of temporality—first a foundation and then a house—Eliot's statement seems to undermine Joyce's fantasy of an author outside of time and a real body. The guide does not, however, contradict Joyce's author-production quite as much as Eliot suggests. By characterizing Joyce's writing process as a simple matter of conceiving and then following through with a plan, the guide disguises the erratic and multifarious path of the novel's composition, recasting in linear terms the time and labor of literary production.[24] Thus this revisionist history of *Ulysses* in fact re-stages the removal of the author from his biography.

While the guide subverts the promotional apparatus of film stardom, subverting the cultural logic of celebrity, it nevertheless functions much like an advertisement to publicize *Ulysses* and enable its circulation, if only within a rarified sphere of the market. The guide, unlike the published complete versions of *Ulysses*, provides the chapter titles that indicate parallels with the *Odyssey*. These parallels helped drum up interest in the novel before its publication.[25] The use of Homer, writes Kenner, easily served "to turn an unwritten book into something that could be talked about" (23). But among whom does this supposed conversation take place? Joyce distributed the guide to sympathetic critics likely to review *Ulysses*, thereby creating authorized readers to publicize the novel according to his own aesthetic strictures. The criticism, in turn, advertises *Ulysses*. Joyce, who "knew the value of informed articles," as Kenner puts it, keeps his own hands clean, and arranges for critics to train their audiences, creating a network of readers, all using the guide. Eighty years later, the guide and the critical works that rely on it are standard apparatus for many readers of *Ulysses*, particularly in university classrooms. The guide has helped turn *Ulysses* into "an icon of literary and cultural sophistication, largely restricted to a Stephen-like audience" (Latham 160). The guide promotes *Ulysses* as an affirmation of the cultural capital of difficulty, elevating both readers and author above the plebeian and infusing *Ulysses* with value by virtue of the restricted community in which it circulates.

Despite the fact that the mere existence of the guide destabilizes the idea of *Ulysses* as a self-enclosed system, the guide reinforces the notion of the author as both origin and end of signification. Recognizing the degree to which the creation of the author as pure subject rests on an ongoing process of interpretation by readers, Joyce famously boasted of cramming *Ulysses* with "so many enigmas and puzzles that it will keep the professors busy for centuries arguing over what I meant . . . the only way of insuring one's immortality" (Ellmann 590). If the act of interpreting *Ulysses* is the act of creating the author, the guide helps Joyce ensure he will be created the right way. The critical debates over *Ulysses* do nothing if not put Joyce, as subject, in play, updating the author for each new critical generation.

The Ghost of the Author

The fact that readers at all levels use the guide attests to the success of Joyce's authorial production, a triumph also apparent from the way scholars refer to chapters in *Ulysses* as if it were a critical necessity to constantly reiterate the novel's links to the *Odyssey*. These links first appeared in chapter titles for the novel's initial, serialized publication; Joyce removed them when *Ulysses* was published in one volume, and subsequently made them the key organizing element of the guide. Although these titles do not appear in any scholarly edition of *Ulysses*, every Joyce scholar is obliged to invoke them.[26] True, the titles provide a handy method of distinguishing the chapters. But they also demonstrate how we willingly participate in a practice that imposes a specific reading on the novel—and not just any reading, but the author's reading. While I am at it, I should point out that the critical treatment of *Ulysses* chapters as individual entities—a tradition I have followed here—is another strange but generally unquestioned, strangely unquestioned, aspect of Joyce scholarship. Once again, Kenner draws attention to this, writing of the distinct "identity each of [*Ulysses*'s] eighteen episodes assumes, by contrast with the relatively anonymous chapters of normal novels" (23).[27]

Because Joyce has become the supreme example of the modernist exception, because his scholarship is the one most under his sway, this chapter closes with a brief rumination on the implications of the celebrity effect within criticism. There was a time when Joyce was dictating explanations of his work to Stuart Gilbert and he thrilled to read reviews and crow: "I see my own phrases rolling back to me" (*Letters III* 69). Since then, Joyce critics have made much progress toward stepping out of the author's shadow. Still, the scholarship has a long history of complying with Joyce's attempt to detach word from world. Indeed, Tim Conley draws recent attention to the fact that critics lament not having more extra-textual help from Joyce (74). The desire manifests in critical limitation. For example, at a 2000 Joyce symposium in London, one internationally prominent Joycean bemoaned the trend toward historically oriented readings of Joyce on the grounds that "we still don't know what everything is in *Ulysses*."[28] This is as much as to say that we need to catalog every detail and allusion Joyce crammed into his novel, every reference to Jesuit learning or Dublin druggists, before we can situate *Ulysses* within its historical moment and see how it reconfigures cultural issues. The durability of criticism that adheres to this Joycean fantasy of self-containment and authorial oversight takes the form of a resistance to critical tactics that might seem to detract from Joyce's achievement or inject what might be considered impure contextual matter, whether drawn from colonialism, gender issues, or popular culture—a defense of high art that resembles Joyce's own defense against popular celebrity.

Such an attitude undervalues the kind of reading this chapter performs. The irony here is that while Joyce's self-fashioning imposes the ultimate recourse to the author that Barthes and Foucault describe, an examination of the self-creation as modernist author can provide a rich critical road. I approach the author much as Hansen suggests we can mobilize the film star, as a presence that "actually undercuts that regime's [the text's] apparent primacy, unity, and closure" (246). The author, too, should be a rhetorical means of illuminating, not resolving, contradictions. The name "James Joyce"—as it appears variously in critical and biographical writings, pops up on hipster T-shirts in urban neighborhoods, enters into Nobel Prize acceptance speeches,[29] or resounds sonorously in reading groups, Bloomsday celebrations, graduate seminars, and all the other institutions of Joyce fandom—is a text. The discourses that attach to that text, such as that of celebrity, reveal what modernism did—and still does—to our world, and illuminate the very reason we continue to read it.

CHAPTER 3

Gertrude Stein,
Everybody's Celebrity

ilde and Joyce help produce the modernist exception, a version of the discrete celebrity as we know it, but celebrity is no longer a discrete phenomenon. Over the last half-century, our media has inundated us with stories and images of celebrity meetings: pairs of practical strangers from different sectors of public life, establishing a mutual link in order to define their own cultural value: Elvis Presley and Richard Nixon might come to mind, or Flavor Flav and Brigette Nielson might.[1] It has not always been a given that this practice would make sense. We can see a preempted rehearsal of it in the encounter between Gertrude Stein and Mary Pickford, who met during Stein's lecture tour of the United States in 1935.

They were a perfect celebrity twosome in their counterintuitiveness: Pickford the silent screen starlet who had been crowned "America's Sweetheart" for both her national ubiquity and her wholesome persona, and Stein the queer avant-garde writer, much celebrated for the latter if not for the former epithet.[2] Despite Stein's celebrity—she scored her *Time* magazine cover story in 1933, six months before Joyce's—American culture seems to have not been ready for the twosome. In *Everybody's Autobiography* (1937), Stein recounts:

> [Pickford] said and suppose we should be photographed together. Wonderful idea I said. . . . Mary Pickford said it would be easy to get the Journal photographer to come over, yes I will telephone said some one rushing off, yes I said it would be wonderful we might be taken shaking hands. You are not going to do it said Belle Greene excitedly behind me, of course I am going to I said, nothing would please me better of course we are said I turning to Mary Pickford, Mary Pickford said perhaps I will not be able to stay and she began to back away. Oh yes you must I said it will not be long now, no no she said I think I had better not and she melted away. I knew you would not do it said Belle Greene behind me. And then I asked every one because I was interested just what it was that went on inside Mary Pickford. It was her idea and then when I was enthusiastic she melted away. They all said that what she thought was if I were enthusiastic it meant that it would do me more good than it would do her and so she melted away or others said perhaps after all it would not be good for her audience that we should be photographed together, anyway I was very much interested to know just what did they think was good publicity and what is not. (7–8)

At issue here is the possibility of a public display in the form of a newspaper photograph of a doyenne of the avant-garde and a film actress known worldwide. The passage depicts Stein as eager to go forward with the public demonstration of their meeting, but thwarted by Pickford's cold feet.

Why Pickford's sudden reluctance? Mary Pickford had already mastered the celebrity association, having married Douglas Fairbanks, the Hollywood leading man par excellence, in 1920. That was one year after forming United Artists with Fairbanks, Charlie Chaplin, and D. W. Griffiths, a business venture that exploited the merging of star capital; Pickford had, indeed, gloried in photographs of the foursome (and their lawyers) celebrating that merger, an image of star power in which her role is to watch over Chaplin's shoulder as he, superstar, about to make legal his participation, looks knowingly at the camera. She had also been willing to pose with non-Hollywood types such as President Herbert Hoover. Pickford had savvy thoughts about publicity; she welcomed the advent of radio, writing in an article for *The Hollywood Reporter*, "Opposition to progress is forever futile . . . the box-office value of every star who appears

FIGURE 3.1. Signing the United Artists contract, 1919. (L-R) D. W. Griffiths, Mary Pickford, Douglas Fairbanks, Charlie Chaplin, attorneys Albert Banzhaf and Dennis F. O'Brien.

to advantage on the air is greatly enhanced, and, potentially speaking, so is the stock of the company to which he or she is under contract."[3]

What Pickford did not foresee, apparently, was the enhanced value of reaching across the great divide to a character of a vastly foreign semiotic code, someone seemingly quite divorced from the "Cinderella-minded" America that Pickford desired (Pickford 234). Stein describes her encounter with Pickford as though the idea of a handshake, particularly, drives the star away. The handshake might be identified as a somewhat masculine greeting; Stein suggests that Pickford's sudden reluctance to having her photo taken with Stein may reflect Pickford's discomfort with how she would look shaking hands with a person who embodies a complicated set of gender signals. Kirk Curnutt reads this moment as one that contrasts Pickford's "calculated attitude toward fame" with Stein's representation of herself as "naïve of the imperative of complimentary press" (305). But surely it is the other way around: Stein casts herself, not Pickford, as the savvy one. Pickford's reluctance is treated with derision. Stein shows her to be a flighty, insubstantial figure quickly and easily manipulated by Belle Greene. Pickford departs by first "backing" and then "melt[ing] away," as Stein emphasizes and pokes fun at her trepidation.

Stein has the last laugh here beyond her subtle satire of Pickford. While this passage occurs early in *Everybody's*, the memoir proceeds to publicize Stein's meetings with a plethora of celebrities with vastly different profiles from her own—Chaplin, Dashiell Hammett, and Eleanor Roosevelt among them.[4] Toward the end of the book the roles get reversed and the Hollywood-types are asking Stein for advice concerning publicity, rather than Stein having to ask them.[5] Indeed, Stein's version of publicity, her public self-construction through a network of celebrity figures, is the version that would prevail, Pickford's rejection notwithstanding. The history of celebrity has borne out Stein's instinct to cross generic boundaries, validating the idea of linking oneself to a celebrity from a separate cultural sphere. Public demonstrations of famous figures attaching themselves to otherwise unrelated famous figures would become the norm of celebrity-production.

Stein, in fact, helped instigate this development. Her writings—and particularly her first memoir, *The Autobiography of Alice B. Toklas* (1932)—produce a system of value predicated on the significance shared among celebrities who are connected by proximity. In this chapter I will read Stein's works, particularly the late, memoir-ish writings, to argue that Stein produces a model of celebrity that, building on Wilde's original model of the celebrity-as-commodity, operates within a differential system, thereby making value depend on the networks that link famous figures. This network, though, requires the central, controlling figure of the modernist author for its ultimate legitimation. Stein's system emerges from her reevaluation of the celebrity name. I intend to show that *The Autobiography* invokes the name's ability to refer beyond the boundaries of the text, toward the discourses that produce celebrity beyond Stein's own pages. In examining the value of the name, Stein ultimately undermines the stability of the name's referentiality, thereby insisting that value be dependent on the system. She thus contrasts the celebrity name with that of the author, which is designated the repository of cultural value. At the same time, Stein recuperates the celebrity name as an appropriately unstable signifier that operates within her idiosyncratic style—the techniques by which she generates her authorial identity.

Prior to *The Autobiography*, most of Stein's voluminous body of work comprises obscure prose that propounds, in Lisi Schoenbach's words, "the power and the importance of repetition, amplification, accumulation, duration . . . the necessity of making things 'a great deal longer'" (251). This distinctive use of language emerges, one might say, as Stein's trademark. Its instantly recognizable quality acts as an insignia that refers to Stein and announces the provenance of her writing, much in the manner of Joyce's manipulations of style and much like a model of Foucault's conception of the author function, as I have been discussing both. In fact, as Leick points out, Stein and Joyce were popularly grouped together "as leading producers of original, if strange, new writing" ("Popular Modernism" 128), a pairing that Stein would note and attempt to negate in her negotiations of celebrity networks, as I will discuss later in this chapter. Stein's own "specific and complex operations" (Foucault 216) also produce the author as discourse. Her stylistic singularity and notorious difficulty render language opaque, referring readers to the idea of an author who creates elite literature for elite audiences, regardless of Stein's claims to the contrary.

That Stein's use of style simultaneously constitutes her identity as author and functions as a kind of trademark is made clear when one thinks of how what she terms "the device of Gertrude Stein"—"a rose is a rose is a rose is a rose"—becomes Stein's "motto," a trademark embossed on her book covers, and eventually appearing in shop windows and print ads during Stein's celebrifying lecture tour.[6] This phrase incorporates the repetition that hallmarks Stein's prose. It can be said to encapsulate Stein's distinct use of language, distilling her writing into a formula. In this way it resembles Wilde's epigrams; thus it is worth again recalling Barthes's comments about Einstein's famous formula concerning the relation of energy to mass: "Through the mythology of Albert Einstein, the world blissfully regained the image of knowledge reduced to a formula... the product of his inventiveness came to acquire a magical dimension" (*Mythologies* 69). As "$E=mc^2$" provides an instantly graspable abbreviation of Einstein's exceptional mind, the Stein "motto" operates similarly, signaling Stein's impenetrable style that, in turn, acts as a signifier of her irreproducibility.

So when Stein conceived of *The Autobiography* as a vehicle for increasing her readership, and thus her fortune and fame,[7] she was confronted with the challenge of how to write in a way that would widen her audience while continuing to present her as a figure of elite culture. That is to say, since Stein severely tones down the idiosyncrasies of her prose and writes *The Autobiography* "in conventional English," as Ulla Dydo puts it (*A Stein Reader* 5), rather than in the language of her previous works, she had to find another means for creating herself as author within the text. Her network of celebrity names becomes just that—an alternate way of producing the self as a subject whose attributes are beyond the conception or capability of ordinary people.

Elite by Association

Critics have been quick to note that *The Autobiography* indeed increased Stein's readership and her fame, and consequently made Stein anxious about her newfound success. Curnutt writes that "she suffered a brief but unexpected bout of writer's block" as a result of her "ambivalence toward her unexpected popularity" (291). Stein admits this herself in *Everybody's:* "Since the autobiography I had not done any writing . . . if my writing was worth money then it was not what it had been" (84). The development seems to have occasioned the spilling of much ink on the subject of celebrity itself; by the time *Everybody's* saw print, Stein was not only famous, but she had also made statements about celebrity that would become famous. Of celebrity, she says, "In America everybody is but some are more than others. I was more than others" (168). Indeed, Stein's trip to America furthered the tradition of Wilde (and Dickens): "I used to say that I would not go to America until I was a real lion a real celebrity at that time of course I did not really think I was going to be one. But now we were coming and I was going to be one."

The critics' and Stein's own takes on Stein's celebrity remain in the background of my thinking in this chapter. As should be clear by this point, my concern is with Stein's stylistic work on the structure of celebrity—how cultural matter passes into her work and becomes transformed into modernist exceptionalism. I will gladly note, however, that if these direct ruminations about fame are prompted by Stein's increased renown then this is only fitting, as *The Autobiography* is where Stein's technique most engages with celebrity discourse.

When Wayne Koestenbaum writes of "the buzz of names in Stein's work" (314), he means the way Stein litters her writings with proper names, a tendency that finds its apotheosis in *The Autobiography*. Stein incorporates names such as Picasso, Eliot, Matisse, Apollinaire, Hemingway, and over a hundred others, to fashion herself as a person of note, as an author and celebrity who absorbs the value of these names into her text. That text is governed by her own name, both within the narrative and—as she is its author—without. Of course, there is hardly anything remarkable about a project of self-aggrandizement simultaneously being a project of name-dropping, of accruing capital by boasting of luminaries that one has met. Stein's name-dropping, though, is characterized by her particular negotiations of referentiality, linguistic proximity, and value. Stein, in contrast to other name-droppers, both enlists and resists the celebrity name's power to refer to the person who bears it.

Stein was aware that the celebrity name gestures beyond the diegesis of a text—beyond the sphere of representation bounded within a world—and toward the real person in the real world, or, considered another way, toward the contextual materials that produce that person as discourse. The very title, or title page, of *The Autobiography of Alice B. Toklas*, announces that the text will invoke this aspect of the celebrity name. The title indicates that this book's writer and subject are one and the same, but they are not. An additional clause, "by Gertrude Stein," contradicts the title, undermining the sense of either the word "autobiography" or the name "Alice B. Toklas."[8] Of course, it is unlikely that anyone still does a mental double take when faced with the inherent paradox on the book's cover; readers probably recognize *The Autobiography* as one of the best known and most popular works of a famously challenging modernist writer. The contradiction of an "autobiography" having been authored by someone other than its subject suddenly seems natural when the work is understood as having been written by an author known to be eccentric and difficult. The words still do not add up, but they make sense collectively as high-art linguistic production that plays with referentiality. This understanding demands a shift in readerly orientation, away from the illogic of the title, and toward the spheres of culture in which Stein's name circulates. As Glass says, the title "strains the autobiographical pact in order to dwell more insistently on the named subject that ratifies that pact in the first place" (115). So while the title and author's name together might seem to subvert language, the author's name, by referring beyond the closed circuit of the book's title to the sphere of public reputation, resolves any ambiguity.

This dynamic of the name echoes the image of the film celebrity and its operations. As Hansen has written, the image of the film star "blurs the boundary between diegesis and discourse, between an address relying on identification with fictional characters and an activation of the viewer's familiarity with the star on the basis of production and publicity intertexts" (246). One could say that the celebrity names in *The Autobiography* similarly activate the extradiegetic discourses that swirl around the famous individual. When Stein writes, "Picasso had just finished his portrait of [Stein]" (6), she invites readers to think beyond her narrative and recall popular texts such as magazine and newspaper accounts of Picasso, in addition to his own artistic output. This type of invocation is a repeated feature of *The Autobiography* and Stein's other "conventional English" writings. In describing Stein's work as "devoid of allusions and the extratextual referents so common to Modernist writing" (157), Shari Benstock misses the repeated gestures beyond Stein's narrative prompted by celebrity names, which actually prove as allusive as anything in Eliot. The difference between Stein's kind of references and those of modernists like Eliot lies in Stein's rampant reference to her contemporaries, rather than the insistent invocation of a literary tradition; her "conventional English" works such as *The Autobiography* situate Stein among texts of her moment rather than of the past, sending readers to contemporary discourse, both popular and elite.

Of course, *The Autobiography*'s names primarily refer to notables of literature and the arts: elite culture. But Stein seems to be using them for the manner in which they resemble the celebrity image, rarely detailing their artistic achievements except in terms of the public acclaim they generate, enlisting the recognizability of the name rather than the works associated with it. This can be understood as Stein's stress on the name's cultural resonance, sometimes referred to as the "aura" of a name. In his examination of name-dropping, Martin Jay writes of "a certain sacred aura clinging to or attributed to" names of celebrated producers of culture (170). These figures, Jay asserts, "are granted an originary power, which surrounds their names with an aura of sanctity." Stein is scrutinizing, and in fact toying with, this effect. In *The Autobiography* she makes use of this sense of "aura" surrounding the name, based, like the celebrity image, on the familiarity of the figure, and on the name's ability to refer beyond the text, toward the fame of that particular producer of elite culture.

Stein transmutes this aura into a kind of cultural capital that attends the author whose narrative incorporates it. *The Autobiography*, in fact, dramatizes this equation of names and value by making name-dropping a form of currency. Early in the book, Stein, in the voice of Alice B. Toklas, depicts the enunciation of a name as a key that provides admission to the Stein salon at 27 rue de Fleurus:

> [Stein] usually opened the door to the knock and the usual formula was de la part de qui venez-vous, who is your introducer. The idea was that anybody could come but for form's sake and in Paris you have to have a formula, everybody was supposed to be able to mention the name of somebody who had told them about it. It was mere form, really everybody could come in ... only those came who really were interested ... Miss Stein once in opening the door said as she usually did by whose invitation did you come and we heard an aggrieved voice reply, but by yours, madame. (13)

Here, a guest's capacity to invoke the familiarity of the name of the person who referred him or her—literally, the guest's reference—functions as the price of admission that allows "anybody" to join a select, if self-selecting, society. (Stein reinforces the exclusionary principle shaping this coterie by announcing that it is both explicitly Parisian and explicitly in the past, and therefore beyond the reach of the American reader of 1932 and later.) The name-dropping here is ritualistic, but also compulsory. "Mere form," it may be, but the one guest who fails to provide a name pays the penalty: the text refuses to grant him a name of his own, reduces him to "an aggrieved voice," and goes on to recount that Stein had once met him and "promptly forgotten" it. Deploring this failure to supply a name apart from that of the hostess, and showing the way names function as currency, Stein casts the act of name-dropping as a sign that reflects value on the name-dropper. The passage allegorizes the process by which Stein stakes her value on her own name-dropping in the book.

An exception to the rule of *The Autobiography*, this passage does not specify any names except Stein's and highlights this absence with its repetitive list of impersonal pronouns such as "anybody," "everybody," and "anyone." The omission of specific names implies that each name is important for its capacity to refer to someone not present in this time and place, its recognizability to its addressee (as the hostess, surely, must know the name in order for it to function in this vein), and, quite simply, for its contribution to the ongoing list of names. Again, the disembodied "aggrieved voice" fails in his duty to establish a link between himself and someone not present, thus failing to prolong the ongoing chain of names. The value of name-dropping, then, lies partly in the linguistic affiliation it creates between guest and host, the sense that they are connected by a chain of names. Value also lies in the way each name prolongs the chain and thus extends the list of names to which everyone in the network can claim to be linked.

It may be that the passage is meant to obliquely refer to the litany of names elsewhere, throughout the book, a nexus at whose center is absolutely Stein. Stein's name has a double valence: she is the hostess within the narrative, and the book's author, without. The idea that Stein presides over the names within both her household and her text is a prevalent aspect of *The Autobiography*. The book's highest concentration of names appears in passages describing those who visit Gertrude and her brother Leo Stein's—later Gertrude Stein and Toklas's—home. (That Leo is absolutely unnamed throughout the volume is a significant omission.) Such sections imply a parallel between the book's collection of famous names and the house's collection of famous guests. Stein writes, "Tristan Tzara came to the house ... Sylvia Beach from time to time brought groups of people ... It was at that time that Ezra Pound came ... Sherwood Anderson ... came with his wife and Rosenfeld ... Man Ray ... Duchamp" and on and on (196–197). The guests bring more guests, conveying the sense of an infinite chain of names, the aura of each adding its value to the whole. Among them is the repeated interpolation of the full name "Gertrude Stein." By granting the author her family and Christian names, the text seems to make this nomenclature metonymically responsible for the chain of impressive signifiers. It is as if she sets that chain in motion while she remains a stable, unmoving figure whom less central personages approach, bringing still others. Thus each name brought into the Stein fold intensifies the burnishing of Stein's own status.

Stein's primary position creates a dynamic by which the famous names not only create Stein's stature by extending their value extradiegetically toward the author, but also reflect value on her name within the narrative as each character comes to meet her. To pirate Jacques Lacan's terminology, itself taken from Ferdinand de Saussure, the names produce value not only "vertically," outside of the "signifying chain" and toward Stein the author, but also "horizontally" toward Stein the character who constitutes the central link of that chain.[9] In the horizontal manner, Stein implies that the equal stature of her name and that of some recognizable luminary allows her to assume some of that celebrity's aura. When, for example, the photographer who has just "finished a series of photographs that he had done for Henry James" wants to photograph Stein for his "volume of prominent woman," Stein claims some of the James aura for herself, the subject of the next portrait (140). As Helga Lénárt-Cheng notes of one moment in the *The Autobiography*, "Stein, as if trying to guarantee the prestige of her portrait, refers to some other famous models of the same artist next to her own name" (125). Stein depicts herself receiving the same treatment as the celebrities, being thought of as an appropriate model for photographs and portraits. She puts her name in places reserved for figures of elite status. By this interweaving of linguistic presence and physical presence, Stein manufactures herself as a person of similar stature.

Unstable Values

Stein's system of accruing value by association and accumulation might seem to suggest that the celebrity names she invokes themselves gain value from this ongoing network—that appearing in such elite company guarantees elite status for all. In truth, the dynamic of *The Autobiography* clearly destabilizes the value of the individual name by placing it within this differential system, in which each name's value is affected by those that either appear in the surrounding sentences and paragraphs or move through the same interior spaces. In one instance, the famous name's linguistic presence might glorify the author by its inclusion in the series, but its referent's absence from the diegesis implies its devaluation. Stein writes, "Kate Buss . . . brought Djuna Barnes and Mina Loy and they had wanted to bring James Joyce but they didn't" (200). Joyce's failure to appear at the salon excludes him from Stein's presence even while Stein includes his name within her set. The omission is a stronger condemnation, one might say, than that of brother Leo, entirely ignored but not disparaged, not deemed worthy of mention. Stein reinforces this subordination of Joyce through her expression of disdain, which she attributes to Picasso, regarding Joyce's work: "Braque and James Joyce, they are the incomprehensibles whom anybody can understand" (212). Although this disparagement seems directed at the writer, the linguistic proximity of Joyce and Braque depreciates the cubist as well. Joyce takes Braque down with him, and, correspondingly, Picasso takes Stein to the top. The remark devalues two rival heavyweight contenders who represent threats to Picasso and Stein's standing as the most important modernists (according to numerous Stein remarks). Thus, even while Stein is basking in the aura of the celebrity names accumulated in the work, *The Autobiography* embeds the names in a relational system, determining the hierarchy of value by proximity.

Picasso's condemnation devalues Joyce's and Braque's artistic productions strictly on the basis of their being intellectually available despite a veneer of difficulty; their names are worth less because their work is understandable to "anybody." (Joyce? Really?) But this seems not to be a directive against accessibility—Stein cohorts like Hemingway and Sherwood Anderson are clearly easier to read than Joyce—as much as it is against having inscrutability be the most recognizable feature of the work, and therefore the feature graspable, or comprehensible, to anybody. Stein reduces Joyce and Braque's standing by positing that their value is based on an illusion—that their names signify a kind of tautological obscurity that is itself totally understandable—unlike the more legitimate inscrutability of Stein and Picasso. That is, the contradiction between public reputation and truth produces Stein's devaluation of these figures.

This disjunction reverberates throughout Stein's treatment of celebrity names in *The Autobiography*. Concerned as it is with the fame of its names, the book often seems something like a 300-page gossip column, portraying private aspects of the celebrities incongruous with their public images. When Pound falls out of Stein's "favorite little armchair, the one [Toklas has] since tapestried with Picasso designs" (202), the undignified incident contrasts with the poet's public reputation. Pound falls out of Stein's favor as well, subsequently.[10] *The Autobiography* continually depicts the unglamorous personal squabbles, the petty rivalries and private affairs of its famous figures, and generally confines them to domestic, interior space. Stein thus undermines the extraordinariness of the celebrities. She sets the connotation of the name as a signifier of its referent's unique qualities in high relief with a picture of ordinariness. Indeed, it may be that the persistent placement of celebrity names within Stein's home not only reflects her central position within the network, but also allegorizes her project of containment—her attempt to limit the name's ability to signify beyond the text, even while her own value relies on that ability. The text thus parallels Stein's situating names within her walls with her undermining the name's reference beyond the narrative, showing both to be ways of destabilizing the name's aura.

The dynamic recalls Benjamin's discussion of the aura that surrounds unique objects:

> Every day the urge grows stronger to get hold of an object at very close range by way of its likeness, its reproduction. . . . To pry an object from its shell, to destroy its aura is the mark of a perception whose "sense of the universal equality of things" has increased to such a degree that it extracts it even from a unique object by means of reproduction. ("The Work of Art" 223)

While Stein's concern is not with reproduction, it is with the recontextualizing of the object, matching Benjamin's anxiety about all objects being made equal when they are removed from their context. In a sense, Stein chooses to "pry" the name from its famous, unique referent. She puts it in "close range" for readers, making it signify an ordinary person within her text as much as it does an extraordinary person in the extratextual world. Benjamin ascribes such treatment of unique objects to a "sense of universal equality of things"—a description that finds its counterpart in *The Autobiography*: Stein portrays herself as "democratic"—someone who believes that "one person [is] as good as another," and who has "deep down as the deepest thing in [her] a sense of equality" (174). This claim correlates with the way Stein treats celebrity names as signifiers of utterly unremarkable people, placing famous figures in familiar, everyday circumstances, and restricting their circulation to domestic spaces, characterizing them as ordinary rather than extraordinary people.

Domestication, in fact, emerges as a key concept in *The Autobiography*, which can be read as a domestic novel of sorts, drawing on a nineteenth-century tradition of chronicling indoor, private doings, filtered through the consciousness of the character who is cast in the role of "wife"—

FIGURE 3.2. Gertrude Stein and Alice B. Toklas at 27 rue de Fleurus. Photograph by Man Ray. The Yale Collection of American Literature, Beinecke Rare Book and Manuscript Library, Yale University.

Toklas. In other words, Stein's interest in the indoor, private rather than outdoor, public affairs of the famous figures can be explained as an affirmation of Stein's and Toklas's supposed positions in their relationship. Stein often uses the typical bourgeois roles of husband and wife to describe her relationship to Toklas. In *The Autobiography* Toklas repeatedly runs interference for Stein, sitting with the "wives of geniuses" (14) so that Stein can monopolize the males. "The geniuses came and talked to Gertrude Stein and the wives sat with me" (87). Catharine Stimpson explains it this way: "the language of self was male and masculine" for Stein, who "was 'husband' to Toklas's 'wife'" (136). We might consider these roles, and Toklas's role as narrator, as a way of accounting for Stein's treatment of the celebrities in *The Autobiography*. That is to say, Stein invokes the wife's traditional view from inside the domestic space at the expense of a perspective from outside the house. Using Toklas as narrator allows her to take names that circulate in the public domain and focus on the private lives of their bearers. We can even see this in the numerous photographs that Stein and Toklas had taken of themselves in their salon: in one famous example, the couple sits opposite one another in the famous Picasso armchairs, between them a coffee table. Above and behind them is the famous collection of works, here relegated to an adornment to the domestic space Stein and Toklas share and control, no more important than the tea service.

In this, Stein echoes the discourses of celebrity that are part of this period's zeitgeist. During the 1920s and 1930s, Joe Moran writes, "celebrity texts began to tease the fault line between the public and private lives of the stars" (62). *The Autobiography* puts stress on that division in its treatment of public figures as ordinary characters. In fact, the roles of husband and wife in the book translate less into gender terms than into categories of public and private. Although, as Benstock argues, "Stein made her homosexual marriage the subject matter for art, describing it in terms that suggested the heterosexual pattern for its roles: Gertrude as husband and Alice as wife" (57), I contend that this pattern is divorced from the body and attached to the idea of celebrity. By situating herself among the husbands, Stein adopts a position that is usually gendered male, thus turning the gendering of that role into a kind of public performance. Throughout *The Autobiography*, Stein categorizes husbands and wives as entities divided into public and private rather than male and female. In terms of *The Autobiography*'s treatment of names, this manifests in Stein's tendency to refer to women only in prename while calling men by their family names, or by both of their names. Picasso is always "Picasso," but his mistresses Fernande and Eve are just called Fernande and Eve. Although we are told that "everybody called Gertrude Stein Gertrude, or at most Mademoiselle Gertrude" (60), Stein, as husband and public half of her marriage, is rarely mentioned as other than "Gertrude Stein" in the text.[11] In *The Autobiography*, then, husbands are celebrities, whose names refer beyond the text to their position in the differential system of the public sphere.

The Autobiography furthers its devaluation of the celebrity name by often throwing out names that are part of Stein's household without differentiating them from the more auratic names. By leaving readers on their own to sort through which names actually have greater value, Stein implies an equality among all the names. Koestenbaum writes of Stein's use of "the proper noun that arrives unexplained, uncontextualized" (313). In *The Autobiography*, this uncontextualized name might refer to Stein's dog, Basket, or to one of the two Stein cars, both of which are given proper names. One of them "was called Godiva because she had come naked into the world" (191). The other is given a proper name after Stein's relative, at the expense of the name of its uncapitalized manufacturer: "Our little ford was almost ready. She was later to be called Auntie after Gertrude Stein's aunt Pauline who always behaved admirably in emergencies" (172). The text operates as if assuming readers will have the same familiarity with names in Stein's domestic space as they do with the names of celebrities; it conflates what is familiar to readers with what is familiar to Stein. Most frequently, Stein's servant Hélène is given treatment resembling that of the more incandescent names, as in this passage:

> It was about this time that Roger Fry first came to the house. . . . Roger Fry had many young disciples. Among them was Wyndham Lewis. . . . Everybody brought somebody. Somebody brought the Infanta Eulalia and brought her several times. . . . Lady Cunard brought her daughter Nancy, then a little girl, and solemnly bade her never forget the visit. Who else came. There were so many. . . . There was Lady Otoline [*sic*] Morrell looking like a marvelous feminine version of Disraeli. . . . There was a roumanian princess, and her cabman grew impatient. Hélène came in to announce violently that the cabman would not wait. . . . It was an endless variety. And everybody came and nobody made any difference. Gertrude Stein sat peacefully in a chair and those who could did the same, the rest stood. . . . As I say everybody brought people. (122–124)

Here, Stein presents the name of her domestic no differently than the royal title of the "Infanta Eulalia." Names such as "Roger Fry" may contribute their particular value to the text, but Stein acknowledges its value no more than she does that of "Hélène." To reinforce Stein's "democratizing" of names, the theme of "everybody brought people" is countered by the refrain of, "Everybody brought somebody and nobody made any difference," which drains each figure of any specific value by announcing that all names are interchangeable in terms of their effect on the events of the salon and on the life of Stein and Toklas.

In this passage, while undermining the value of the celebrity name, Stein plays with its referentiality. She shows that proper names are not always quite fixed to their referents. Here, Wyndham Lewis and Nancy Cunard have not, one might say, grown into their names. Cunard's name refers to a child rather than the journalist she is to become, or, for that matter, the line of ships her famous family owns. Similarly, "Wyndham Lewis" refers to a "disciple," who "used to come and sit and measure pictures"—a habit whose eccentricity his later achievements mitigate (122). Stein plays with the disparity between this Lewis and the 1932 edition, the stridently avant-garde anti-modernist gadfly writer and artist of the year of *The Autobiography*'s publication. These proper names emerge as slippery, representing incarnations of Cunard and Lewis that contrast with their public identities. Compounding this indeterminacy, Stein smuggles the name "Disraeli" into the passage to use as a simile for Lady Morrell. She invokes Disraeli, perhaps the best known of all these names, a name that refers to a long-dead historical/political/literary figure, in order to describe someone else, making one name's meaning depend on another. Furthermore, the names Disraeli and Wyndham Lewis, when coupled, constitute an inside joke. It is a documented fact—one certainly known to Stein—that in 1839 Benjamin Disraeli married a woman whose name was Mrs. Wyndham Lewis. It also seems that Lady Morrell, whose presence in the text incurs the reference to Disraeli, was on friendly terms with Lewis;[12] one can only guess what Stein is insinuating by means of this multilayered linguistic linkage. In any case, Stein shows that when reference beyond the narrative emerges as unstable, the horizontal links between names can create their own counter-narratives.

That Stein should suggest an unstable connection between celebrity names and their referents, or words and their referents, while signaling the system of interdependence that governs value, is not wholly surprising. Saussure, in his lectures of 1906 to 1911, views language itself similarly, arguing, "Language is a system of interdependent terms in which the value of each term results solely from the simultaneous presence of the others" (114). Value, to Saussure, is determined by exactly that relationship between signifiers: "Values remain entirely relative, and that is why the bond between the sound and the idea is radically arbitrary" (113). Saussure's point that words depend on other words, not referents, for significance, explains Stein's tendency to structure names relationally in *The Autobiography*. Saussure imagines the primacy of the relationship among signifiers, relegating as secondary the relationship of signifier to signified. This formulation of language squares with Stein's attempts to reveal the unstable connection between the celebrity name and its extradiegetic referent, her focus on the linkage between the names themselves.

In fact, given that Stein and Saussure were participating in the same historical revision of language, it follows that Stein specifically supports Jean-Joseph Goux's claim that money is the root of all such revolutions. Goux writes:

> The profound rupture in semiotic (Peirce) linguistic (Saussure) or aesthetic (cubism, abstract art) conceptions at the end of the last century and the beginnings of this one—all of which involve an attempt to found meaning on the reciprocal and differential relations between a signifier and another signifier, in an indefinite play of deferrals and referrals, instead of on the

direct relationship between a sign and the thing it signifies or represents—is indeed perfectly congruent with this socio-symbolic transformation of the monetary status of the sign. (118)

Goux shows that the system in which monetary signifiers (cash) signify only credit infinitely defers any direct exchange. This "dematerialization" of money, he argues, correlates with an entire generation's revolutionary emphasis on the horizontal links between signifiers, suggesting that these historically new cultural concerns result from a shared anxiety over whether value inheres in an object or results from exchange. Stein's differential network of names, and her portrayal of name-dropping as currency in the example, early in *The Autobiography* (13), that omits the names, support Goux's supposition that systems of aesthetics and systems of currency are manifestations of the same cultural problem.[13]

In turn, Goux demonstrates that, despite Stein's "rupture" between celebrity name and referent, the constellation of names in her text still, like money, represents a form of capital. But this capital relies on the establishing of an authorized position within the network. Perhaps this is best seen in a passage in which a domestic scene explicitly confounds the name's referentiality. In an episode concerning the fame of Marcel Duchamp, Stein portrays a name as having two contrasting referents, one that is outside the narrative, one within:

> Everybody loved him [Duchamp]. So much so that it was a joke in Paris that when any american arrived in Paris the first thing he said was, and how is Marcel. Once Gertrude Stein went to see Braque, just after the war, and going into a studio in which there happened just then to be three young Americans, she said to Braque, and how is Marcelle. The three young Americans came up to her breathlessly and said, have you seen Marcel. She laughed, and having become accustomed to the inevitableness of the American belief that there was only one Marcel, she explained that Braque's wife was named Marcelle. (134)

At the expense of the tourists, Stein depicts a relationship between the name and its referent that depends on intimate knowledge of Braque's domestic arrangement. When Stein voices the name "Marcelle," she and Braque understand her meaning. By contrast, the Americans mistake the French feminine "-elle" for the masculine "-el"—suffixes pronounced practically identically—and, in their lack of cosmopolitan sophistication, suppose that Stein is referring beyond the immediate context to the famous "Marcel." Under the sway of Duchamp's intense fame in the United States, those with only public knowledge of the celebrities "breathlessly" assume that in Paris the name Marcel (or Marcelle) always refers to Duchamp. The orthographical difference between the two names, of course, lets the reader in on the joke, if not into the group. Stein blocks the tourists' attempt to establish their own link with Duchamp, creates a situation that delegitimates the name's gesture beyond the context for its meaning, and satirizes both the presumptuous invocation of Duchamp's prename and the presumption of the celebrity name's singularity. In this instance, the preoccupation with the domestic is revealed as a preoccupation with the clique. The domestic sphere becomes a kind of coterie, imbued with its own cultural capital, of greater value than that of public knowledge. One must have a view from the inside in order to recognize that the name being pronounced is that of Braque's wife rather than that of a celebrity. Even Stein's readers, accessing these events through this memoir qua tourist guide, are distanced from them by, in many cases an ocean's span, and in all cases more than twenty years of time. One cannot feel a part of an artistic scene from the past, and "in this spring and early summer of nineteen fourteen the old life was over" (142). The referentiality of the name depends on whether one is positioned inside or outside the network.

The Trademark of Time

Stein continues to suggest that whereas the individual name, removed from the network, can be devalued, the nexus of names in her text accrue value that extends to the author. As I have shown, she does so by establishing herself as the central figure of the coterie. Stein also subsumes the value of the celebrity name by integrating its instability into her aesthetics. Her treatment of proper names turns them into a literary device, in keeping with Stein's project of making all linguistic signification temporary.

Stein's use of the proper name to proclaim an unstable connection of signifier and signified contrasts with her view of noun usage in nonliterary linguistic production—knowing that nouns and names derive from the same etymology. In her 1935 lecture "Poetry and Grammar" she disparages journalism for its treatment of nouns. In "newspapers . . . nouns tell it to us that is they name it, and in naming it, it as a telling of it is no longer anything . . . a noun is a name by definition" (*Writings* 334). Here, Stein asserts that in other idioms, the bond between name and referent is closed, final in a way that completely negates the referent. Accordingly, she claims to avoid writing "anything just and only as a name." This account of the name places Stein within a venerable philosophical tradition, Plato having once written, "the name being an instrument, what do we do when we name. . . . Do we not teach one another something, and separate things according to their natures? . . . A name then, is an instrument of teaching and separating reality" (17). Whereas Plato extols the fact that names delineate categories and divisions, clarifying reality, Stein bemoans that very effect, wondering, "If [the name] is adequate then why go on calling it, if it is not then calling it by its name does no good" (313). She writes that by referring to its referent, the name as much as substitutes for it, and she asks, basically, what the point of this is. In other words, the name, by "tell[ing] it to us"—exhibiting a direct correlation of signifier and signified—makes language undesirably transparent.

While it is critically risky to take Stein's theorizing of language at face value,[14] Stein apparently backed these words with actions, or more accurately, with more words: Dydo documents that Stein's manuscripts reveal something of a vendetta against the proper noun. Stein frequently revises proper names into pronouns, "in order," Dydo claims, "to prevent attention from shifting to the references" (*Language* 39). Indeed, Dydo writes of Stein's "insisting that definitions distort by freezing what is constantly evolving and simplifying what is complex" (296). According to this evidence, Stein views proper names—unlike the more indeterminate pronouns—as too fixed to their referents for her taste and her impulse toward difficulty.

Stein disdains the determinism of the proper name, apparently, because it runs counter to the prose style by which she produces her originality and thus her identity as author, a style—Matei Calinescu calls it Stein's "note of undecidability"—that casts all signification as unstable. Primarily, Stein generates this note by emphasizing the process of time in language, by her so-called continuous present. She posits that the gradual unfolding of time diffuses meaning that otherwise seems unshakable. In *The Making of Americans*, one of her earliest attempts at literature, she claims, "this is very true then that to many of them having in them strongly a sense of realizing the meaning of the words they are using that some words they once were using, later have not any meaning" (441). Though she is writing specifically of love letters at this moment, Stein's remarks expose her conception of words as shaking free of reference over time, thus going beyond even Saussure.

Stein's differential view of language depends on time and repetition, both of which change the context of a word. Time alters the horizontal links of the signifying chain by situating each iteration of the word differently, providing different words around it, which, as we have seen, destabilizes signification. As she explains in her 1926 lecture for an Oxford audience:

It is understood by this time that everything is the same except composition and time, composition and the time of the composition and the time in the composition. Everything is the same except composition and as the composition is different and always going to be different everything is not the same. Everything is not the same as the time when of the composition and the time in the composition is different. . . . The time when and the time of and the time in that composition is the natural phenomena of that composition. ("Composition as Explanation," *A Stein Reader* 497)

Here, Stein makes time a crucial component of changes in "composition" that place words in a differential network. The composition creates a time-sense that allows for the generation of linguistic meaning independent of the link between signifier and signified. According to these principles, nouns whose referents are too fixed eventually lose all meaning unless they are repeated in varying combinations with other words. For example, the word "composition" in the passage from the lecture seems to first mean the context of an art object, and then that object itself. The repetition of the word places it in different linguistic positions and thus produces Stein's differential linguistic system.

Indeed, the phrase "a rose is a rose is a rose" demonstrates Stein's claims regarding time and composition. Stein's motto, seemingly tautologically closed by the end of its first clause, is made more ambiguous by an unusual addition, the repetition of "is a rose," which continues the phrase beyond its logical end. This repetition of the clause prolongs the sentence, adding the element of time. It thus allows for multiple readings of the phrase, multiple understandings of which noun or noun clause constitutes the grammatical subject, and which the object. Of course, this diffuse quality of the sentence reminds us that it alludes to Shakespeare's "a rose by any other name," and thus invokes Juliet's question immediately preceding that phrase—"What's in a name?" (*Romeo and Juliet* II. ii)—turning the motto itself into a questioning of all referentiality associated with names.

As the motto demonstrates, Stein attempts to evoke the process of time within her writings as a way of conceiving of language as in flux. This project correlates with the hallmark features of her prose such as repetition, accretion, and the preponderance of gerunds and coordinating conjunctions that always point readers beyond the "current" word or clause and on to the next, which repeats the process. Much critical ink has been spilled in assessments of that style. Stein writes, according to Jonathan Levin, as if "nothing is ever said just once because consciousness does not register anything in isolation: it works by slow and steady accretion"

(153). That is, having iterated something merely once in the past fails to represent a world in which meaning is engendered through process. Most critics, indeed, consider Stein's repetition and accumulation her attempt at a kind of mimesis: prose that captures experience. As far back as 1927 Wyndham Lewis was writing that Stein's style "is intended to convey, with its endless repetitions, the monstrous *bulk* and vegetable accumulation of human life in the mass, in its mechanical rotation" (56). More recently, critics such as Sara Ford have investigated the influence on Stein exerted by the writings of William James, Stein's onetime teacher. Ford writes that Stein kept in mind James's concept of passing states of consciousness, the idea that "once we can see the differences in the self as it exists in different experiences, our need to base our knowledge on an abstract, single, and unchanged self becomes highly suspect" (5). She argues that Stein follows this version of consciousness, attempting to express the temporal movements of the changing self in her prose.

These critical accounts correctly link Stein's rejection of absolute meaning to her conception of the instability of perception and consciousness, but fail to see the implications of this project. Stein's linguistic play is but an aspect of her project of accruing cultural capital. She destabilizes meaning to produce herself as an author who rejects linguistic or cognitive convention. As Koestenbaum writes, Stein "made language's slipperiness seem a reflection of her own psychological and stylistic eccentricity" (318). This idea that an aesthetic of uncertainty finds explanation in authorial psychology, of course, perfectly matches what Foucault points out about the author function, writing, "The author is also the principle of a certain unity of writing" that inspires readers to rationalize anything irrational about the text by imagining the author's complex psychology (221). Stein's aesthetic serves to continually point readers toward the author whose use of language must reflect such a unique and mysterious consciousness.

In most of her work Stein is circumspect about proper names that might fix meaning and undermine her project of self-production. But unlike those unremarkable, unknown proper names that Stein erases from her notebooks, celebrity names can be incorporated into this system. *The Autobiography* destabilizes the referentiality of the name, partly through the manipulation of time. As examples, we may consider the references to Wyndham Lewis and Nancy Cunard in the passage I cited earlier. These figures are shown in an immature stage of development—a stage that will culminate in the popular correlation of character to celebrity only later in *The Autobiography*. Stein invokes these names to put in play their dual meanings, which are separated by time. In other words, to refer, in 1932, to Wyndham Lewis as an "apprentice" is to show that the passage of time has altered the name's reference. Similarly, in a description of Ford Madox Ford, Stein suggests that the passing of time changes the name's reference and the name as well. She writes, "Ford Madox Ford had started the Transatlantic Review some months before. A good many years before, indeed before the war, we had met Ford Madox Ford who was at that time Ford Madox Hueffer" (215). In this instance, the shifting identity of the referent over time is matched by the shifting of the name. Celebrity names, then, do not disrupt Stein's signature indeterminacy. Stein incorporates time into her system of treating the value of names relationally.

Stein establishes early in *The Autobiography* that time will figure prominently in her work on the celebrity name, through Hélène's musings on the fame achieved by those whom she once served omelets. "Isn't it extraordinary, all those people whom I knew when they were nobody are now always mentioned in the newspapers, and the other night over the radio they mentioned the name of Monsieur Picasso. Why, they even speak in the newspapers of Monsieur Braque" (8). These figures were once "nobody" to Hélène, but years later their names are seen and heard in popular culture. Here, the celebrity name as it appears in the press seems to mean someone entirely different from the person once situated within Stein's house. Hélène's wonder gives expression to how celebrity names, over time, change their referent. Of course, these names refer to a different iteration of the celebrity not only because of the passing of time, but also because the celebrity is outside the domestic space, outside of Stein's sphere, outside the network that can stabilize value.

Name of Constant Value

Stein's manipulation of time helps us understand why the celebrity name becomes such a prominent figure within her writing and also reveals the way that Stein can destabilize the value of other names while maintaining the constant value of the author's. Time's effect on the name is instrumental to what is possibly *The Autobiography*'s most notorious moment: Stein's claim to the status of genius through association with others. Recounting her initial encounter with Stein, Toklas says, "Three times in my life have I met a genius and each time a bell within me rang and I was not mistaken, and I may say that in each case it was before there was any general recognition of the quality of genius in them" (5). Toklas's insight produces a rarefied club of three geniuses: Stein, Picasso, and Alfred Whitehead. What I would like to point out here is that while Picasso's and Stein's stars remain ascendant now, more than seventy years after the publication of *The Autobiography*, Whitehead's reputation now probably pales in comparison. Even though Whitehead made his influential mark on twentieth-century philosophy, his name no longer excites the public recognition it once did. At the time of *The Autobiography*'s publication, though, it was Stein who trailed Whitehead in renown. Placing herself alongside Picasso and Whitehead in a triumvirate of genius may have been an act of chutzpah on Stein's part in 1932. The intervening years have dulled that effect, though. The time "outside" of Stein's composition—though a function of her text—has changed the value of the name "Whitehead."

Despite the name's instability of reference, at this one moment the sense of value shared among celebrity names seems more stable than it does in the longer lists of names, because here Stein makes the set of geniuses finite. By mediating this assertion of genius through Toklas, specifically through Toklas's interior, physical response, Stein ends the chain. Indeed, the ability to immediately perceive genius is what distinguishes the narrator. Stein grants Toklas, one of the novel's few major characters not engaged in artistic production (the others are all wives, too), an instinctive and sensory recognition of genius. In fact, one might argue, as Barbara Will does, that through Toklas's receptivity the novel imagines "the dialogic nature of the capacity of genius," which emerges as "a shared phenomenon" between Stein and Toklas (140). Most certainly, it is Toklas's particular gift of insight that justifies her role as narrating voice, and allows her to be positioned at the center of the text alongside Stein, physically closest to the famous individuals with whom the couple socialize.[15] While Toklas is not included as a genius, she is linked to the trio of geniuses through her role as the narrating "I" of *The Autobiography*.

But we should ask, what does the pronoun "I" really signify in this book? Aside from the diegetic character of Toklas, we are informed by the book's cover, and told within its pages,[16] that it refers extradiegetically to Stein, who is practicing authorial ventriloquism through Toklas. Dydo calls this Stein's "joining the substance of Stein to the voice of Toklas" (540), but surely Stein the author overwhelms Toklas the diegetic figure. Famously, the book ends with Stein's declaration that she is going to write the autobiography, and Toklas's parting remark, "And she has and this is it" (252), which erases all pretense of keeping the authorship secret. In Stein's manuscript these words are followed by a crossed-out signature, "Sincerely yours Alice B. Toklas" (Dydo 537). The conscious erasure of the narrator's name testifies to the fact that the work's narrating consciousness inevitably points back to Stein. And of course, the "I" of Toklas allows the name "Gertrude Stein" to appear in the text. So the closed circuit of genius that seems to be circumscribed by Toklas, unsurprisingly, refers to Stein's authorship, further adding luster to her name.

Furthermore, the fact that Toklas's main attribute is her appreciation and understanding of genius, and that her name and every enunciation of the first-person pronoun invoke the author, creates yet another circuit. Toklas's physical response demonstrates a structural link to Stein's claim to be investigating "the insides of people" (*The Autobiography* 119). "Alice B. Toklas" may refer to Stein, but "Gertrude Stein" does not refer to Toklas. So the proximity of Stein and Toklas, and Toklas's recognition of Stein's genius, produces a stable value for the name of the author as it appears both in the text and in its extradiegetic incarnation. The name of the author, within and above the signifying chain, filtered through Toklas's body, acquires the status of genius even within the relational system that governs the text. Stein is making the value of an object understood when it is consumed by another—when it passes through the body of another.

That Stein locates Toklas's radar for genius inside the body suggests that the object's importance is dependent on the subject. It makes the highest possible value, however, dependent on physical proximity as well. Recalling the importance of domestic space in *The Autobiography*, Stein makes genius depend on one who shares its physical space—Toklas. Similarly, Stein construes identity from a circuit between herself and another. She repeatedly makes the assertion, "I am I because my little dog knows me"—in "Identity, a Poem," (*Reader* 589); in *Everybody's* (297); in "Henry James" (*Writings* 149); in *Geographical History of America* (*Writings* 464); and in "And Now," her article published in *Vanity Fair*.[17] Identity, according to this assertion, depends on not only Stein's dog recognizing her, but also Stein recognizing that her dog recognizes her. In other words, Stein is Stein because her dog knows her and because she knows that her dog knows this, a back-and-forth that is enacted by the repetition of the first-person pronoun in the words "I am I." I think that my dog thinks therefore I am.[18] This chiasmatic movement—from one person to another and back to the first—incorporates the motion, and thus the time, that forms Stein's aesthetics. In so doing, the movement parallels Stein's use of the celebrity name.

This movement between bodies that Stein repeatedly describes helps explain the devaluation of visuality in Stein's work, particularly in comparison with the celebrity name. In *The Autobiography*, Stein says, "the human being essentially is not paintable" (119). But Stein says a lot of things. She provides more specific contrasts between words and images throughout her writings, often in relation to celebrity. A moment in *Everybody's* emblematizes how the celebrity name can invoke the circuit between the body and the object. Stein visits New York with Toklas and, first, hears her name spoken aloud by a stranger and, second, sees her own name in lights, a public display of the celebrity name that elicits her mixed reaction of disquiet and gratification:

> How do you do Miss Stein, said the man, how do you do I said. . . . He was so natural about knowing my name that it was not surprising and yet we had not expected anything like that to happen. If anything is natural enough it is not surprising and then we went out again on an avenue and the elevated railroad looked just as it had ever so long ago and then we saw an electric sign moving around a building and it said Gertrude Stein has come and that was upsetting. Anybody saying how do you do to you and knowing your name may be upsetting but on the whole it is natural enough but to suddenly see your name is always upsetting. Of course it has happened to me pretty often and I like it to happen just as often but always it does give me a little shock of recognition and non-recognition. (174–175)

This passage contrasts the "natural" and thus un-disturbing use of the name with the perturbing sight of the name. The reference to the el, "look[ing] just as it ever had," emphasizes the spectacular quality of this moment. Stein's simultaneous "shock of recognition and non-recognition" indicates acceptance and rejection of the name as a publicly available, visible signifier of her identity.

Stein dwells on visuality throughout her writings. Especially in composing numerous literary portraits of famous artistic figures, invoking a genre that implicitly compares images to language, Stein mostly eschews the language of visual description, holding "the idea of representation in complete disregard," as Ulla Haselstein puts it. Stein instead creates "abstract word collages as conceptual equivalents for the subjects in question" (724–725). Critics commonly compare Stein's literary portrats to painting, for obvious reasons: Stein's critical and curatorial interest in the Paris art scene, coupled with the fact that many of her portrait subjects were artists, invite the comparison between cubist and fauvist works and Stein's own writing.[19] To compare Stein to those painters such as Matisse and Picasso with whom she aligned herself, though, is to base criticism only on the celebrity network she was producing. I would like to suggest that Stein's exploration of the celebrity name is at least as much of a key to understanding Stein's portraits as her interest in painting is.

Stein claims that her portraits reflect her "desire to express the rhythm of the visible world," which cannot be represented in a static image (*The Autobiography* 119). Her goal is to convey the back-and-forth intersubjective movement between her interiority and that of her subject. "I must find out what is moving inside of them that makes them them, and I must find out how I by the thing moving excitedly inside in me can make a portrait of them" (*Writings* 298). An interior component of identity transfers between the author and her subject and passes through the border of the body. This, we should note, recalls the referential movement of the celebrity name beyond the border of the text, reflecting value on the author in whose work they appear through an intersubjective transference, the inside of the person-as-object generating the inside of the person-as-subject.

In a portrait of Hemingway, however, what traverses the distance between author and subject is simply more text, taken from another source entirely. Stein is making the construction of identity dependent on the movement between author and subject in such a way that is set in obvious contrast to the image. "He and They, Hemingway" absorbs extratextual material drawn from the very paper on which Stein penned it, a French school notebook celebrating Victor Hugo. The first five lines of the portrait run:

> Among and then young.
> Not ninety-three
> Not Lucretia Borgia.
> Not in or around a building.
> Not a crime not in the time. (*Reader* 449)

About this strange text, Wendy Steiner points out, "the second to fifth lines take up each of the four works of Hugo mentioned on the cover" (113).[20] What seems to me to be most significant about the appearance of the schoolbook material is what it says about Stein's concept of portraiture, specifically Stein's shunning of visuality and her emphasis on the permeability of textual borders. With the appearance of material from the notebook, the private matter of the author—not the celebrity—becomes absorbed within the portrait. Furthermore, although Steiner writes that the works of Hugo are "mentioned" on the schoolbook cover, this is inaccurate. The cover features tableaux representing episodes from Hugo's oeuvre: visual translations, in a sense, of four of the French novelist's works. In the portrait, the "not" that precedes Stein's references to these pictures suggests her rejection of the visual.

The sense that Stein shuns the pictorial here is enhanced by the function of the famous name. Stein does not even mention Hugo. Hemingway is instead compared to Lucretia Borgia, whose mention is spurred by the illustration of Hugo's story. It might be said that illustrations of written texts form a generic counterpart to literary portraits, a genre that traditionally "had to compete with painting, and to emulate the individual life-likeliness of visual representation" (Haselstein 725). If we think of Stein's portraits this way, we can see that she takes these visual translations and translates them back into language. This gesture enacts a similar chiasmus, the same movement back and forth, to the one that Stein constructs between herself and her dog in the "I am I" statement. This movement, furthermore, replicates the way the extratextual material of the Hugo notebook filters through the portrait of Hemingway but comes to rest by defining Stein's authorship. In other words, the supposedly external texts pass through the scene of composition as Stein incorporates them into her writing, and appear in (negative) relation to the portrait's subject, Hemingway. This material contributes, in its obscurity, to Stein's trademark prose style, and, in its allusiveness, to the unstable division between Stein's text and the texts in its proximity. Stein reveals that the intersubjective movement between bodies we have seen in her writings is actually an intersubjective movement between texts. It turns out that the things "moving inside of them [her portrait subjects]" and "moving excitedly inside" of Stein are composed of language. In this model, Stein's portraits can embody the textual three-dimensionality that visual texts cannot.

The proximity between different texts, rather than between different bodies, emerges as the essential aspect of Stein's portraits. Stein posits that the portrait subject's value lies in the transformation of that person into a combination of words connected to other texts that filter through the author's scene of composition. In this treatment of celebrity portraiture, Stein is not alone. Nancy Armstrong, writing of Alfred Stieglitz's celebrity photographs, argues, "such portraits insist that *they* have conferred uniqueness on the celebrity rather than the other way around" (*Fiction* 259). In both cases, the celebrity emerges as an object recognizable only as a sign of the value of the author. The difference is that Stein, unlike the modernist photographer, rather than playing against realism, has disavowed representational techniques as being only external, having no "inside," as it were. In *Paris France* she writes, "out of doors is made up of air and a painting has no air, the air is replaced by a flat surface, and anything in a painting that imitates air is illustration and not art" (4). Illustration, here, suggests exactly the inadequacy of the visual medium—its two-dimensionality that prevents the author's own inside from infiltrating it, keeping the author's private, textual matter out of the portrait. Stein dismisses visuality in favor of the written text—and the name—that can make the interior available from the outside.

Through the celebrity name, Stein introduces the sphere of the private, of the interior, into her differential system of value. In other words, Stein turns the inside out, making a public display of the texts that comprise a person's interior. The clearest illustration of this is the collection of art and artists that comprise her salon. As J. Gerald Kennedy writes, in Stein's writings her Paris home constitutes a "sign of identity, a projection of personality" (68). But while Kennedy attributes this function to "the stable details of place," it is precisely, I would argue, the instability of the place, the changing cast of characters who arrive and depart, and the rotating set of art objects on display for these guests, that makes her home such a significant part of Stein's self-production. *The Autobiography* makes clear that this changing collection of objects functions similarly to the network of celebrity names for Stein; Stein refers to paintings by the name of the painter: "At that time there was a great deal of Matisse, Picasso, Renoir, Cézanne but there were also a great many other things. There were two Gauguins . . ." (10). Of course, it is hardly unusual to speak of paintings this way. This book's fascination with the celebrity name, though, sheds particular light on this linguistic formulation, indicating an interchangeability of painter and painting. As Stein has defined her value by those names on display within her pages, here she defines it by those objects on display within her walls. They constitute her inside.

At the same time, Stein, and Toklas as narrator, constitute the inside of the coterie. In the voice of Toklas, Stein says, "And now I will tell you how two americans happened to be in the heart of an art movement of which the outside world at the time knew nothing" (28). The two women are at the center of this clique (described, significantly, as a "movement," as if to locate it within Stein's ethos of instability). Stein conceives of herself as containing the network of objects and names, as the book's author, and contained within this network, as the book's centerpiece.[21] In both ways she asserts that all value ultimately depends on its relation to, and creation of, herself.

A Democracy of One

In *Everybody's* Stein writes of celebrity as if it is both universal and a phenomenon of degree:

> I used to say that I would not go to America until I was a real lion a real celebrity at that time of course I did not really think I was going to be one. But now we were coming and I was going to be one.
>
> In America everybody is but some are more than others. I was more than others. (168)

We might assume that to assert that "everybody" is a celebrity is either to elevate all people or to level the playing field that constitutes celebrity, two moves that would tally with the rhetoric of equality that permeates Stein's writings. Yet Stein's somewhat Warholian gesture is undermined by her somewhat Orwellian language of all people being created equal but some being more equal than others. Furthermore, the book's title casts a particular light on Stein's use of the indefinite pronoun; since *Everybody's* is a narrative, not of everybody, but of all those with whom Stein comes in contact, we can take "everybody" in this passage to mean something to the effect of "everybody who comes within Stein's orbit," if not, in fact, "everybody who is Stein." While Stein seems to be celebrating America as a place that confers celebrity democratically, she essentially withdraws value back into herself.

This is the effect of Stein's late writings. Through the accessibility of a more realist mode of narrative, Stein coaxes readers into the atelier, invites them to look around at the famous objects she has collected, but then, when it comes to allowing them into the inner sanctum, she slams the door shut. Stein's ardent critical supporters tend to disavow *The Autobiography* and all of Stein's works composed, as Dydo says dismissively, in "conventional English" (*Reader* 5)—including Stein's memoir-ish writings of the 1930s that have comprised my object of scrutiny here. As Will writes, *The Autobiography* "has long been considered by Stein's most attentive readers as the least 'Steinian'[22] text she wrote—a book about genius but certainly not of it" (138). I have tried to argue in this chapter that it is exactly this less "Steinian" aspect of the writing that reveals Stein's project of self-creation and self-valuation, her use of the celebrity name to construct a system of value that ultimately depends on the last word of the author. The flattening of celebrity throughout Stein's works masks the final authority of the name that appears the most—that of Stein herself, physically positioned in the eye of the storm, a stable figure amid the swirl of names, as if to allegorize both the author's textual control and her function as axis linking all of these names whose value is accrued within her own. Thus these are, in fact, the most crucial Stein texts, the place where Stein is most Steinian.

The crux of Stein's work is that, despite its appearance of making all objects equal, it does so in order to elevate one name above all the others; the apparent leveling of hierarchy does not level Stein herself. Dydo demonstrates how Stein's authorial self-production encourages the view that her aesthetics are liberating and democratizing, writing that in Stein, "nothing is absolute, hierarchies are not respected, roles and identities can change, and the only authority is in the wide democratic freedom of the word that can move, make, and remake itself. It is the world of here and now, which does away with all authority by asking, 'What's in a name?'" (*Language* 18–19). What Dydo misses here is that this "only authority" that resides in "the word," resides in certain words more than in others. Those words, of course, are the words that, in Stein's work, achieve the only semblance of constant value—not only the proper name that refers to the author, but also all the accumulated value of all the celebrity names in *The Autobiography*. The name comes to stand for a quite particular form of democracy: the democracy of Gertrude Stein, everybody's celebrity.

CHAPTER 4

Charlie Chaplin, Author of Modernist Celebrity

Charlie Chaplin is thought to have been the most famous person in the world during the 1920s,[1] and his films show him to be very much a modernist, fashioning himself as an exceptional figure, a high-culture author embodied in an object. His high modernism displays itself most clearly in *Modern Times* (1936), which features what is surely one of the strangest endings in Hollywood history. The film concludes with its otherwise nameless protagonists the Tramp (Chaplin) and the Gamin (Paulette Goddard) walking down a dusty road, east toward the sunrise, away from the camera, penniless. They leave behind the city, their hopes for employment, and, it seems, civilization itself. The iconography is clear: it is 1936, millions are unemployed, and to march into the Great Depression and the Dust Bowl means destitution if not death. Chaplin invokes a familiar trope of 1930s texts, that of the "marginal men," for whom "life on the road is not romanticized" and who "do not participate in any culture," as Warren Susman puts it (171).

FIGURE 4.1. Still from Charlie Chaplin's *Modern Times*. United Artists, 1936. Charles Chaplin/Photofest.

The Tramp and the Gamin seem destined for this non-existence. For the duration of the film they have tried to live and work within society, but now they are cast out.

Happy Endings

This is supposed to be a happy ending, however. Before pressing on into poverty, the Tramp whistles a tune and tells the Gamin to "buck up" and smile; the soundtrack's string section swells around them. The film is sure to show us the illogicality. Before they walk down the country road away from the camera, the Tramp and the Gamin walk toward us. The camera is positioned so that the pair can march forth with their optimistic and determined smiles fully visible. As they approach the apparatus, the fantasy becomes obvious. The machinery of cinema stands in their path; the audience's own spectatorial position is impossible, makes it impossible to accept the narrative. Only when the pair have nearly walked into the apparatus does the film cut to the rear view, showing the characters walking away from their audience. Why, exactly, does this cynical take on transcendence, and the resulting signal of poverty and despair, encourage any optimism? How do we resolve these contradictory signs?

The answers to these questions lie outside of the narration. There is another iconography at work here; the rearview silhouette of the Tramp strolling down the road, in the foreground against a natural vista, complete with bowler hat, baggy pants, and duck-toed walk, recalls previous Chaplin films, including *The Tramp*, which was named for this shot. By invoking similar moments in his oeuvre, Chaplin prompts recognition of the Tramp not merely as a movie character, but also as the mass-reproduced trademark image of Charlie Chaplin, multimillionaire entertainer and worldwide celebrity. This figurative double exposure, the overlaying of the character with the performer/filmmaker/celebrity, reconciles the contradictions between the cheerful atmosphere and the grim story by alleviating the suggestion that the protagonists are doomed. Rather than being reduced to one of the "marginal men"—in Susman's terminology—the Tramp is heading for the Hollywood hills, where Chaplin, far from "not participat[ing] in any culture," engages in one of the most prominent and widespread forms of cultural production—making hit movies for huge audiences.[2] Nice work if you can get it, indeed. *Modern Times* thus provides resolution by overriding narrative logic with celebrity logic, shifting the attention of the audience from the story to the producer of that story. Chaplin's celebrity is encoded within the text.

By mobilizing celebrity in this manner Chaplin intensifies the effect

FIGURE 4.2. Still from Charlie Chaplin's *Modern Times*. United Artists, 1936. United Artists/Photofest.

FIGURE 4.3. Still from Charlie Chaplin's *The Tramp*. Essanay, 1915. United Artists/Photofest.

of the typical Hollywood star, as it is described by Miriam Hansen: "The star's presence in a particular film blurs the boundary between diegesis and discourse, between an address relying on the identification with fictional characters and an activation of the viewer's familiarity with the star on the basis of production and publicity" (*Babel and Babylon* 246). That is to say, the cinematic image of the star gestures beyond the plot to invoke a discourse that transcends the diegesis—that space of fictional people, places, things, and events. Chaplin, however, seems to have raised the stakes here. He makes the filmic resolution of *Modern Times* not only induce, but actually require, recognition of the extradiegetic figure, the real person beyond the text. The film proposes that abandoning plot and leaving the Tramp and the Gamin to their fates is the only way to make sense of otherwise contradictory semiotic material.

This radical change in focus from on-screen image to off-screen celebrity makes meaning dependent on the historical Chaplin, the celebrity. Thus, Chaplin, like the modernist version of authorship I have been tracing through Wilde, Joyce, and Stein, recalls post-structuralist theories of the author. For if, in Foucault's idea of the "author function," the production of the author organizes a text's meaning, that organization matches the Chaplin effect. For Foucault, the author is "the principle of a certain unity of writing—all differences having to be resolved" by reference to the author's life and subjectivity (215). Chaplin, similarly, proposes himself as the key to the text's coherence by reconciling narrative contradictions through the individual who is not only the film's star but also its producer, writer, and director—the author. Again, this dynamic inflates the standard star treatment. In Chaplin's case the presence of the author constitutes an attempt to "impose a limit on that text, furnish[ing] it with a final signified," in the words of Barthes ("The Death of the Author" 147). *Modern Times* evokes the logic of celebrity by relying on recognition of the image, but enlists that recognition to reaffirm the text's unity and closure. As we have seen celebrity discourse operating within the modernist text, through Chaplin we see modernist discourse operating within popular media.

By merging early twentieth-century celebrity with the operations of authorship, Chaplin combines discourses that are structural bedfellows. Chaplin's most productive years, 1914 to 1939, roughly match those of Joyce, years when celebrity was exploding as a popular phenomenon, as Marshall notes (8–9). Celebrity discourse of the period is generally understood to comprise star images and their corresponding publicity and advertising materials, which collectively act as "discursive practices that produce the star's identity," as Richard deCordova puts it (12). This description echoes Foucault's contention that the production of the author signals beyond the narrative: "The text always contains a certain number of signs referring to the author" (215). The celebrity and the author emerge from these arguments as parallel productions of an individual whom the text produces, but produced as if they are located outside the narrative.

In this chapter, I will depict Chaplin as uniquely revealing the commonalities of popular celebrity and modernist authorship. I want to show how Chaplin uses the logic of celebrity to create the author, enlisting the familiarity of his Tramp image to produce himself as the creator of the film, an idealized subject who authors textual signification. While Chaplin mobilizes his celebrity image, he also delineates a distinction between the image and the author, as the conclusion of *Modern Times* exemplifies. Chaplin's work thus signals its distrust that visuality can adequately represent the subject—a paradoxical distrust, perhaps, for a filmmaker, but not for a modernist. With the image stripped of the subject yet remaining on display, however, Chaplin recuperates the Tramp, wielding it as an emblem of his mass audience. The Tramp's universal familiarity, Chaplin suggests, authorizes the image to represent its historical moment: the Age of Chaplin. Celebrity, in Chaplin's work, becomes a way of narrating history.

An Author Is Born

Characteristics of Chaplin's improbable early celebrity established the foundation for the later division between image and subject that marks his particular combination of celebrity and authorship.[3] Chaplin broke into moving pictures in 1914 as an ensemble performer in Mack Sennett's Keystone Studios, a company that churned out slapstick cinema with unparalleled success. This was an arena supposedly resistant to the star system that was taking over Hollywood. As Douglas Riblet writes, Sennett's studio differed from the rest of the film industry in that it "promote[d] its stock company and studio formula over individual stars" (184). Furthermore, the slapstick genre itself constitutes a type of production that leaves little room for its performers' individualization. Slapstick stages "clashes between human beings turned into things and objects assuming a life of their own," as Hansen describes it (Introduction to Kracauer xxi). Indeed, Sennett first hired Chaplin on the grounds that the comedian was "a man who claims that all inanimate objects are perverse" (Dale 31). That is to say, slapstick films put both people and things at the mercy of seemingly unpredictable physical laws, showing scant difference among objects animate and inanimate.

Within this genre Chaplin's characters are often barely able to control their body's movements. A scene from Sennett's only feature-length work, *Tillie's Punctured Romance* (1914), offers a typical example. Chaplin, fleeing the jilted Tillie (Marie Dressler), almost runs full tilt into a police officer, slowing himself with a cartoonish form of braking, a hopping stutter-step. He repeats this motion three times, using it to counter his momentum as he careens into the street, trips and falls over the curb, finds another police officer looming above him, rushes in the direction of the camera, reverses direction, and rushes back. Susan McCabe describes Chaplin in such moments as having an "elastic body [that] is never rendered entirely volitional" (437). The film grants Chaplin a limited degree of agency—only imperfect authority over the body's movements. It reinforces this lack of control by bouncing Chaplin's image between bodies that are either larger (Tillie) or bearing insignias of power (the policemen).

By reducing Chaplin to an automaton, Sennett's films recall Henri Bergson's understanding of physical comedy as depicting a gulf between body and mind. Bergson describes the comedian's "lack of elasticity . . . absentmindedness and a kind of physical obstinacy" (14). Such depictions of the individual elicit laughter "*as a result, in fact, of rigidity or of momentum*, the muscles continu[ing] to perform the same movement when the circumstances of the case [call] for something else." To Bergson, physical humor is rooted in the spectacle of a body limited in its responses to the world because it is emptied of a complete consciousness, and therefore complete agency. In *Tillie's Punctured Romance* and the other Sennett films, Chaplin's performance enacts this division between mind and body. According to Gerald Mast, "There is never a sense of the Sennett characters as people . . . their individuation is strictly in terms of physical type" (92). Sennett produces characters that are physical, rather than psychological entities. Thus Chaplin's image at the outset of his career makes him more object than subject.[4] That this becomes the source of humor—and in fact, of Chaplin's celebrity—will color his entire public life.

With the image of his body devoid of agency and subjectivity, Chaplin's rise to stardom belies most accounts of early Hollywood celebrity. Whereas the initial screen appearances of Chaplin in no way suggest that his body contains a fully realized subject, other Hollywood stars of Chaplin's day are thought to "reveal purified feelings within [the body]" and provide "models of the well-integrated self," as Jib Fowles writes (27). Richard Dyer has written perhaps the most influential analysis of this logic, arguing that stars "articulate what it is to be a human being in contemporary society; that is, they express the particular notion we hold of the 'individual'" (*Heavenly Bodies* 8). This star-function relies on "the idea of the separable, coherent quality, located 'inside' in consciousness and variously termed 'the self,' 'the soul,' 'the subject' and so on" (9). Early film stardom, in these accounts, proposes that the celebrity images articulate, in fact incorporate, a coherent interiority, a fully realized subject.[5] In this way, celebrity addresses questions about how to establish individuality in the face of modernization. As Charles L. Ponce de Leon writes, "Given the growth of cities and the impersonality of the new urban-industrial social order, how could an individual distinguish himself from the crowd and have his unique attributes recognized by others?" (36–37). In these critical accounts, celebrities offered both a reaffirmation and an embodiment of the subject to a culture beset by these anxieties concerning justification of the self. While these scholars establish a basis for understanding the rise of mass-mediated celebrity, they do not entirely explain the particularities of a figure like Chaplin.

For example, according to such accounts, a major component in the production of early Hollywood film stardom is the close-up, the moment when the actor's face fills the screen and dominates the audience's sight. That close-ups were nearly a ubiquitous component of the production of stars during this period is noted by Mary Ann Doane, who writes, "with the formation of a star system heavily dependent upon the maintenance of the aura, the close-up became an important means of establishing the recognizability of each star" (46). Scott J. Juengel describes this cinematic device as "a fetishization of the face" that creates "an intense manifestation of subjectivity" (353). Indeed, the close-up was conceived from the start as a way to make a person's interior life visible; D. W. Griffiths, credited with popularizing the technique, claimed that with the close-up he was "photographing thought" (Schickel 47).[6] Such remarks underscore the critical consensus that early film stardom relies on a notion that images reveal the subject within the body, proposing an interrelation of surface and depth that is at least correlative, if not actually indexical. In other words, the image is proposed as a sign by which the subject, housed within, can be read and understood.

But the close-up is completely irrelevant to Chaplin's celebrity—or, rather, it is only relevant in negation. By eschewing the close-up, Chaplin's initial screen appearances diverge from these scholarly accounts of celebrity-production.[7] *Tillie's Punctured Romance*, for example, unfolds almost entirely in medium-range shots, with a glaring absence of close-ups even at moments when the narrative seems to call for one. In one scene, Chaplin and his partner in crime (Mabel Normand) escape to a movie house that is screening a film called *Double-Cross—A Thief's Fate* depicting a con-artist at work. While watching the film-within-a-film the two characters fidget and exchange glances, exhibiting traces of self-reflection. The frame, however, includes other audience members; the film does not isolate one character's image. Even during this reflexive moment, the film remains barely concerned with creating the interior life of the characters, severely restricting the sense that these images can be considered to represent subjects. That this is the style of film in which Chaplin's star is born foreshadows that Chaplin's treatment of his image will complicate the version of celebrity attributed to his contemporaries.

When Chaplin writes and directs his own films,[8] he transforms his image into an emblem of control, thus dramatizing the production of an author who generates and governs meaning. Chaplin manipulates the very generic materials of slapstick to establish the image as less interchangeable with the other characters or objects, and to cast the Tramp in a new role in this revised slapstick universe. For instance, Chaplin's characterization of the Tramp in *The Vagabond* (1916) contrasts with his limited physical control in the Sennett films. The Tramp, embroiled in a barroom brawl, runs toward the saloon's swinging doors and neatly sidesteps before reaching them; there is no call for the cartoonish stutter-step now. The Tramp's pursuer, naturally, is unable to stop, so his momentum carries him through the doorway. This moment, like the scene in *The Rink* (1916) in which the Tramp literally skates circles around the other characters who slip and fall all over the ice, grants the Tramp a degree of volition that marks him as different from the other images. Other characters are holdovers from the slapstick genre that treats bodies as objects, but the Tramp seems to exist in a less chaotic genre of film. These treatments of the celebrity image announce that the films are controlled by one unified subjectivity.[9] Gilbert Seldes comments on the change in Chaplin's films in a 1924 article: "It was foreordained that the improvised kind of comedy should give way to something more calculated" (40). Seldes refers not only to the more controlled universe of the films but also to Chaplin's involvement with practically every aspect of film production. The Tramp, acting as a fulcrum of control, obliquely but unmistakably refers to the author who has created the text.

This treatment of the image is an instrumental part of the creation of Chaplin as exceptional entity; it makes visible the machinations of authorship identified by Foucault, who writes, "We are used to thinking that the author is so different from all other men, and so transcendent . . . that, as soon as he speaks, meaning begins to proliferate, to proliferate indefinitely. The truth is quite the contrary: the author does not precede the works" (221). Instead, the author is defined by "a series of specific and complex operations" (216). In this formulation, authors do not create meaning; rather, formal attributes of the text create the author. In Chaplin's combination of author and celebrity, the text in question consists not only of the film but also of any place where Chaplin's name or image appears. As deCordova writes, "discursive practices produce the star's identity, an identity that does not exist within the individual star . . . but rather in the connections between and among a wide variety of texts—films, interviews, publicity photos, etc." (120). Chaplin's films, increasing in length and complexity, increasingly gesture beyond the diegesis toward the figure of Chaplin as author of the film, known from previous films and intertextual discourses.

In *Modern Times*, for example, the use of sound incorporates the extra-diegetic Chaplin by invoking Chaplin's famous reluctance to use dialogue. Chaplin's production methods therefore comprise part of the film's meaning. Although the talkies started to appear in the late 1920s, Chaplin held out against dialogue throughout the 1930s.[10] Charles Maland writes, "Chaplin's refusal to make a dialogue film, nearly a decade after sound films were introduced, made *Modern Times* a stylistic anachronism" (157). The film eschews dialogue except for the two moments when a voice emanates from the radio or from the factory boss's giant two-way screen—two moments, that is, when voices are mediated through technology (within the diegesis, as well as without). These instances bear sinister implications in light of the film's obvious distaste for the mechanization of society.[11]

Furthermore, the plot of the film, and Chaplin's author-production, reach a catharsis when the moment comes for the Tramp to perform the singing half of his job as a singing waiter. The film has provided quite a build-up to this. The Tramp needs work to survive, and needs to sing in order to keep his job. Chaplin's voice, of course, has never been heard within a film. When the manager asks, "Can you sing?" the Tramp touches his neck as if wondering whether there is a voice in there at all, a motion clearly invoking the extradiegetic figure of Chaplin and his resistance to sound. As the big moment finally arrives, the Tramp loses his lyrics sheet, stalls for as long as he can, and finally sings nonsense words, making his gestures convey the meaning (though his intonation participates in this as well). The significance of this entire sequence—of sound in *Modern Times*—lies in its insistent invocation of the author beyond the events of the narrative.

While Chaplin relies on the familiarity of his celebrity image to produce the author, he maintains a separation between the Tramp and the extradiegetic Chaplin, using the image only to connote a subject located elsewhere. For instance, Chaplin usually places the Tramp in the role of the protagonist—in fact the hero—of his narratives, a gesture that elevates the image in relation to the other characters. He does so, however, without endowing the Tramp with the particular physical abilities that distinguish the hero of other genres of film; the Tramp rarely performs deeds with guns, swords, or fists. The Tramp's brand of heroism corresponds to Siegfried Kracauer's argument that slapstick makes the hero a figure of luck. Kracauer writes that slapstick does not "highlight the performer's proficiency in braving death and surmounting impossible difficulties; rather, it minimize[s] his accomplishments in a constant effort to present rescues as the outcome of sheer chance" (*Theory of Film* 62).[12] In other words, where Douglas Fairbanks dons the mask of Zorro and swashbuckles around with swords and guns, producing a hero with superior physical attributes, the slapstick hero achieves success without his abilities having had much bearing on it.

North, reading silent film comedy from the perspective of cinematic technology, notices this dynamic: "the more helpless a comedian is in the role of dramatic hero, the more skillful he has to be in handling the technical demands of filmmaking" (*Machine-Age Comedy* 11). North sees the failings of the fictional character as revealing cinematic technique; he suggests the crossing from diegesis to extradiegesis. In Chaplin's films, the Tramp's "luck" invokes the superior physical attributes of the extradiegetic Chaplin. For example, in *The Circus* (1928), the Tramp finds himself performing a high-wire act without the hidden rope he had meant to attach. The Tramp, in Slavoj Žižek's description of this scene, "starts to gesticulate wildly, trying to keep his balance, while the [diegetic] audience laughs and applauds, mistaking this desperate struggle for survival for a comedian's virtuosity" (4). The irony is that this performance does, of course, represent a comedian's virtuosity: Chaplin's. Though the circus audience wrongly identifies the Tramp's actions as a demonstration of his abilities, their response invokes the Chaplin situated outside of the narrative. This scene withholds physical prowess from the character, displacing it, extradiegetically, onto the celebrity. To be sure, the virtuosity of Fairbanks similarly gestures toward the celebrity's real body. Fairbanks's physical skill, however, plays a diegetic function that suggests no separation between celebrity and image; Zorro's abilities have an indexical relationship to Fairbanks's abilities, matching them exactly. Chaplin's ironic play with the Tramp's clumsiness while the circus audience cheers for a virtuosic performance activates an extradiegetic space in the text by invoking Chaplin, beyond the diegesis, and by delimiting the character's capacity to represent him.

Chaplin, indeed, enforces the separation of image and subject inherited from Sennett's films, continually demonstrating that the Tramp is not to be equated with Chaplin. As Devin Anthony Orgeron and Marsha Gabrielle Orgeron argue, "Chaplin produces a double discourse: as the Tramp he is the unknowing, perhaps ambiguous sign, but as Chaplin the director he is creating a critical and specific reading of that sign" (91). In other words, the Tramp figure is treated in the films as an object that points to an author outside of the text.

For instance, *The Idle Class* (1921) casts Chaplin in two roles in order to signal the inadequacy of either as a location of the subject. Chaplin plays, and the title refers to, both the penurious Tramp and a wealthy, tuxedoed alcoholic named Charles. Although Maland contends that these dual personas allegorize Chaplin's biographical contradictions as a rich celebrity born into the working class (60), the film does not merely provide two separate images of Chaplin; it complicates the notion that images have a direct correlation to a subject located inside the body. The plot of *The Idle Class*, stemming from a case of mistaken identity (the revelers at a masquerade ball assume the Tramp is really Charles in costume), thematizes the question of which image contains which identity. The film only shows both images on screen simultaneously when Charles dons a suit of armor whose helmet visor is jammed shut, masking his face. Trying to prove his identity as the real millionaire, Charles enlists the Tramp to help remove the helmet, resulting in the evocative sight of two supposed images of Chaplin trying to wrestle the disguise off of one of them, struggling to remove the exterior in order to verify the interior. Once the visor is lifted, with the Tramp still visible, the film provides a brief glimpse of Charles's face—but only from medium-range, as a close-up of Chaplin at this moment would literally reaffirm the correspondence of the image to the subject in a way that the film is resisting. *The Idle Class* makes use of the celebrity image to question the stable relationship of exterior and interior, staging a separation between the image and the extradiegetic Chaplin, registering suspicion that a single image adequately represents a single subjectivity. Although North considers *The Idle Class* one of Chaplin's "allegories of unwilling reproduction, Chance dropping the tramp into situations in which he must face and in some cases fight his mirror image" (*Reading 1922* 168), he misses the way the film is always sure to reject any assertion that the images on screen contain the subject. In this way Chaplin devises a metonymic relationship between author and image; the Tramp cannot encompass the author, only refer to him. Chaplin's films exhibit a distrust, if not actual rejection, of the idea that an image can embody the author.

This suspicion toward the image reverberates in critical reception of Chaplin's work. This particular kind of critical treatment tries to transform the films by establishing their credentials as art rather than mere entertainment. At the forefront of these commentators is Benjamin, whose newspaper writing regarding Chaplin simultaneously lauds Chaplin's elite qualities and re-enacts the division between author and image. He compares Chaplin with Shakespeare, arguing that, as Shakespeare's stage acting is the least important aspect of his work, so the image of Chaplin on screen is less noteworthy than his writing and directing:

> Chaplin's relationship to film is fundamentally not that of the actor-protagonist at all, let alone that of a star . . . one can almost say that Chaplin, seen in his totality, is as little a performer as the actor William Shakespeare was . . . he is the poet of his films, that is, as director. ("A Look at Chaplin" 309)

Benjamin opposes the "star" that performs to the "poet" who composes. The comparison to Shakespeare specifically, and poets generally, proposes that true artists work off-stage or off-camera, not as figures of display. (There is no audience for watching someone write.) The image of Chaplin's body disturbs Benjamin to the extent that he tries to wish it away altogether. Reviewing Philippe Soupault's treatment of Chaplin, he writes,

"Soupault, unlike virtually all previous commentators, sees the peak of Chaplin's work in *L'Opinion Publique* [*A Woman of Paris* (1923)], a film in which, as is well known, Chaplin himself did not appear at all" (310). Benjamin emphasizes the irreconcilability of author and image implied by Chaplin's works. His gesture suggests that in order for a work to achieve elite status its author must remain invisible. This movement away from the body, toward an intangible construction of the subject, suggests the "purification" of the subject described by Herbert Marcuse as a self-legitimating staple of bourgeois capitalist society. "This noncorporeal being of man is asserted as the real substance of the individual," he writes (104). Society maintains itself through this "affirmative culture" that makes matters of the subject transcend the body. In the case of Chaplin and his interpreters, the insistence on separating the author from the image performs the impulse toward this purified version of the subject.

Chaplin's uneasy negotiation among celebrity, author, and image finds a perfect dramatization in the opening moment of *Shoulder Arms* (1918), a short film that makes a bold claim. The film's title card displays a cartoon sketch of the Tramp in doughboy garb alongside the printed title, and the words "written and produced by" above a blank area. Then a real (celluloid) human hand (Chaplin's) appears, points to the drawing, elaborately signs "Charles Chaplin" in the blank space, and pantomimes shooting a gun at the Tramp. The film announces itself as a product of a single author, represented by a giant, disembodied hand. The hand provides an inimitable signature of the author—a literalizing of Jaffe's idea of the imprimatur of the author—while the Tramp, disfigured by the uniform but still identifiable, provides an inimitable signature of the celebrity. The relationship between the image and the "writer" is codependent but antagonistic: the same hand both signs Chaplin's name and mimes shooting the Tramp. The moment consolidates Chaplin's author-production and his resistance to the image as representation of the subject.

Sign of the Times

The opening of *Shoulder Arms* reminds us that despite Chaplin's conception of himself as an author whose subjectivity transcends the image, the icon of the Tramp remains present in the film, and not quite accounted for. Here Foucault's theory of the author finds its limitations. It cannot completely explain the operations of an author-production that relies on the image even as it situates the author outside the narrative, and that uses the image to connote the author but simultaneously empties the image of subjectivity. For Kracauer, the Tramp image prevents a complete separation of Chaplin's corporeal and idealized identities, writing, "Perhaps Chaplin's triumph rests in conclusively demonstrating, for the first time in recent memory, that this 'person-as-such' is not an abstraction but walks among us, in the flesh" ("Two Chaplin Sketches" 119). To buttress his point Kracauer recounts an anecdote about Chaplin throwing an ostentatiously lavish banquet at which trappings of his Tramp image, instead of appearing on Chaplin's body, adorn the pastry, and are thereby distributed among the partygoers. "The cane and the hat—the badges of his rank as beggar—are still there to be seen: the cooks at the Carlton Hotel carved them out and put them on the frosting, so that the guests could really savor this unusual event" (118–119). The celebration of Chaplin, Kracauer points out, would be incomplete without this revision of Holy Communion, in which the guests take the trademarks of the celebrity host into their mouths.

The Tramp, which Benjamin wants so badly to get rid of, seems to get in the way of the idealized model of the author, whose subjectivity cannot be limited to one image. To Žižek the Tramp is "the remainder" of the text— "left over" from the narrative (7). Žižek notes that in *City Lights* (1931) the Tramp is "always interposed between a gaze and its 'proper' object ... [and] occupies a place which is not destined for him." When discovered, the Tramp "turns into a disturbing stain one tries to get rid of as quickly as possible" (4). *Modern Times* follows a comparable pattern, continually altering the Tramp's station in relation to social institutions. For example, the Tramp repeatedly shifts from one side of the law to the other, enduring two prison sentences, preventing a jailbreak, and briefly finding employment as a security guard.[13] The film characterizes the Tramp as a problem, continually repositioning him within the social structures as if to indicate the uncertainty of his textual function.

At the same time, Chaplin shapes this "remainder" as an image that is recognized even when reduced to its simplest components of mustache, bowler, baggy pants, splayfeet, and some combination of cane, tails, and plaid waistcoat. For example, the plot of *The Kid* (1921) hinges on the need of the Mother (Edna Purviance) to track down the Tramp. To this end she places a personal ad in the newspaper (depicted in a close-up) that announces her search for a "little man with large flat feet and a small mustache." The narrative depends upon whether characters will identify the Tramp using these clues, and it therefore invokes the image's recognizability—its ubiquity within Chaplin's films and intertextual discourses. *Sunny Side* (1919) unfolds similarly, opening with the Tramp in bed, encased in a nightgown that, it turns out, he wears over the baggy pants and waistcoat. Gradually removing the outer garment to reveal his outfit, Chaplin jokes that he sleeps dressed this way, and thus reinforces this image's trademark quality.[14] Furthermore, the appearance of these garments announces the familiar character Chaplin will play in the film, providing a key to the ensuing plot, and incorporating the trademark into the film's system of signification by keying audiences in on how the story should be understood, much in the manner of, oh, a chapter-by-chapter guide. By enlisting his image's familiarity, Chaplin insists on it, making the image recognizable by assuming its recognizability.

Chaplin thus makes his image into an icon, a "universal symbol" as Seldes calls it (35). "The iconic quality of any celebrity is also the zenith of a career," writes Marshall, adding, "what the icon represents is the possibility that the celebrity has actually entered the language of the culture and can exist whether the celebrity continues to 'perform' or dies" (17). Chaplin's films promote his Tramp as an image that represents more than himself; rather, it becomes an emblem of the collective experience provided by his films, proposing that his work unifies everyone in his audience, possibly the largest viewing audience in the world. Chaplin's "immediate recognizability" in his Tramp guise is not only "the very basis of his appeal,"[15] it actually composes the insignia of the masses that consume his films.[16] In other words, while granting the image only a metonymic relation to the author and leaving it over as "remainder," Chaplin also asserts that the celebrity image makes legible his mass audience.

As an emblem of the masses, the icon becomes, in *Modern Times*, a way of telling history. More than most of Chaplin's films, *Modern Times* is set in a specific moment, the 1930s; this moment is indicated by the title, the indexical word "modern," and the film's striking scenes of social unrest. The narrative unfolds against a backdrop of historical change, onto which Chaplin superimposes the Tramp, who exists, as usual, somewhat apart from the diegesis. Chaplin withholds the icon during the first section of the film, putting the character in factory clothes. When the Tramp emerges in his trademark regalia after a stay in the "hospital," his appearance has the effect of those moments in *The Kid* and *Sunny Side*, invoking the familiarity of the icon. In this case, the arrival of the icon coincides with the arrival of a new historical stage. Chaplin indicates the temporal transition through a montage of filmmaking techniques: abrupt crosscutting between shots at tilted angles, superimpositions, and crowds of people and cars moving rapidly through the city, all set to jarring brass-wind music. The film then situates the Tramp contiguously with signs of social upheaval, first placing him against a backdrop of a closed factory, and then putting him at the vanguard of a socialist demonstration (to which he remains oblivious). This sequence unites signs of social upheaval, technological advancement, and Chaplin's heavy-handed but non-transparent cinematic style to indicate that the film has entered "modern times"—all spurred by the appearance of the celebrity image and its unaltered and unaltering appearance.

In fact, some of the most vivid and famous scenes of the film, such as when Chaplin is subjected to the feeding device and takes a trip through the giant gears of the factory, are firmly established as the film's past, a period prior to the modern times and social unrest that ensue.[17] *Modern Times* thus uses the icon as a marker of historical change. The celebrity image becomes at once a universally identifiable emblem of Chaplin's mass audience and a sign of that audience's moment in history. The ongoing reflexivity of the film adds to this sense. Chaplin's recycling of his earlier work forms part of North's reading of *Modern Times*, which he calls "a massive anthology of Chaplin's favorite devices," in order to argue that Chaplin is disavowing his previous aesthetics (*Machine-Age Comedy* 188). North is astute to note that the intertextuality conveys cultural transition; he thus supports my reading that the references to prior films proffer the idea that the Tramp has become a transcendent historical icon. Among the pat routines *Modern Times* incorporates is Chaplin's skating, previously seen, as I note above, in *The Rink*. But where the 1916 skating shtick alludes to an author among images, a subject among objects, the 1936 edition features the Tramp skating by himself, as now the audience is made visible in his body.

The logic behind this gesture is clarified by Benjamin's concept of the dialectical image that furnishes a culture with a method of identifying itself:

> What distinguishes images from the "essences" of phenomenology is their historical index.... For the historical index of the images not only says that they belong to a particular time; it says, above all, that they attain a legibility only at a particular time.... Every present day is determined by the images that are synchronic with it: each "now" is of a particular recognizability.... Image is that wherein what has been comes together in a flash with the now to form a constellation. In other words: image is dialectics at a standstill. For while the relation of the present to the past is purely temporal, the relation of what-has-been to the now is dialectical: not temporal in nature but figural. (*Arcades Project* N2a,3–N3,1, 462–463)

Benjamin argues that although images and time are in a sense opposed—as images are static but time moves from the "what has been" to the "now"—images can provide a static figure of temporality. In this system images achieve "a particular recognizability" at a specific historical moment and define that moment by crystallizing the dialectical relationship between past and present. That is to say, instantly identifiable images put temporality in stasis. Clearly, Benjamin and Chaplin articulate similar lines of thought in different cultural spheres. In Benjamin's terms, *Modern Times* elevates Chaplin's icon to the status of historical emblem by suggesting that its familiarity makes it a static figure of his moment, defined against and incorporating the "what-has-been" of the past. Justus Nieland, in his assessment of Chaplin as modernist, sees Chaplin in a similar way. He writes that Chaplin constitutes "a story of the modern person's relationship to temporality and historicity . . . that is everywhere synonymous with the potential—and threat—of Chaplin's eccentric personality" (252). Though Nieland's goal is to identify modernism's insistent (and critically overlooked) reliance on affect, his analysis supports my purpose. To Nieland, Chaplin's identification with his moment is exactly what constitutes his modernism.

Benjamin and Nieland provide the basis by which we can see Chaplin's work demonstrating that celebrity images, specifically, those legitimated by the audiences that grasp their meaning instantly, act as transcendent signs of their times. They can be removed from context because they incorporate that context, like Chaplin's skating moment in *Modern Times*. Chaplin thus assigns celebrity the social function of emblematizing history. Schickel has retroactively identified Chaplin with the inception of this version of celebrity. He calls the celebrity image "a walking context [that] we apprehend instantly" (*Intimate Strangers* 70). These images contain their own historical backdrop and become figures for their eras, tokens of their historical moments. That all starts in the 1920s: "In the 1920s, the media, newly abustle, had discovered techniques whereby anyone could be wrested out of whatever context had originally nurtured him and turned into [celebrity] images . . . for no previous era is it possible to make a history out of images . . . for no subsequent era is it possible to avoid doing so. For most of us, now, this *is* history" (70–71). Schickel proposes the 1920s as a moment that provides the techniques and the logic to treat the celebrity image as history. Considered alongside this argument, Chaplin appears to be participating in a broader cultural imperative of distilling the passage of time into an image that, by virtue of being ubiquitous during a particular era, now embodies that era. Nieland is correct to think of this as a modernist effect. Modernism's very appellation promotes it as fixed in a historical period and simultaneously looking to the future, always able to carry that moment forward in time. Similarly, Chaplin's *Modern Times* claims both Chaplin's representative power for his moment and his ability to signify that moment to later audiences. Modern times, we are told, are Chaplin's times, the time of Chaplin and his audience. Chaplin authorizes the celebrity icon to function as a sign of history.

By gesturing beyond the boundary of the text, toward Chaplin's audience, the Tramp image makes legible that significant portion of the masses unified in recognition of Chaplin's celebrity, thereby affirming that the celebrity sign depends on its wide circulation to attain significance. As Marshall writes, "The celebrity's power is derived from the collective configuration of its meaning" (65). The image's connotative function requires collaboration with the audience, and the Tramp's recognizability to that audience as it moves through scenes of historical change, whatever other discourses may attach to it. North writes that, to critical admirers, "Chaplin appealed as the symbol of a symbol, one so purified of the abstract and arbitrary that it could be read and understood universally" (*Reading 1922* 166). Chaplin's universality was understood as encoded within the Tramp image, turning the icon into a figure around which a culture organizes itself and then communicates itself to subsequent generations. The durability of this effect is testified to by the ongoing appearances of that image, edited and refined, in what would be considered the most unlikely places—on the cover of salsa legend Hector Lavoe's 1978 album *Comedia*, in IBM commercials, everywhere in the world on October 31 of each year—were it not for the point that there are no unlikely places. The effort to separate subject and image that permeates Chaplin's work thus enables the creation of this principal role of the celebrity.

The Object of Celebrity

We return to the conclusion of *Modern Times*, and specifically to the background music that clues viewers in to the happy ending. Chaplin composed this score. Years later, John Turner and Geoffrey Parsons adapted the theme and added lyrics. Titled "Smile," the song has become an American standard, and has been performed by professional crooners and jazz musicians worldwide.[18] Turner and Parsons's lyrics to "Smile" illuminate Chaplin's legacy:

> Smile though your heart is aching.
> Smile even though it's breaking.
> When there are clouds in the sky, you'll get by.
> If you smile through your fear and sorrow,
> Smile and maybe tomorrow,

You'll see the sun come shining through for you.
Light up your face with gladness.
Hide every trace of sadness.
Although a tear may be ever so near,
That's the time you must keep on trying.
Smile, what's the use of crying?
You'll find that life is still worthwhile,
If you just smile.[19]

These words re-enact the separation of subject and image found in Chaplin's films by enjoining the listener to smile, to change countenance, in the face of the despair afflicting the self. And yet, in a way, the image has control over the self. To smile—to "hide every trace" of the subject on the image—is to bring about a desirable change in attitude. The changed image changes the self. That change, furthermore, is located within neither the image nor the self divorced from the body; it is found in the sun, "shining through." Here, the idea of a disembodied subject is supplanted; the lyrics assert that the image's relation to the surrounding world is a manifestation of subjectivity.

Numerous moments of Chaplin's career illustrate the way that, by establishing his icon in metonymic relation to his self, Chaplin created an image that ultimately controlled his identity as surely as Valentino was sure that his life was controlling him. One example of this is Kracauer's anecdote about the Tramp dessert. Another is Chaplin's appearance, after twenty-five years as a political exile from America, at the 1972 Oscar ceremony, which the audience deemed incomplete until the eighty-three-year-old donned a hat and cane and performed his famous bowlegged walk (Maland 347). In a similar vein we have North's report that Chaplin's public appearances without his trademark accouterments were often met with disappointment. North explains the dynamic this way: "The crowd seems spellbound by the aura of the famous individual, and yet it also seems intent on destroying that aura, so much that it resorts to duplicating him against his will and then taunting him with its power to possess his duplicates" (*Reading 1922* 167). These moments each pinpoint the particular inescapability of the Tramp icon for Chaplin, and the way his trademark seems to displace some of the agency of the subject.

A telling example of this effect exists in the form of *The Great Dictator* (1940), a satire of Hitler, and Chaplin's last film featuring the Tramp. Once more, Chaplin appears in two roles, playing both a Jewish barber (in recognizable Tramp mode), and a fascist dictator named Adenoid Hynkel.

In most accounts, the film is an expression of both Chaplin's repugnance toward the Nazis' campaign of genocide and world domination and his irritation toward Hitler's own production of the icon as an embodiment of the masses.[20] Chaplin invokes his famous resistance to synchronized dialogue in *The Great Dictator* as he does in *Modern Times;* while his Hynkel speaks in a pidgin German, the barber remains mostly silent throughout the film. Only at the finale does the audience hear, for the first (and last) time, sustained speech from the Tramp's mouth: he delivers the homily to peace and hope that was to be roundly dismissed by viewers and critics after the film's release.

Yet the main result of this speech, and of *The Great Dictator* in its entirety, is to reaffirm Chaplin's icon as the inescapable object that generates his identity. The speech seems anticlimactic precisely because the spell of silence that has accompanied the Tramp throughout Chaplin's career is suddenly broken. The moment suffers in contrast with Chaplin's renown as a universal figure who transcends language.[21] In a different vein but to similar effect, the contrast between the virtuous barber and Hynkel, whom Chaplin portrays as a frothing lunatic, leaves no doubt as to which image is authorized to represent the figure of mass adulation. While denigrating Hitler, Chaplin does not denigrate the idea of elevating the icon above the masses. Rather he condemns that it should be put to such perverse use. At the same time, the public outcry about the film from an America not yet committed to war was very much an outcry about a movie star overstepping his bounds and venturing into the realm of international politics — however quaint that objection now seems. The reaction to *The Great Dictator* thus emblematizes how Chaplin's public image confined his capacity to produce his own self. Having established his identity as a function of the mass audience's familiarity with his image, the meaning of his work becomes subject to that response.

Indeed, Chaplin's work formed evidence against him in trial much as Wilde's work was used against him. In the case of Chaplin, this trial was held less in a court of law — Chaplin's various legal troubles notwithstanding — and more, as the cliché would have it, in the court of public opinion. Nieland writes: "the comedian's star image in the 1930s became increasingly wedded to those progressive political commitments expressed in his most celebrated satires," by which he means *Modern Times* and *The Great Dictator* (257). In the post-modernist, post–World War II, early Cold War United States, the fact that Chaplin's image was readily identified with the ideals of progressivism made him an easy and popular target of anti-communist paranoia, landing him in political hot water. If those dangerous pre-war ways of thinking were to be eradicated, Chaplin would have to go. Of course, what developed around Chaplin—his catching the panoptical eye of J. Edgar Hoover's young Federal Bureau of Investigation and eventually being denied re-entry into the United States on the specious grounds of subversion[22]—testifies to the immensity of his effect, the intensity of the changes he wrought, on the perception of celebrity. That Chaplin's popularity seriously ebbed in the 1940s was beside the point. It was, in other words, Chaplin the icon of his historical moment, Chaplin the individual whose image subsumes the idea of mass resistance, that was considered a threat.

By denying Chaplin his visa in 1952, Hoover was performing an astute, if misguided, anti-celebrity polemic. This was nine years before Daniel Boorstin published his famous condemnation of the celebrity as "*a person known for his well-knownness*" (56). Perhaps it is no coincidence that just two years before Chaplin was exiled, Billy Wilder's *Sunset Boulevard* had similarly expressed the fantasy of removing a 1920s film icon from society and from sight. But, in one of the film's memorable moments, before Nora Desmond can be finally removed, she is sure to don hat and tails and perform a Chaplin impersonation. Apparently, the role of celebrity Chaplin embodied, as icon of history, was almost ready for its close-up, and institutions of culture from government to fiction to cultural criticism stepped forward to express their ambivalence.

> Back in touch with literary London she [Rhys] heard those rumors again: Jean Rhys was dead.
>
> CAROLE ANGIER, *JEAN RHYS: LIFE AND WORK*

CHAPTER 5

Rhys, the Obscure: The Literature of Celebrity at the Margins

In 1956, Francis Wyndham, having not yet become one of Jean Rhys's most ardent professional supporters and friends, published an essay referring to its subject as "the late Jean Rhys." Ten years later Rhys completed work on and published *Wide Sargasso Sea*. Rhys's obscurity, that which prompted Wyndham's erroneous assumption and epithet, would seem to be the very opposite of fame. The obscure, far from indicating an apotheosis of the individual subject, represents a state of being in which one's very existence is called into question. Accordingly, of the various figures this book examines in the light of celebrity and modernism, Jean Rhys is most likely to induce raised eyebrows. After all, Rhys's self, not entirely self-fashioned, seems to read quite differently from that of the celebrity, especially when compared with those grandiose textually constructed identities of Wilde, Joyce, Stein, and Chaplin. The Rhys biography and oeuvre, though, share important characteristics with the other figures analyzed here.

Ella Gwendolyn Rees Williams was born in Dominica of Welsh and

Scottish-Creole ancestry in 1894. She became an unrestrained practitioner of modernist aesthetics during her early, expatriate publishing career (1926–1938), one that immediately followed the high modernist moment. Her representational techniques, often elliptical and often nonlinear, certainly can be considered obscure. I use the term obscure here not only for its meaning as something unknown, but also because of the notion of a literary work that is difficult to penetrate for its unconventional style and thus contributes to constructing the modernist author. Delia Caparoso Konzett writes of Rhys's "conscious deployment and appropriation of modernist stylistic techniques" (133). Rhys's style, in other words, conforms to those modernist gestures that I have shown to correspond with the creation of the celebrity.

Thus end the major parallels. For over a decade during and after World War II, at the chronological midpoint of her literary career, Rhys lived in virtual anonymity. Rhys never generated an image that became famous, never produced a style that became famously associated with her, never investigated the semiotics of famous names, and never, by twentieth-century standards, became terribly well-known—although eventually the splash made by *Wide Sargasso Sea* (1966) established her literary reputation and returned her earlier writings to public circulation. Rhys's history suggests a chronicle more of obscurity than of fame.

Yet the obscurity Rhys lived in, an obscurity that finds its counterpart in the abject position of Rhys's protagonists, can be seen as a defining obverse of the cultural currency that constitutes celebrity. Rhys offers glimpses of not only the way celebrity discourse appears in the most unlikely places during the modernist period, but also how intersections between celebrity and modernism have permeated literary culture since the end of the modernist period. In this chapter, I will argue that the syncretism between Rhys's life and work demonstrates that the literature of celebrity underwrites her career, and that Rhys's works figure anonymity into the structures we have seen more aurified writers using to think through the idea of celebrity.

Rhys's protagonists—Mary Cantwell calls them all "the same woman although she bears different names" (21)—are marginalized by gender, geography, nationality, and age. They are marked anonymous by the same tokens that render fame: they are objects on display—distinct, irreproducible, and non-reproducing. But they remain powerless, residing below rather than above the crowd. In Rhys's writings, the materials of celebrity construe not the modernist exception but the abject, which in turn becomes another way of articulating the individual in the face of mass culture. Marginalization creates not Barthes's "Platonic Idea of the human creature," but a dystopic idea, and one that does not even always seem human. Rhys participates in a mutually defining production of the individual with the figures I examine in my earlier chapters by offering up an idea of the obscure, the anonymous, as a figure just as incompletely comprehensible as the celebrity.

By reading Rhys in this vein I argue that celebrity provides explanatory power for texts of modernism besides those that explore celebrity most prominently, and besides those whose personalities loom above (or within) their writings. I begin by treating the works Rhys published in the first phase of her career, the short stories and four novels published between 1926 and 1938, touching most emphatically on the last of these, *Good Morning, Midnight* (1938). These writings, I argue, constitute an odd but undeniable entry in the literature of celebrity. They explore the structures of individual display in relation to the anonymous crowd, and they deploy autobiographical material to generate a figure of the author; thus they construct the desire to rise from the abject position in order to enter, rather than rise above, the masses. From these early writings I move to a re-reading of *Wide Sargasso Sea*, which, I contend, continues Rhys's exploration of the abject's relation to the mass. Finally, I look at one of Rhys's final stories, "Sleep it Off, Lady" (1976). Rhys's late works, I note, demonstrate a particular concern with vermin: pests. I read Rhys's repeated interest in her protagonists' relation to non-humans that feed off human civilization as her final expression of desire to resist extraordinariness. My argument in this chapter ultimately points beyond modernism and celebrity. Here, not only do I stress that celebrity helps us understand Rhys, and that Rhys reinforces modernism's engagement with celebrity, but I also argue that Rhys reveals the ways celebrity, by the time of *Sargasso*'s publication, could already be seen as a dominant subtext of the Anglo-American literary tradition, proliferating beyond the modernist era, making a cunning passage into the postcolonial field.

That Obscure Abject of Desire

Anonymity, obscurity, abjection: these terms frequently arise in commentary about Rhys because they characterize dynamics particular to practically every Rhys text, including that of her life. Rhys's work constructs people, almost exclusively women, who generally reside not exactly at the bottom of the social system, but rather outside of it altogether, maintaining no fixed role. Rhys renders them in their own way "extraordinary"—as Mr. Blank calls Sasha Jensen in *Midnight* (27). Their lowly and often irrelevant positions comprise, but are ultimately unlimited by, their gender, class, economics, age, marital status, sexual mores, occupation, nationality, and dipsomania. As they reside outside of the social system, they disrupt the semiotic one. Abjection, according to its foremost theorist, Julia Kristeva, is related to "what disturbs identity, system, order" (4). "When I am beset by abjection," she writes, she experiences and perceives something that "is not an ob-ject facing me, which I name or imagine" (1). The abject has no power to name. In Rhys, this unnamable abjection is accompanied by an exploration of anonymity, which emerges as both condition and desire; the protagonists occupy a status so illogical that they are both stripped of an identity and simultaneously unable to physically place themselves somewhere they can avoid notice—despite a constant effort to do so. Rhys's characters would like nothing better than to dissolve into the mass, but they cannot. *Midnight*'s Sasha repeats to herself, "Faîtes comme les autres—that's been my motto all my life" (106). Act like everyone else, she exhorts herself. The deployment of French while in Paris—she does this regularly—underlines Sasha's desire to blend in during her two-week Paris retreat that constitutes the novel's time frame. Of course, the untranslated French that peppers Rhys's writings from the outset of her output establishes her ideal readership as not unlike that of Stein's memoirs. Her audience is cast as the expatriated or otherwise cultivated elite and the middlebrow pretenders either stuck at home or traveling on a tourist visa. In *Midnight*, though, this gesture is turned on its head; the intrusion of foreign words makes Rhys's implied audience exceptional, but it simultaneously suggests Sasha's desire for a lack of exceptionalism.

More frequently, though, such desires cast identity in terms of visual exchange, which Rhys usually links to marketplace culture. Sasha silently pleads, "Please, please monsieur et madame, mister, missus and miss, I am trying so hard to be like you. I know I don't succeed, but look how hard I try. Three hours to choose a hat; every morning an hour and a half trying to make myself look like everybody else" (106). Sasha asks that she be looked at for her unexceptionalism. Individual appearance becomes a tool by which to render oneself less visible, more anonymous. Here, specifically, the hat, a vexed accouterment for modernist-era European women,[1] is chosen so its bearer can avoid being the object observed by the nameless crowd.

What is most significant in such moments is the way the world of Wilde has turned inside-out. Rhys reveals the idea of the carefully cultivated public image, one that refracts through *Dorian Gray* and all of modernism as a failed method of avoiding the gaze. Sasha, one might say, parades through *Midnight* as if one of the "grotesques" from Wilde's *De Profundis*. Thus, when visiting the studio of a Jewish painter, Sasha sees herself reflected in the portraits of those whose appearances mark them as living on the societal margins. Her response is to remove the images from circulation (think of Dorian's portrait remaining hidden from the world) and attempt to incorporate those images into her own consciousness. She buys a painting of "an old Jew with a red nose." Upon leaving she thinks, "The pictures walk along with me. The misshapen dwarfs . . . the four-breasted woman . . . the old prostitute . . ." (100–101). Sasha identifies with these figures to the degree that she imagines them accompanying her in the street, suggesting a desire to hide the grotesqueness within her, invisible. In *After Leaving Mr. Mackenzie,* George Horsfield, watching Julie Martin, thinks to himself, "People ought not to look obvious; people ought to take the trouble to look and behave like all other people. And if they didn't it was their own funeral" (92). If celebrity, standing out from the crowd, is immortality, then abjection, standing out from the crowd, is as funereal as death.

These moments encapsulate the version of Rhys I am putting forth in this chapter: always stressing the need to hide one's difference. That need, Rhys shows, is a staple aspect of the urban scene. Rhys's work is often recognized for its "persistent focus on objectification and spectacle as central to metropolitan culture" (Britzolakis 459). Indeed, from "Illusion," the story that kicks off Rhys's first published volume of fiction, onward, Rhys can be seen to question whether it is better to be looked at or looked through as one moves through early twentieth-century cities. This issue is certainly corollary to that which concerns Wilde's, Chaplin's, and Stein's play with public images; to Joyce's manipulation of hypervisual literary style in *Ulysses;* and to the idealized individual consciousness in those texts that creates the idea of the celebrity. Conversely, visual culture condemns Rhys's protagonists to a lack of identity by objectifying those who stand out. In Rhys, the literature of celebrity is put to the service of portraying those who stand out from the mass by virtue of their abject position.

The abject make strange bedfellows; for context and a point of reference we might compare the Rhys protagonist to Franz Kafka's story "The Hunger Artist" (1924), a work that itself delves into the correlation between display, celebrity, and abjection. In a story that seems to owe a debt to Barnum, Kafka writes of a character who publicly performs his fasts. His career consists of being put on display, in stage exhibitions, doing exactly nothing—his extraordinary talent being the ability to not eat for the biblical number of forty (or more) days at a time. But the Hunger Artist's once real popularity has now waned, and he is "regarded as a publicity seeker" or "fraud" (139). Booked as a circus sideshow, he becomes a pathetic figure whose main selling point is "his long-famous name" rather than his actual act. He is eventually ignored by all, even management: "The colorful posters [his advertising] became dirty and illegible, they were torn down and no one thought to replace them" (144). He wastes away, forgotten. Here Kafka teases the fault lines between extraordinariness and abjection, showing that celebrity and obscurity can settle on the same figure in equal order, all the while keeping the figure in question in full display of the public.

Rhys, too, uses the idea of display to spotlight the obscurity of her protagonists. Her persistent return to spectacle explains why *Midnight*'s plot weaves through the 1937 *Exhibition Internationale des Arts et des Techniques Appliqués à la Vie Moderne*,[2] which Sasha first dreams about and then visits. It is why, as Rishona Zimring notes, Rhys's writings of the 1920s and 1930s extensively examine women's makeup, which Zimring calls "a means by which to display, exaggerate and distort the construction of beauty during the cosmetics industry's rapid rise and transformation of modern femininity" (220). It is why Rhys zeroes in on scenes of shopping for clothes and being watched in cafés, and why, for Sasha, the most utopian public moments occur in the cinema. The cinema offers for Sasha a mode of public consumption both communal and anonymous; in a darkened theater she is invisible while the crowd sits facing the same direction, eyes trained on the illuminated screen. There, Sasha reacts in accord with the audience: "Everybody laughs loudly at this, and so do I" (108).

Sasha's laughing along with the crowd at a common target resonates particularly as it is set among frequent scenes where she considers herself the source of amusement. A few pages earlier, she enters a *tabac* to escape the rain. There, she becomes immediately legible to the employees. First, "The woman at the bar gives me one of those looks.... We don't cater to tourists here" (104). Then, a waiter "looks at [her] in a sly, amused way." Sasha thinks, "God, it's funny being a woman! And the other one—the one behind the bar—is she going to giggle or to say something about me in a voice loud enough for me to hear?" Sasha sees herself as the visible object of laughter for both male and female. Clearly, though, her use of "woman" in both the description of the barmaid and the rumination on femininity, plus the term "the other one," suggest Sasha's desire for identification with the woman whose place this is.

Though an actual character in the world of the novel, the woman behind the bar recalls Manet's impressionist icon, the unhappy employee in *Un bar aux Folies Bergère* (exhibited at the *Paris Salon*, 1882). There, a dour-eyed Parisian barmaid returns the viewer's gaze while the nightclub audience is visible in the background via what appears to be either

Figure 5.1. Edouard Manet, *Un bar aux Folies Bergère*, 1882.

a distorted mirror or more space behind a circular bar. Manet's painting suggests an ambivalent approach to the effects of display. The crowd's attention should be on the performing trapeze artist whose feet appear in the top left corner; but, our spectatorial focus is on the bar, and the barmaid looks back. Her uniform both articulates her body and makes her indistinguishable from the other employees. The bar itself physically insulates her from the crowd but simultaneously marks off her lower status. Reinforcing the connection to Rhys, placed on the bar are two bottles of Bass Ale, with that trademark triangle, which not only invoke the idea of visual recognizability but also signal that this nightclub indeed caters to tourists. That *Midnight* assimilates Manet's vexed look at display within the description of the woman at the *tabac* suggests just how much Sasha desires any form of anonymity, any escape into the crowd, any chance to be the observer, instead of the observed. But the cultural conditions that have made her an exceptional, readable figure in the 1930s of *Midnight* preclude this possibility.

As the crowd in *Un bar aux Folies Bergère* is an impressionistic blur, in *Midnight* Sasha recognizes the masses themselves, the other denizens of her grey world, as indistinct and unparticular. She narrates herself returning to her temporary residence: "Back to the hotel without a name in the street without a name. . . . This is the Hotel Without-a-Name in the Street Without-a-Name, and the clients have no names, no faces" (145).

To Sasha, this utter anonymity seems achievable by the suppression of the interior. "Isn't there something you can do so that nobody looks at you or sees you? Of course, you must make your mind vacant, neutral, then your face becomes vacant, neutral—you are invisible" (19). The vacantness—the performance of having no interior—constitutes an attempt to deny one's subjecthood and therefore become invisible on the exterior. Susan Buck-Morss, in her discussion of female commodification in modern metropolitan culture through Benjamin's *Arcades Project*, states that "viewing oneself as constantly being viewed inhibits freedom. As with all surveillance, it is a process of censorship" (125). Rhys's protagonists, aware of their visibility, limit their interiority in attempts to mitigate their visual distinctiveness.

Desire for visual anonymity, linked to that denial of a mental and psychological life, reflects in perhaps the most recognizable trait of Rhys's fiction. In Rhys, while character consciousness serves as the guiding principle of the narrative, the writing severely restricts representation of the interior life. Her character's internal monologues emerge as replete with gaps, ellipses, and non-sequitorial turns to objects of popular culture. These traits, of course, help categorize Rhys as a part of her historical moment, a participant in the modernist project; they befit her for modernist syllabi. But Rhys's ellipses—both the aesthetic ones that Emery names "silences, inactions, or even formal flaws," and the typographical ellipses that proliferate in her prose—mark her eschewal of character motivation, a resistance to allow for the complex negotiations of various options that fill the prose of contemporaries such as Woolf and Joyce.

This passivity that marks the Rhys characters, their lack of desire, stems from their powerless position. An early Rhys story, "Discourse of a Lady Standing a Dinner to a Down-and-Out Friend," literalizes this suppression. The narrative comprises speech of the "Lady" while the thoughts of the protagonist, a supplicant, are literally parenthetical; again, punctuation plays a part (*Collected Short Stories* 45–46). Sometimes, when faced with a dilemma, Rhys's protagonists will simply wander to less particular, more external concerns. "She began to think how ridiculous it all was, that it was chilly," Marya thinks in the midst of a tense moment between herself, Lois, and Heidler (*Quartet* 128). The weather is of course something over which no person can claim control. Frequently, such moments portray the character as stripped of agency, particularly when it comes to sexual relationships. In *Voyage in the Dark* (1934), Anna recounts her first evening with Mr. Jeffries: "I hated him. 'Look here let me go' I said. . . . But as soon as he let me go I stopped hating him" (22–23). The text provides no explanation for Anna's change in attitude, nor has it heretofore represented Anna as being attracted to Mr. Jeffries, nor has it offered any consideration of what Anna's involvement with Mr. Jeffries might mean. Yet after this incident she unhesitatingly complies with his arrangements for their affair. A similar unexplained change of heart characterizes the start of Marya's relationship with Heidler in *Quartet*. Marya initially rejects Heidler's sexual advances and calls him "rude and unkind and unfair," yet, without any apparent change in opinion, she thinks of herself as being "lost before she knew him" a mere ten pages later (83). Sylvie Maurel writes of *Quartet* that Marya "no longer reacts, even silently. Her mind has gone blank. Her objectifying reaches a climax in abjection, a state in which Marya is no longer a subject or an object but an amorphous entity" (22). The romantic plots in Rhys's work are cast as overdetermined, contributing to a construction of character independent of desire. Even sex, in Rhys, as Elaine Savory writes, is "a matter of absence, inertia, coldness, or distraction" (60).

In Rhys's pre–World War II writings, this dynamic reaches its apex in the conclusion to *Midnight*. Sasha, drunk in her hotel room, abandoned by her gigolo lover, is visited by the nameless neighbor she has taken to calling "the commis"—a man she has feared throughout the novel. She says, "I look straight into his eyes and despise another poor devil of a human being for the last time." Next she draws him to her, saying, "Yes—yes—yes . . ." (189).³ While initial responses to this moment might be to ask why Sasha would act against her earlier impulse and what it means that she does, we might be better served asking why it is that Rhys is concluding this narrative with an obvious allusion to the acquiescent words ("yes I said yes yes") that Molly Bloom addresses to her husband at the end of Joyce's *Ulysses*. The answer, I propose, is that Rhys is making sure to distinguish between two kinds of identity and two kinds of writing. The Molly Blooms of the world (of fiction), ensconced within their domestic arrangements, are granted at least some agency over their desires, a freedom of choice (however delimited by societal norms, gender and class positions, and more) that constructs the narratives of their interiors. In *Quartet*, Marya sizes up Lois Heidler as, "Obviously of the species wife" (97); meanwhile her own marriage to Stephan Zelli is spoken of as if no one quite believes it (7). Rhys negatively implies that her protagonist is distinctly not of that species—not the type to be granted the ruminations that accompany secure social status.

The Marya Zellis and Sasha Jensens choose without considering, act without narrating; they cannot afford otherwise. Again, Kristeva's words are apt. She writes of the abject: "it means that there are lives not sustained by *desire*, as desire is always for objects. Such lives are based on *exclusion.* . . . Their dynamics challenges the theory of the unconscious" (5–6). The ellipses of modernist interiority can thus be seen as finding a correlative in the "exclusion" marking the thought of Rhys's protagonists. The representative techniques of high modernism are employed to efface the interior life rather than emphasize its shifting focus in the name of mimetic realism. In other words, stylistic devices that in other contexts generate the idea of the author as extraordinary individual, here turn the very idea of character into a vacant signifier, pointing to nothing. Structures that elsewhere build the celebrity here fall short, building the unremarkable.

Bildung *in the Dark*

That Rhys particularly mimics Joyce, who, already by the time of *Midnight*, was acknowledged in *Time* as an international literary giant, suggests the contrast between her version of modernist technique and his. That is, this allusion makes sense in numerous ways aside from the telling differences between Molly Bloom and Sasha Jensen. Rhys's and Joyce's oeuvres share the dynamic of seeming to suggest biographical exegesis, and each has an attendant critical bibliography taking them up on the invitation. Rhys, like Joyce, may be said to establish a particular distanciation between her characters, who are beset with autobiographical trappings; thus she also mines the idea of the author beyond the text. Rhys's protagonists are often understood as living fictional versions of Rhys's own experiences, but unlike Stephen Dedalus, they are never portrayed as literary progenitors, never seen writing. This is particularly noteworthy in light of the fact that Rhys's protagonists are often depicted in jobs of the sort that Rhys apparently did have, according to the biographical information—mostly jobs related to commerce and display (e.g. mannequin, chorus girl).[4] So while Rhys puts these characters in professional occupations with which she has experience, she does not show them engaging in writing, as she was doing during the corresponding periods of her life. That they do not write, and are never suggested as having the power to rewrite the script of their own histories, both affirms their abject position and serves to highlight their distance from the authorial consciousness.

The lack of literary production is matched by the lack of biological reproduction. Rhys's fictions repeatedly stage scenes of reproductive failure. The most famous of these is Anna's pregnancy and abortion that concludes *Voyage*, a scene to which I will attend shortly. In *Midnight* Sasha recalls her son's death shortly after birth, a fact she barely comprehends: "Ought a baby to be as pretty as this, as pale as this, as silent as this?" (60).

As they do not bear healthy children, neither do the Rhys protagonists have parents; as with Wilde's Dorian, and many of his stage characters, the previous generation is all aunts and uncles. The notable exception to this is Antoinette of *Sargasso*, who is referred to as an "infamous daughter of an infamous mother" (110)—an epithet that manages to incorporate both *Ulysses*'s treatment of fatherhood and, of course, Rhys's source material—Brontë's *Jane Eyre*, a *Bildungsroman* prototype.

I have suggested in my treatment of Joyce that in the twentieth century the literature of celebrity replaces the *Bildungsroman/Kunstlerroman* as the primary literary form for envisioning the individual. Thus it is particularly telling to see Rhys willfully avoiding hallmark signs of *Bildung* while employing autobiographical material. In addition to noting the absence of scenes of writing or even the idea of writing as an option, and the precluded possibility of biological reproduction, we might think of her protagonists' lack of individual progress. Rhys signals this restriction on development, as readers often note, by the literal and metaphorical "impasse" where Sasha begins *Midnight* (9). Indeed, after Sasha's child dies in infancy she notes that she herself remains physically unchanged, "with not one line, not one wrinkle, not one crease . . . without one line, without one wrinkle, without one crease" (61). The repetition drives home her lack of development; she is as she was. A more widespread signal of protagonist stagnation would include the characters' general under-realized subject-formation, their lack of reflexivity that I discuss above. These characteristics add up to a sense of anti-*Bildungsroman*, demonstrating the inapplicability of the *Kunstlerroman* to the modernist subject.

Furthermore, if we note that Rhys's first four novels are roughly linked in a chronological narrative that parallels Rhys's life, then the repetitive circumstances among Rhys's various protagonists also denote the forestalled *Bildung*. That is, since Rhys's works center on women of different ages but similar in material circumstance, temperament, and appearance, they can be and sometimes are considered of a piece. But instead of showing their respective protagonists' gradual transformations into socially integrated subjects, they each conclude with women in no better condition, economically or emotionally, than they were at the novel's outset. Thus the start of each subsequent work cycles the Rhys protagonist back to the material circumstances where the last one began, but moves her forward in age, as if to highlight this psychological and economic stagnation.

Taking this approach to Rhys requires, I should note, keeping in mind that *Voyage*, though published third in the sequence, was composed earlier than *Quartet* and *Mackenzie*. Thus Anna's youth fits into the overall picture of Rhys women advancing in age but achieving no progress. In the case of *Voyage*, the protagonist's final condition, lying sick as a victim of a botched abortion, is significantly worse than her place at the start of the novel. Anna's fate, however, was not necessarily so. *Voyage* was in fact originally to end with her death:

> And the concertina-music stopped and it was so still so still and lovely like just before you go to sleep and it stopped and there was a ray of light along the floor like the last thrust of remembering before everything is blotted out and blackness comes . . . (Scott 389)

If the question posed by much of Rhys's work is that of what to do with the abject figure, here Rhys offers this solution: kill her. The idea has arisen in Rhys before. In *Quartet*, Lois expounds on "Prostitutes, and Sensitiveness . . . Clergymen's daughters without any money. . . . Those sort of people don't do any good in the world." To this Marya responds, "Don't worry. . . . They're getting killed off" (61). *Quartet* trots out a system in which unproductive women of society are erased, and the first *Voyage* ending mobilizes it. The mercy killing not only removes Anna, it erases her and her memories, blotting out her consciousness. The fact that Anna is the youngest version of the Rhys protagonist suggests that part of the fantasy here is that obliterating Anna would, according to some models of time travel, prevent the struggles of later Rhys characters by having them never exist.

But this fantasy is unrealized. The publication of *Voyage* in fact became dependent on Rhys's agreeing to change this ending,[5] despite her protests. "I *know* the ending is the only possible ending," her June 1934 letter to Evelyn Scott insists (*Letters* 25). In Rhys's posthumously published memoir *Smile Please*, she recalls the publisher exhorting her to "give the girl a chance" (127); and so Anna does in fact survive the published *Voyage*. However, Rhys's rewritten ending retains much of the language of the original passage and uses it to depict Anna's waking death, a refiguring of the later protagonists' destinies.

> When their voices stopped the ray of light came in again under the door like the last thrust of remembering before everything is blotted out. I lay and watched it and thought about everything starting all over again. About being new and fresh. And about mornings, and misty days, when anything might happen. And about starting all over again, all over again. . . . (188)

The "ray of light" does not rescue Anna by ending her suffering. Rather it returns her to her repetitive, unproductive existence. Despite a momentary sense of rebirth sparked by the words "new and fresh," one would have to read this passage through seriously rose-colored lenses to conclude that Anna will transcend her marginalized state. Even the hope of "starting all over again" is not Anna's unambiguous expression of regeneration. Rather it mimics the language of the doctor's cynical suggestion that Anna will soon recommence her sexual activities: "'She'll be all right,' he said. 'Ready to start all over again in no time, I've no doubt'" (187). Rhys's revised conclusion to *Voyage* produces no change in Anna's circumstances; it resists the idea of *Bildung* as surely as does the initial version.

Here, as throughout Rhys's early novels, the construction of the protagonist as subject never gets off the ground. Similar dynamics in Wilde and Joyce, as I have shown, operate as part of the self-construction of the author as exception. I would argue, though, that Rhys's author-production differs from that of the paradigmatic modernist exceptions. True, Rhys trades in style; her narrative techniques force readers to cognitively piece together the fictional world in a way that draws attention to the author who choreographs this world. However, Rhys's repeated use of the motifs and developments that afflict her characters and point to her lived experience do not generate her extraordinary originality; they suggest the opposite. That is, the intertextual aspects of her work may point to a textualized version of the author, but the repetitiveness of these moments actually produces a sense of creative incapacity. Rhys's recycling of material among her writings reinforces the idea that her ability to generate or procreate is limited. (This is unlike Stein, who incorporates stylistic repetition to suggest the genius of the unique voice). However withering that may sound, readers should note that I am not deprecating Rhys's writings on these grounds, merely assessing the authorial identity they suggest.

One might say that Rhys's final work, her memoir *Smile Please*, re-emphasizes the persona of the *un*original author insofar as it reworks much of the material of her earlier novels. Critics have indeed accepted the unoriginal author persona; Paula Le Gallez notes that those approaching Rhys in terms of her biography have a tendency to "reduce what is complex and particular in Rhys's writing to a simple formula" (2). Critics are insightful to do so, in a sense. The Rhys formula, contrapuntal to those authors who create their exceptionalism, produces the author as having no distinct value in relation to the system. Thus her author-production reflects the fantasy of anonymity that guides her plots. Her ambivalent use of autobiographical matter pronounces the Rhys author as not the apex of individuated subjectivity, but instead as an unexceptional subject of a bland and repetitive world.

The Hidden Rhys

While Rhys's early writings both court and curtail the principles of *Bildungsroman*, the sense of autobiography pervades her work partly because her lived experience illuminates so much of the cultural material present in her work, particularly the celebrity discourse I have been treating. Rhys's biography—which was published most voluminously by Angier in 1990 and has been an inescapable component of Rhys criticism since—itself suggests a treatise on anonymity, abjectification, and, finally, celebrity.[6] In treating Rhys's own experiences, I intend not to simply note direct correspondences between fiction and nonfiction, but to consider how the celebrity narrative—the narrative of the exceptional individual—underwrites cultural narratives outside of fiction. Rhys's life allows for this approach. As a teenager in England, Rhys began a career of putting herself on display: on stages as a chorus girl, in clothing boutiques as a mannequin, and, briefly, on-screen as a movie extra. In 1919 she escaped to the European continent. There, Rhys's 1920s life reads like a Bizarro-world version of modernist coterie fame. Rhys coincided in Paris with Joyce and Stein, but her experience there sings counterpoint to the avant-garde expatriate experience chronicled in works such as *The Autobiography of Alice B. Toklas* or Kay Boyle and Robert McAlmon's *Being Geniuses Together*.[7]

Rhys established contact with high modernist circles primarily through her association with Ford Madox Ford, whom she met while down on her luck in 1922 Paris, and whose relationship with her is popularly understood as the basis of her first novel *Quartet* (1928). Indeed, Ford, while taking carnal advantage of Rhys's supplicatory position, was significantly responsible for the eventual publication of her first collection of short fiction, *The Left Bank and Other Stories* (1926). However, while entering a chain of celebrity signification can enable a figure to share in the aura of the celebrity name—as I have argued in the context of Stein—Rhys seems to have been a rather unmentionable figure in expatriate Paris. Her name does not arise in any of the central chronicles of the artistic life of those heady days. She managed to avoid serious involvement in any literary group. We can imagine her there, perhaps in the scene depicting a party thrown by the Braddocks (the characters representing Ford and his common-law wife Stella Bowen) in Hemingway's *The Sun Also Rises*. Rhys would be an appropriate extra, anonymous but present, in Jake Barnes's psychodrama—particularly because of her acquaintance with Ford and her cosmopolitan life. However, she remains absent or unnamed, or both. The abject is not "which I name," says Kristeva. In other words, getting involved with Ford and hanging around Left Bank cafés did not make Rhys's a name worth dropping for the other modernists.

This period and the years that followed—the 1920s and 1930s—comprise the bulk of Rhys's publishing career. *Quartet* was followed in short order by *After Leaving Mr. Mackenzie* (1930). After writing *Mr. Mackenzie* Rhys labored to produce *Voyage in the Dark*, which she had started fifteen years before its 1934 release, and then *Midnight* (1938). Her output to this point, the four novels and the short fiction, earned her minor critical appreciation, including the praise of Rebecca West,[8] but few readers. Still, modernist reputations (e.g. those of Joyce and Eliot in the early stages of their careers) had been forged on less, and Rhys's writings are invested with and invigorated by enough modernist thematic concerns and stylistic tics—they would have to be, for Ford to act as patron—that one could imagine her being conferred with greater repute, elevated as Djuna Barnes was, through her association with one of the high modernists (Eliot) and through her literary voice. Far from becoming a *cause célèbre*, though, Rhys, as World War II worked its way toward France, England, and American involvement, was almost completely forgotten as a literary figure. Not long after *Midnight*, she was assumed to be dead, even by many who had known her well. Of course, during these years the modernist celebrities whose lives she strangely echoes were dying: Joyce in 1941, Stein in 1946. Rhys's presumed decease parallels the actual ones of the figures she shadows.

Rhys is far from the only author, or even the only modernist novelist—Nella Larsen springs quickly to mind—to live in obscurity and only later achieve canonical status. What distinguishes the Rhys history is how the utterly abject, obscure position Rhys occupied contrasts with the intense public acclaim of the last decade of her life. In Angier's account, during the war and in its wake Rhys struggles to survive, living penuriously and peripatetically in remote British suburbs. When she does achieve some public notice, in 1940 and again in 1946, it results not from her writing but from her becoming a social pariah, a local terror. A violent altercation with neighbors leads to her entry into official record—local newspapers and legal documents—as a diagnosed hysteric who is convicted of assault (Angier 442-446). Rhys as a literary figure lurks in the background here, but stays there. The newspaper refers to her as "a writer," and Rhys defends herself in court by arguing, as Angier notes, that she thought the accusation of hysteria "rather odd" because "she wrote books" (446). Her case, noticed only in the local periodical *Bromley and West Kent Mercury*, is a far cry from the celebrity trials of Wilde, and of *Ulysses*.

This story takes a gradual turn—one now quite famous among scholars—that leads to Rhys's emergence into the spotlight. Rhys's rediscovery occurred in fits and starts. In late 1948 the actress Selma vas Dias, planning a radio adaptation of *Midnight*, attempted to track Rhys down in order to obtain legal rights to the book. Her initial inquiries were met with the report that Jean Rhys had died in Paris (449). Eventually, vas Dias placed a newspaper advertisement requesting information on "Jean Rhys (Mrs Tilden Smith)," Tilden Smith being Rhys's former legal name. Word successfully reached Rhys, who was thus rediscovered—but only for a while. The radio production was never realized and the disappointed Rhys slipped immediately back into obscurity. Such was this obscurity that history had to repeat itself for Rhys to emerge again. In 1956, once again, the BBC planned an adaptation of *Midnight*, and once again searched Rhys out, and once more, she was brought back into the public sphere. This time she would not disappear again. Her continued visibility was effected as Rhys began to circulate among her acquaintances and supporters the news that she was working on a new novel, had been for some time actually, and that it was a revision of and a prequel to a classic English novel: *Jane Eyre* by Charlotte Brontë. We might ask, what better way to get one's forthcoming novel discussed? (Aside from spreading word that one is writing a book set in modern-day Dublin but based on the wanderings of Odysseus, of course.) From the darkness of obscurity Rhys had cannily begun a project perfectly made for publicity, perfectly suited to be discussed with anticipation.

It is with the composition and publication of *Sargasso* that Rhys's life and art synch most uncannily. The strangeness stems from the fact that the parallels are not due to Rhys's use of biographical material, but rather to a correspondence between the internal structures of the book and Rhys's subsequent experiences, two separate narratives in which the concealed is made visible. Via the novel's pronounced success, Rhys bursts into public glare. She does so with a work that thrusts into visibility the most famously hidden character in English fiction, Bertha Rochester née Cosway, formerly Bertha Mason, that attic madwoman, she who in Brontë's novel is sequestered from society and kept in darkness as a secret shame. The character had been "silenced in *Jane Eyre*" says Emery (15), an aural description that reminds us that Bertha Rochester's confinement coincides with her speaking no words in Brontë, having been granted no language by Victorian society. But Rhys draws attention to the fact that Brontë's Bertha is not seen, rather than not heard. She explains her plans for the character in a 1958 letter to vas Dias: "In *Jane Eyre*, Bertha is '*off stage.*' In *Sargasso* she will be 'right *on stage*'" (*Letters* 156). By placing the spotlight on this character, Rhys probes the dynamics of hiddenness and exposure. Her literary strategy in turn illuminates that this set of concerns reverberates through Rhys's entire output. Moreover, though Antoinette is the first protagonist in a Rhys novel to be removed from the times and places through which Rhys herself lived, her hidden status suggests that Rhys was still, in this novel, reckoning with and using the stuff of autobiography. While Rhys could not have known the changes to her own person that would result from *Sargasso*, she writes the novel as if considering what it would mean to reveal the figure who was previously in darkness. The materials of celebrity provide the system that delineates what it means to emerge from such obscurity.

Wide Sargasso City

That *Sargasso* reads as technically continuous with the modernist style of Rhys's earlier publications is argued by Konzett, who analyzes Rhys as a modernist stylist, and by Emery, who writes that to read *Sargasso* one must "recognize the formal ruptures of convention that cultural difference may introduce to modernism" (16). Indeed, in bringing Antoinette out of the attic and into the light, Rhys constructs a narrative that may be said to be full of holes, gaps, ambiguities, and indeterminacies. What I would like to suggest in this section is that despite its setting—the bulk of the plot transpires in the Caribbean—the novel concerns itself with the structures of public display and exhibition that characterize the modernist city; in this way *Sargasso* reads as continuous with the tropes of Rhys's earlier work. And if those writings are beholden to the structures that produce celebrity, then *Sargasso* is as well.

Rhys's pre-*Sargasso* oeuvre rarely engages with spaces outside of the capitals of European modernism. *The Left Bank* digresses only momentarily from its bohemian Parisian milieu, and it does so in a manner that heightens the sense of Rhys's fiction matching her lived experience. First, the speaker of "Trio" observes a Caribbean family and announces, "It was because these were my compatriots that in that Montparnasse restaurant I remembered the Antilles" (35). This statement is one of the few overt suggestions that a single narrative consciousness exists throughout the volume, as it seems to prompt a pair of stories set in the Antilles: "Mixing Cocktails" and "Again the Antilles." *Voyage* also incorporates an extended sequence depicting Anna's childhood in Dominica. But mostly, Rhys's 1920s and 1930s fiction conforms to the salient modernist trait of chronicling urban processes, illustrating what Raymond Williams calls the "decisive links between the practices and ideas of the avant-garde movements of the twentieth century and the specific conditions and relationships of the twentieth-century metropolis" (37). Indeed, the dynamic of visuality in Rhys's work—the crowd and the display—clearly registers as a depiction of urban existence in the high modernist period.

One critically unexamined aspect of *Sargasso* is the degree to which it is continuous with Rhys's earlier writings in its concern with the street and the individual's relationship to the crowd. In other words, whereas critics have examined its formal qualities to consider it a modernist novel, *Sargasso* also revisits the thematic concerns that emerge out of the metropolitan picture of Rhys's previous work. That *Sargasso* registers as a work incorporating the culture of the modernist city emerges from a comparison of one of its signature moments—Antoinette's first encounter with Sandi Cosway, later to become her paramour—with scenes from the earlier works. Throughout her work, Rhys depicts street scenes in which women are watched, approached, or followed by strange men—scenes that highlight the protagonists' alienation and vulnerability in public, and suggest that solitary women will indeed be taken for prostitutes.[9] In *Mackenzie*, Julia experiences two such encounters, both in Paris. One example: "That night, coming back from her meal, a man followed her. When she had turned from the Place St Michel to the darkness of the quay he came up to her, muttering proposals in a low, slithery voice. . . . She wanted to flay at him and strike him, but she thought that he would probably hit her back" (59). The detail of the man's serpentine voice, of course, heightens both the seductive and the phallic danger of such moments. Or, as Christina Britzolakis puts it, Rhys depicts "the street itself as an ambiguously gendered, treacherous and possibly even sadistic lover" (471).

These encounters, however sinister at first, and however tinged with eroticism and violence, seem to offer redemptive potential. Consider one of Rhys's early stories, "In the Rue de l'Arrivée." This sketch briefly depicts the archetypical Rhys protagonist, an initially anonymous "Lady" who is "down on her luck," and lacks "strength of character." The peripatetic Miss Dufreyne, as she is eventually named, moves among and drinks cognac at various Paris cafés. Trying to escape attention, she is sure to rotate her patronage so as to "avoid the curious stares of the waiters" (50). To return to her hotel after these nights Miss Dufreyne must travel down a dark street—"A street of sordid dramas and horrible men who walked softly behind one for several steps before they spoke." And sure enough, she notices one man "slinking up not quite alongside, a little behind her" (53). From feeling initially threatened, however, Miss Dufreyne goes to feeling "soothed and calmed." The story concludes with her dream that the man is an angel leading her to the afterlife, which may be hell, but may be heaven. Walking the streets is a necessary aspect of urban existence that holds both the threat of danger and the promise of transformation. Indeed, both Anna and Sasha are chatted up in the street by the men who will become their romantic partners, if only for a while.

When Rhys makes her literary reappearance, publishing her first novel in twenty-eight years, the street encounter also reappears. *Sargasso*, which is mainly set in and around the estates owned by Antoinette's family, features this early public scene:

> The first day I had to go to the convent, I clung to Aunt Cora as you would cling to life if you loved it. At last she got impatient, so I forced myself away from her and through the passage, down the steps into the street and, as I knew they would be, they were waiting for me. (29)

The word "street" here is remarkable. It is the first time it appears in the novel and it repeats twice in the passage; Only one other thoroughfare in the work merits such an urban-sounding word. There is a "road" in the opening passage, a road (badly in need of repair) that once linked Antoinette's family to white Jamaican society but now represents the Masons' marginalization. In several ways, then, the street into which Antoinette is pushed by her Aunt Cora signals a new beginning: Antoinette is leaving the comfort of childhood and isolation and entering public spaces alone for the first time, emerging, visible, onto the street, and about to join a convent. The convent itself suggests a liminal place: Antoinette will remain hidden there from the public gaze, but there she will also be schooled and prepared for public life and marriage. Thus her initial steps are fraught with terror, promise, and, ultimately, the disaster that awaits her after her marriage.

The terror is provided by the "they" who lie in wait. Once again, a Rhys woman will be menaced in the street, though this time by a boy and girl. This pair clearly mirrors the sexually abusive caretakers of Antoinette's mother, a man and a woman, who are described in the passage immediately prior to this moment. Antoinette's antagonists are equally sinister, first following Antoinette, next issuing insults and threats, and soon thereafter jostling her as they walk alongside. At the moment of physical contact the menace hints of sexual violence: the boy says, "one day I catch you alone, you wait, one day I catch you alone" (30). Before her Antoinette sees "a long empty street" in which she will be exposed and unsafe, and thus powerless. However, the street holds the promise of redemption, as well. Antoinette sees "a tall boy who was walking along the other side of the street," first watching the scene, then running over to shoo away the others; her savior's "feet hardly touched the ground." The boy turns out to be Sandi, Antoinette's mixed-race cousin, actually her father's grandson. Later in the narrative, an adult Antoinette will recall the period in which he had been her lover, and their parting when she refuses to run away with him, a choice that dooms her to an unfortunate marriage. This street scene emerges as implicated in Antoinette's fate as subjugated wife and eventual prisoner of the nameless husband figure who stands in for Brontë's Edward Rochester.

As is characteristic of Rhys's street encounters, this moment depicts visual exchange as underwriting social interactions. Antoinette first notes her danger from the boy's gaze: "They looked so harmless and quiet, no one would have notice the glint in the boy's eyes" (29). After she manages to "walk past without looking," the girl tells the boy to "look the crazy girl." She announces that both Antoinette and her mother have "eyes like zombie," and she asks, "Why won't you look at me?" The language of looking overwhelms the narrative. After the rescue by Sandi, Antoinette runs to the convent, a place where women are sequestered, hidden from public eyes, the place where Antoinette will be prepared to become someone's wife, which is not only a domestic role, but also a social one—an acceptable position within the patriarchal system that does not stand out or draw attention to itself.

The scene engages in play with the ideas of public/visible and private/hidden. This is, it turns out, characteristic of the entire novel. Indeed, while *Sargasso* chronicles very different characters in very different places than Rhys's previous work, it continues Rhys's intense concentration on display and visual exchange as the dominant forms of social interaction. For example, the novel starts by depicting the Cosway family as unaligned with either white or black society, and therefore scorned and spurned by both; their marginalization is repeatedly expressed by their being on display. One of the first descriptions of Antoinette's mother Annette states, "My mother walked up and down the *glacis*, a paved roofed-in terrace.... Standing by the bamboos she had a clear view to the sea, but anyone passing could stare at her. They stared, sometimes they laughed" (11). The novel is strewn with moments that couple being on display with being laughed at, redolent of both *Midnight* and, again, Wilde's grotesques. Antoinette, finding herself the object of the gaze, attempts to mask her emotional response. She recounts her childhood experiences to her husband in the section that he narrates:

> The people came to see us again and though I still hated them and was afraid of their cool, teasing eyes, I learned to hide it.
> 'No,' I said.

'Why no?'

'You have never learned to hide it,' I said.

'I learned to try,' said Antoinette. Not very well, I thought. (79)

Antoinette, her abject position visible, tries to disguise her interior, an attempt that the husband, from his more dominant position, deems a failure. *Sargasso* might be a story of the disasters of colonial subjugation in the nineteenth century, but its most basic gestures depict society in terms that govern twentieth-century cities.

Sargasso's continual return to the visual is highlighted by the way visuality underwrites major plot developments, such as Antoinette's meeting with Sandi and, crucially, the household fire that drives Annette over the brink of madness and constitutes Antoinette's childhood trauma that Bertha Rochester attempts to recreate years later in England. The Mason family (Antoinette's mother has by now been remarried and renamed) is burned out of its home by resentful former slaves. As they escape the fire Aunt Cora says, "They are laughing at you, do not allow them to laugh at you" (25). The family, in its moment of despair, is exhibited before the assembled, antagonistic crowd, which is cast in terms of anonymity. "I recognized no one. They all looked the same, it was the same face repeated over and over, eyes gleaming."[10] The crowd starts yelling "look" repeatedly, and their flaming torches illuminate the night, making it "light as day," and rendering the family even more visible. In the most spectacular detail, the parrot Coco momentarily draws the attention of everyone assembled when, aflame, wings long since clipped, he falls from the *glacis* to his death. The scene suggests that Antoinette/Bertha Rochester, in her pyromaniacal actions represented in the final pages of both *Sargasso* and *Jane Eyre*, is re-enacting Coco's fiery death-leap, identifying herself with the captive parrot whose end is remarkable for its display. Rhys, in her account of the West Indies under European dominion, continues to explore the kind of individual produced by a social system that is dominated by visuality.

Posthuman Beings

As the *Sargasso* fire scene sputters out, Antoinette suddenly wants to immerse herself in the anonymous crowd, leaving her own family to join that of a local girl named Tia. Tia has formerly been Antoinette's friend, but eventually turns on her, calling her—the novel's first of many instances of it—"white nigger" (14). It is Tia who first literalizes Antoinette's abjection; she steals Antoinette's clean clothes and leaves her own dirty dress in exchange, leading to Antoinette's attempt to hide her shameful appearance. But at the moment of intense trauma caused by the crowd's attack on her house, Antoinette disregards all that. Despite their ethnic and social differences, she thinks of herself and Tia as equals: "We had eaten the same food, slept side by side, bathed in the same river. As I ran, I thought, I will live with Tia and be like her" (27). By living and being with Tia, she thinks, and by joining the popular culture of Jamaica, she will avoid scorn and the public disdain toward her appearance. Bursting from her family and running toward Tia, she expresses this desire in a short series of phrases: "Not to leave Coulibri. Not to go. Not." Tia throws a rock at her to keep her at bay.

Antoinette's internal monologue as she runs toward Tia, her mantra of negativity with its odd infinitive aspect, has a literary precedent in what might seem an unlikely location: *The Island of Doctor Moreau*, H. G. Wells's 1896 science-fiction novel chronicling the titular character's experiments in vivisection. Certain of Moreau's creations—those that the doctor has deemed insufficiently human to stay within his household, those that have been cast out of Eden, so to speak—have formed their own civilization in the woods. In their yearning to be more human than beast (to use the text's way of thinking), they have taken to repeating the following:

> Not to walk on all-Fours; *that* is the Law. Are we not men?
> Not to suck up Drink; *that* is the Law. Are we not men?
> Not to eat flesh; *that* is the Law. Are we not men?
> Not to shed blood; *that* is the Law. Are we not men?
> Not to hunt other men; *that* is the Law. Are we not men? (59)

Now, I do not know of any historical evidence that Rhys was purposely parroting Wells. But Rhys was a well-read writer and Wells was an oft-read writer. Superficial similarities (island setting, characters who have been exiled from their more civilized homes) and the question of intention aside, the implications of *Moreau*'s presence here are manifold. Philip Armstrong has called *Moreau* a novel about the desire to "transcend and mould the limitations of fleshly, instinctual, beastliness" (90). We might use these terms to think of Antoinette in *Sargasso*. At the moment when Antoinette longs to merge with the anonymous crowd, she echoes Wells's creatures in their attempt to establish their humanity.[11] In other words, Antoinette's behavior suggests that to be truly human one must be unexceptional. That there is an underlying nineteenth-century racial teleology here is unmistakable: the former slaves have already been likened to "animals howling" (23). At the same time, Antoinette's putting herself in the place of a hybridized animal-human attempting to maintain its humanity echoes other moments in the text when she and her family are referred to as vermin, usually by the local community. "They called us white cockroaches. Let sleeping dogs lie. One day a little girl followed me singing, 'Go away, white cockroach, go away.... White cockroach, go away'" (13).

These moments when Antoinette is categorized as one of the untouchables of the animal kingdom might seem to be exclusively readable in terms of ethnic and class categorization, were it not for the constant appearances of vermin throughout Rhys's work, frequently used in ways that signal the degradation of her protagonists. As one of many small examples, in *Midnight* Sasha recalls living in a destitute hotel room "covered with bugs, crawling slowly" (125). Mostly, Rhys uses insects to illustrate individuals' inconsequence. One example of this is her story "The Insect World" (1976) whose protagonist thinks of people traveling via the London Tube as pests: "No, they didn't *look* like large insects: they were insects" (356). While "The Insect World" employs the word "jiggers" in an extended metaphor that denigrates mass society, her next story foregrounds how Rhys uses vermin to cast characters as abject. "Sleep it Off, Lady" (1976) validates reading these moments in the context of Rhys's critique of human society. "Sleep" depicts a territorial dispute between its protagonist, Miss Verney, and a rat—actually a "Super rat." Miss Verney loses. She tries and fails to enlist the aid of the community of the local village where she resides, and she actually dies as an indirect result of her attempts to foil the rat.

That is, in one of Rhys's final fictions, she casts her protagonist as lower down in the pecking order than vermin, having less cultural power, less of an identity. As Savory points out, the rat scares Miss Verney "to death, in effect," and produces a narrative switch from her consciousness "to an objective narrator's account" (166). Not only is Miss Verney terrified by the rat to the extent that she loses the ability to think, but her pleas for help against it result in ridicule. When she tells Tom, her house's caretaker, that the rat is still alive although Tom has already put out rat poison, he assumes she has drunk too much and hallucinated. His eyes (of course Rhys puts this in terms of vision), formerly "honest eyes," turn "sly, mocking, even hostile" as he asks Miss Verney, "Are you sure it wasn't a pink rat?" (379). In response, Miss Verney speculates that the rat might be one of the species of "Super rats." The "super" adjective emphasizes that Miss Verney understands that the rat is, in a sense, above her.[12] Miss Verney feels so socially inferior to the rat that she describes it this way:

> *I'm the monarch of all I survey.*
> *My right, there is none to dispute.*
> That was the way the rat walked. (378–379)

The lines in verse are taken from William Cowper's 1782 poem "Verses Supposed To Be Written By Alexander Selkirk, During His Solitary Abode In The Island Of Juan Fernandez." Miss Verney attributes to the rat a monarchial (and thus divine) right to roam the grounds surrounding her cottage. By citing the poem, Rhys puts the rat in the place of Cowper's speaker, Selkirk, a conqueror surveying his island—an island otherwise inhabited only by animals. Rhys inverts the poem's roles of human and animal, making Miss Verney a victim of a rat's colonial conquest.

In contrast with the territorial rights of Selkirk and the rat, Miss Verney becomes a virtual shut-in; she almost entirely stops leaving her cottage or communicating with other people via letter or telephone. What little energy she has is dedicated to keeping her house free of debris—her way of discouraging the rat from penetrating her space further. One day she finds that Mrs. Randolph, the local woman who normally empties her garbage, has failed to leave the dustbin in its customary spot. When Miss Verney attempts to move it, she collapses beneath its weight. Her cries for help are rejected—most notably by the neighbor girl Deena, who, assuming Miss Verney is drunk, disrespectfully utters the story's title phrase. Rhys's protagonist resigns herself to defeat: "Miss Verney waited in darkness for the Super Rat" (386). She is eventually found, unconscious, by her postal worker and shortly thereafter dies. The mailman's delivery of books arrives too late to save her. Though the doctor's diagnosis is heart failure (perhaps code for alcoholism), the narrative is clearer: Miss Verney has been killed because society valued her as less than vermin.

Kafka provides a noteworthy comparison to Rhys's manipulations of exhibitionism, one that illuminates Rhys's use of vermin as a way of signaling abjection. Kafka's most widely read fiction, "The Metamorphosis" (1915), turns its protagonist Gregor Samsa into a dung beetle. Samsa is depicted as having been relatively ordinary before his transformation: he is a salesman, a functionary of commodity culture. Unlike Rhys's characters, it is his participation in the system of exchange, rather than his existing beneath it, that seems to justify equating him with an insect. In other words his participation in the status quo qualifies him as vermin. With "The Hunger Artist," however, Kafka gets closer to Rhys. The Hunger Artist, in his final days of circus life, fails as an object of display. He becomes so abject that he offers "no more than an obstacle in the path to the animals" (144). After his death, he is replaced by one such animal. The circus uses his cage to house an exquisite panther who garners the admiration of the audiences and the circus keepers: "He lacked for nothing" (145). The panther is not vermin, of course, but he is not human either; his triumph over the story's protagonist signals the Hunger Artist's extraordinary irrelevance in the system of visual exchange.

Rhys likewise signals her characters' abjection through their relation to animals, an ongoing motif that may be complexified by a small sampling of animal theory, critical writings that consider animals as a form of discourse. Derrida, in his legendary lecture-essay "The Animal That Therefore I Am (More to Follow)" theorizes the unjust treatment of animals in post-Enlightenment civilization: "no one can deny the *unprecedented* proportions of this subjection of the animal." For Derrida, though, the meaning of animals is inflected not only by human practices regarding them but also by the aspect of denial involved. He argues that "no one can seriously deny, or for very long, that men do all they can in order to dissimulate this cruelty or hide it from themselves" (394). This remark finds correspondence in Rhys's work. It suggests that animals strike a singular chord for Rhys because their subjection is achieved matter-of-factly and anonymously, while the Rhys protagonist is made the object of scrutiny and gossip as part of the process of abjection. It recalls *Midnight*, and Sasha's objection to her boss Mr. Blank: "Let's say you have this mystical right to cut my legs off. But the right to ridicule me afterwards because I am a cripple—no, that I think you haven't got" (29). Sasha accepts her subjugation but resents the public attention it draws. The tirade, forming Sasha's interior monologue, argues that the inhumanity of social structures resides in its displaying its victims' powerlessness, which contrasts with the covert exploitation of the animal kingdom.

But further implications of Rhys's treatment of animals can be seen in exactly the limitations that animal theory runs up against. As Armstrong points out, recent scholars in the field of animal studies have critiqued the idea that "animals mean whatever cultures mean by them" and have striven "to go beyond the use of animals as mere mirrors for human meaning" (2–3). An obstacle to this admirable goal, of course, is that "scientists and scholars can never actually access, let alone reproduce, what other animals mean on their own terms" (2). That is, a non-linguistic consciousness cannot be rendered or understood in language. This inaccessibility, the very obscurity of animal consciousness, animals as subjects, seems to filter into Rhys's treatment of the non-human. Can the inhuman speak? No. Can the abject? It need not. Rhys puts a patriarchal poem from the British imperialist canon in the mouth of a rat to show the rat's dominance over Miss Verney, true, but in this way Rhys also suggests that society can only project culture onto the animal as if onto a tabula rasa. However, representing an animal's thoughts—making them visible—is ultimately impossible. This itself, in contrast to a human culture that holds its bottommost members up for ridicule, can be an enviable state of affairs.

Celebrity on the Margins

The mail-ordered books arrive too late to save Miss Verney from the rat. Rhys, on the other hand, laments that her literary renown arrives too late for her to enjoy it.[13] The success of *Sargasso* led both to the re-emergence of Rhys's entire body of work—first Deutsch, then Penguin, put her early novels back into print—and to intense recognition for its author. Rhys was eventually (1978) awarded the honor of Commander of the British Empire (CBE). By 1970, critic A. Alvarez was proclaiming her the "best living English novelist" in a plaudit that has been the starting point, and in some cases the straw man, for numerous discussions of whether Rhys should be thought of as English at all. The phrase strangely echoes a moment in *Midnight*. A Russian student studying English tells Sasha, "I think Oscar Wilde is the greatest of English writers," and goes on to excoriate "English hypocrisy," presumably in reference to Wilde's incarceration. Sasha thinks to herself that the Russian is "preaching to the converted" (131-132). The text registers Sasha's resistance to the dominant British culture in which she has lived and to which she will presumably return after her Paris sojourn. She herself finds Wilde "sympathetique," indicating her appreciation for Wilde's work but also her sympathy for the person, Wilde, who was, of course, not exactly English, and of course, a victim of unjust laws that punished him for inadequately concealing his erotic preferences. In having the Russian call the colonial subject not Irish but English, Rhys indicates that the dominant culture has the capacity to absorb the voices at its margins. Alvarez's comment might be said to enact the same dynamic. What heightens that idea is that Alvarez was writing in praise of *Sargasso*—the only Rhys novel set in the Caribbean (parts of *Voyage* excepted), and the novel largely responsible for her frequent if vexed classification as a West Indian writer. Indeed, if Rhys had stayed "dead" it is quite possible that her fiction, if read, would never be considered in light of colonialism, and today she might be remembered, if at all, as a curiosity: an ethnic modernist whose ethnic-ism formed only an occasional aspect of her writing.

In the novel that would lift her out of the shadows and into lasting fame, Rhys draws from a canonical English work a character who is himself famous: Edward Rochester. She strips him of his name and sets him in a slightly different era, but he remains recognizable as an element of discourse that refers beyond the text, the husband of Jane Rochester née Eyre, here depicted in his life preceding Brontë's narrative. This persona, of course, personifies dominant culture—the patriarchy and rule of law that emigrate from the heart of the British Empire to its colonial holdings. Although the empire's patriarchal hereditary law has placed the husband, a second-oldest son, in a troubled financial position, he exists in marked contrast with Antoinette, who, despite her inheritance, is shown to be powerless in the face of patriarchal rule. The fact of being known by the general public—visible, intertextual, and able to be recognized without being named—becomes intertwined with the idea of social control. After the husband asserts his dominance, the character linked to obscurity is systematically deprived of agency, "her face blank, no expression at all" (100), even as the novel itself represents Antoinette's emergence into the light. While *Sargasso*, in its telling, might constitute a symbolic gift of a voice to one perceived as voiceless, it nonetheless equates recognizability, the fact of being a known quantity, to social power. This power extends to Antoinette, who is just as intertextually identifiable as her husband, as well. Antoinette is granted the novel's final narrative voice and actions; *Sargasso*'s story is ultimately the story of Antoinette's revenge. Bringing the powerless into the light makes her a celebrated victim.

If giving a voice to those perceived as voiceless can be seen as a cornerstone of postcolonial writing, it is noteworthy that Rhys's rehearsal of that gesture is thematically continuous with the reflections of celebrity culture that mark her earlier writings and her hidden years. In *Sargasso*, which is often deployed as a seminal text of the field of postcolonial studies, celebrity becomes a way of rewriting what constitutes cultural power. But the novel is not so easily situated, and neither is its author. As Konzett writes of Rhys, "Critics and readers have particular difficulties in classifying her work as that of a European modernist, feminist, expatriate, or, more recently, postcolonial and West Indian writer" (130). The very act of classification, of course, fixes the identity of its object, incorporating it within the dominant culture's system. And thus we may say that the emergence of postcolonial literature as an idea integrates the discourse of celebrity, as surely as, Konzett also points out, postcolonial writers appreciate the market value of ethnic narratives (167).[14] Lorraine York has noticed this about Sri Lankan–born Canadian Michael Ondajtee; she writes of "the exoticizing of his public image" as a key component of his marketing. Postcolonialism gives a hybrid writer such as Ondajtee or Rhys a designation that supplants an allegiance to a dominant, colonizing nation. In this way celebrity makes its cunning passage into one, if not the, predominant literary current that has followed modernism. While, or rather, since modernism is the literature of celebrity, modernism's successor has retained the structures it inherited from a previous half-century's genre; it has used celebrity to symbolically (at least) upend the structures of authority.

Sighting *Rhys*

That Rhys's fictions focus significantly on display has underwritten this chapter's argument. The dynamic also infiltrates Rhys's last work, *Smile Please*, nowhere more than in the title and opening passage. There, a camera operator takes Rhys's portrait as a young girl, exhorting her, "Not quite so serious" (13). The resulting photo will be displayed in the family household so as to distinguish her among her relatives: "it pleased me that it was by itself, not lost among the other photos in the room, of which there were many." But this representation soon becomes foreign to the child Rhys, and, indeed, a way by which she understands her degraded position. She later looks at it, "realising with dismay that I wasn't like it any longer.... The eyes were a stranger's eyes." Rhys commences this narrative of her life, then, with an anecdote about how visual objectification, separating an individual from the crowd, can obscure a person's recognizability to herself.

Indeed, photographs of Rhys in her post-*Sargasso* years make particularly rich reading. The cover of the 1990 edition of Rhys's *Letters*—writings that are at least theoretically not intended for publication—features a photograph, taken by Bill Brandt, of Rhys in her final years, slightly smiling, gazing congenially out from a window in her house. The window frames the writer, as if to emphasize that while she is looking out at the camera, the audience is very much able to look into her home. Yet there is another, parallel, photograph of Rhys, likely taken at a proximate moment in her life.[15] This picture is less warm; Rhys stands behind a French window that is only half open. Squinting out at the viewer, she pushes the curtains partially aside with one hand. (The other dangles a cigarette.) A look of ill favor marks her face, as if she views the camera as the apparatus of an unwelcome paparazzo. Yet she holds the curtain aside as if understanding the necessity of being the object of the gaze, especially during these, her years of triumphant renown. The photograph summarizes the contradictions of Rhys's late celebrity, arriving as it does at the tail end of a career in which Rhys has continuously represented the desire to be anonymous, to be a member of the crowd. That authorship and celebrity are intertwined, she knows. That she could recede into the unexceptional, she wishes.

Epilogue

"Everybody who was anybody was there": After Modernism, After Celebrity, John Dos Passos

By using pivotal aspects of this book's argument to re-read Rhys, whose works have a less overt engagement with celebrity discourse than do the works of Wilde, Joyce, Stein, and Chaplin, I have hoped to suggest a productive way of reassessing all modernist writing. Once we understand celebrity discourse as the creation of an idealized object that collapses interior and exterior, subject and object, it can be used as a reading approach that both clarifies and adds critical complexity to modernism, and to the cultural movements that follow. This is true even, or rather especially, when the lens is trained on works by authors whose names are rarely seen to evoke the aura of celebrity, regardless of whether the writer's work specifically creates the author as that brand of modernist exception, or whether, on the contrary, it undermines the modernist, self-fashioned version of authorship. In this epilogue, John Dos Passos is my case in point.

Actually, because his writings are gradually fading from the modernist canon,[1] it may seem strange to recall that, like Joyce and Stein, Dos Passos once merited his own *Time* cover, published in 1936 after his trilogy of novels, *U.S.A.* (1930–1936). Still, Dos Passos's writings and Dos Passos as a figure have failed to grip the public imagination the way Wilde, Joyce, Stein, Chaplin, and even Rhys did—and continue to do. This failure likely stems from both his under-choreographed self-promotion and his post–World War II politics that dismayed the academic left. As I will show, however, celebrity discourse animates his writing; this is my impetus in reading Dos Passos to conclude this book.

The precise nature of this animation provides the stronger impetus. Dos Passos was pointing out the interweaving of modernist styles, modernist networks, and celebrity discourse while modernism's imprint was still fresh. We can see this at work in the trilogy, a text arriving at the tail end of high modernism. Dos Passos does not seem to be grouped among the "late modernists" as named by Tyrus Miller and others, nor among Rosenquist's "modernist latecomers"—those writers of the 1930s reacting against the towering explosion of modernist writing during the previous decade that reconfigured English letters. However, *U.S.A.* reassesses modernist style, and the ideological implications of that style, from the perspective of a slightly later moment and slightly jaundiced eye, with that eye trained on the structural parallels between celebrity and modernist exceptionalism. It is, quite literally, a postmodern and post-celebrity work. For these reasons, my treatment of Dos Passos, of his reconsiderations of modernist style, and, briefly, of his textual relationship to Ernest Hemingway, will serve as the epilogue to this study. By analyzing *U.S.A.*, I wish both to remind readers that modernist authorial self-fashioning is made legible by the discourse of early twentieth-century celebrity culture, and to re-assert that the formal characteristics that constitute the modernist legacy are one manifestation of the general cultural impulse to grasp at forms of individualism in the face of mass-visual society.

The Camera, I

U.S.A. features, among its four narrative modes, sections labeled "The Camera Eye" that spur my reading of Dos Passos. These passages are written in what might be considered a generically modernist style: they move through time elliptically and associatively, and they eschew, in varying degrees, traditional punctuation, syntax, grammar, and typography—all in the service of an impressionistic depiction of events focalized through their nameless narrator(s). They bear significant resemblance to prose that can be found in Joyce, Woolf, Stein, and Dorothy Richardson. Turn to one "Camera Eye" section at random and you might read:

when the telegram came that she was dying the bellglass cracked in a screech of slate pencils (have you ever never been able to sleep for a week in April?) and He met me in the grey trainshed my eyes were stinging with vermillion booze and chromegreen inks that oozed from the spinning April hills (*1919* 6; unorthodox spacing in the original)

This typical sample unleashes the tics of modernist style: consciousness represented as pure, metonymic textuality. To pick one characteristic: it is worth noting that although compound words proliferate in Dos Passos's work, here, the word "chromegreen," in tandem with the actual narrative events, creates a specific reference to Joyce, highest of the modernists. In *Ulysses*, Stephen recalls the telegram informing him that his mother is dying; the word "snotgreen" rewards readers who make it through the first two pages (1.79). The modernist exception par excellence makes its cunning passage into this iteration of "The Camera Eye."

Each of these sections is closed within a single consciousness, a record of individuated experience. "The Camera Eye" was famously called by its author a way of maintaining "the subjective" apart from the rest of his panorama of early twentieth-century United States life[2]—that is, apart from the other three narrative styles in *U.S.A.*: the media collages of the "Newsreels," the naturalist prose narratives of ordinary Americans, and the biographies of historical figures that appear more or less as prose poems. In other words, the stated goal is to craft a version of modernist interior monologue or stream of consciousness, and thus keep such impressionism from contaminating Dos Passos's attempt to objectively represent cultural history through the trilogy. That this attempt at a purified objectivity is a fantasy is hardly worth mentioning, and that these quarantined expressions of subjective experience are named for the photographic machinery that many people at the time considered the key to wholly objective representation creates an obvious irony best focused on elsewhere.

What is also obvious is that with the title "The Camera Eye," Dos Passos names his supposedly subjective sections after the technology of visual reproducibility, though he has given that device a biological organ. The photograph—whether moving or still—is the modernist period's dominant form of mass-visual reproduction. The name of these sections combines with their formal qualities, their generic modernism-ness, to give the lie to the very idea of authorial originality. If a literary style associated with individual consciousness has generic components that make it reproducible, then that individual consciousness cannot be terribly individuated. Despite these contradictions the critical tendency seems to have been to read the "Camera Eye" sections as unironic transcriptions of an individual consciousness. Scholars such as J. N. Westerhoven and Tim Armstrong consider these passages Dos Passos's way of announcing the author's voice.[3] Armstrong writes of the choice to "split public and private voices ... in John Dos Passos's *U.S.A.*, in which the subjective 'Camera Eye,' representing an authorial interiority, alternates with passages of conventional narrative and the 'Newsreels' which chronicle public events" (10). To Armstrong, "The Camera Eye" locates the narrative within the mind of the author, contrasting with sections that chronicle characters in more traditional languages or represent the broader drifts of history. If these passages represent subjectivity in a way associated with authorial consciousness, then that association can also be thought of as foregrounding the idea that "The Camera Eye" shares the characteristics of modernist writing. These aspects combine to invite a reading of this style as parody, or, if that word conjures up an overdetermined intentionality, an imitation, or, if nothing else, a deployment of the specialized but communal language of modernism that draws attention to that language's stylistic traits. Authorial reproducibility is set alongside authorial originality. Visibly a manifestation of genre, a variation on a theme, a participation in a trend, the "Camera Eye" passages weaken notions of modernist authorial individuality, much as Wilde's emphatic appropriations subvert Victorian notions of the self—though Wilde offers a new version of originality to supplant the old.

As the generic mimicry of "The Camera Eye" questions authorial individuality, its contrast with the other sections of *U.S.A.* emphasizes that sense of interrogation. Most directly, "The Camera Eye" complements *U.S.A.*'s prose-poem biographies of figures such as Theodore Roosevelt, William Jennings Bryan, Eugene Debs, etc. These sections mostly narrate the lives of famous movers and shakers of the period whose repute stems from the pre-modernist version of renown, the version that Brady categorizes as "fame" rather than "celebrity." Formally, the blank verse prose-poems that chronicle the men of history are unrestricted and typographically playful at moments. However, they are essentially transparent rather than opaque, neither elliptical nor reflexive in technique. The first biography, about Debs, begins:

> Debs was a railroad man, born in a weatherboarded shack in Terre Haute.
> He was one of ten children.
> His father had come to America in a sailingship in '49, an Alsatian from Colmar (*The 42nd Parallel* 19)

This narrative, ignoring character interior, moves through time and space traditionally and factually, clearly denoting temporal and geographical contexts. In fact, Dos Passos's nonfictional figures act as historical markers. Such men, "forces in a nation ... not merely victims of its times" (Ludington, "Explaining Dos Passos's Naturalism" 39), indicate what moment in history the novelistic characters or the "Camera Eye" individuals are experiencing. They serve as chronology for the sections that read more obviously as fiction (as do the "Newsreel" sections). The subjects of the biographies are thus designated as figures through which history is told — more than when the narrative sections briefly refer to historical names, such as the momentary and orthographically incorrect cameo of "Charley Chaplin" in the narrative section of Janey Williams (*Parallel* 119). Such a stylistic divergence from "The Camera Eye" befits the representation of figures from traditional societal roles, who denote official historical time.

The contrast between these two particular styles exemplifies how Dos Passos's varying modes recast the "Camera Eye" idiom. If critics are correct to argue that "The Camera Eye" generates an authorial consciousness, thus diverging with the narratives of society writ large, then this separation of the individual from the mass signals that the modernist writings of "The Camera Eye" are merely one communicative technique among many, rather than one particularly authorized to represent Dos Passos's fictive world. The effect is similar to how Joyce's stylistic pastiches in *Ulysses*, in Moretti's words, emerge as "equally *irrelevant* as interpretations of reality" (*Signs Taken for Wonders* 206). But while Joyce is attacking literary history, revealing the ideological underpinnings of historical literary styles, Dos Passos tackles modernism itself. Dos Passos engages in, if not an outright critique, then at least a reconsideration of the modernist aesthetic — whether one considers "The Camera Eye" stream of consciousness, interior monologue, or simply modernist style. He thus undermines its claim to cultural authority.

The In Crowd

That Dos Passos should cast modernist stylistic innovation as a fashion, and perhaps as a fad that by 1930 has passed, may not be altogether surprising. Cartoons in the *New Yorker* were doing so as well, as Hammill has chronicled (43–54). But two aspects particularize Dos Passos's treatment of modernism, as I will show. One, he pairs modernist style with celebrity style, and two, his stylistic mimicry worries the ideology of the aesthetic. Indeed, *The 42nd Parallel* includes a crucial instance, "The Camera Eye

(26)," which not only directly connects formal aspects of literary modernism with a turn to celebrity concerns, but also constitutes an ideological critique of modernism on the very grounds of this connection. Beginning with scenes of the collective political energy of the sort that fired both Dos Passos's progressive politics and most of his writings throughout the 1920s and 1930s, it eventually descends into individuated private life. Dos Passos's prose, simultaneous with this transition, adopts a cadence and phrasing that seems to ape the writing of the two perhaps most famous American modernists: Stein and Hemingway. The text links these writers to the shift from political action to individual inaction.

The section, set during the early years of World War I, prior to United States involvement, is rare among the "Camera Eye" passages in that it depicts a day of leftist activism: first an anti-war, pro-socialist rally at Madison Square Garden, and then an Emma Goldman address at the Bronx Casino. These events can be historically pinpointed as occurring in the spring of 1917; they in fact coincide with what Dos Passos claimed as the moment of his political awakening. In his 1966 autobiography *The Best of Times: An Informal Memoir*, a different Dos Passos writes of the spring of 1917 as a time when socialism and activist politics became part of his life:

> We protested night and day. We were carried away by a brilliant speech of Max Eastman's at a mass meeting in Stanford White's Madison Square Garden; we approved the shrill denunciations of Emma Goldman. We read each issue of *The Masses* damp from the press. . . . Suddenly I believed I was a socialist. Even then I think I marveled a little at the suddenness with which passionate political convictions develop in the youthful mind. (45)

In *U.S.A.*, Dos Passos uses this moment of his own initiation to directly challenge, and ultimately chastise, modernist writing's production of the individual. In "The Camera Eye (26)," the narrator is an anonymous first-person who actually begins as a plural—much like the "we" in the passage from Dos Passos's memoir. He is a member of a nameless cadre that attends these momentous events but is kept at their periphery—first by the impenetrable crowds, and subsequently by the police:

> we couldn't get a seat so we ran up the stairs to the top gallery and looked down through the blue air at the faces thick as gravel. . . . I didn't know who was speaking somebody said Max Eastman and somebody said another guy but we clapped and yelled for the revolution and hissed for Morgan and the capitalist war and there was a dick looking into our faces as if he were trying to remember them (272)

On display here are the obvious elements that make this writing a recognizably modernist medium—for example the experiments in grammar, syntax, etc. But here, though the prose might privilege individual experience, the descriptions resist the dominance of subjectivity. Dos Passos keeps identities indistinct; even the figure on stage might be the famous socialist and former editor of *The Masses*, Max Eastman (a seminal figure in Dos Passos's political progression, as noted in his memoir), but then again, it might not. An attempt to establish fixed identity is actually condemned through its association with surveillance by the state apparatus— the "dick" who is cataloguing people, attempting to understand the crowd as distinct entities despite the smoky air and the groupthink behavior.

In contrast with the indeterminate identities in the rally, the narrative links one renowned person, J. Pierpont Morgan, with the war. This prompts the crowd's collective disparagement. To the activists, the famous figure of Morgan represents capitalism and its ill effects; he embodies the larger principle of villainous United States capitalism. Literally, the audience's negative response is to the idea of the war and its meretricious motivations, of course. However, the passage simultaneously seems to condemn the way the war is identified with one famous figure. Its specific diction— "we . . . hissed for Morgan and the capitalist war"—suggests a critique of the very act of associating the celebrity with a historical moment.

Law enforcement breaks up the Goldman meeting and disperses the crowds that have congregated in the public space outside the Garden. So the narrator and his companion(s) retreat to the interior space of the Breevoort Hotel (here called the "Brevoort"), a well-known gathering spot for the political left, where they engage in celebrity-gazing:

> we went to the Brevoort it was much nicer everybody who was anybody was there and there was Emma Goldman eating frankfurters and sauerkraut and everybody looked at Emma Goldman and at everybody else that was anybody and everybody was for peace and the cooperative commonwealth and the Russian Revolution (273)

Their revolution held at bay for the nonce, the would-be agitators head indoors to eat and gawk at one another and at, particularly, the sight of a cultural figure such as Goldman engaging in the simple pleasures of the frank, that American culinary staple that comes from Germany. Dos Passos indeed seems to have attended such a meal and noted Goldman's celebrity aura. In an April 1917 letter to his friend Rumsey Marvin, he writes, "Did I tell you about sitting next to Emma Goldman's table in the cafe at the Brevort [sic] some time ago? It was wonderful—the people I was with knew lots of her myrmidons, and we were the outer circle of her glory" (*Travel Books* 661). Goldman, iconic in her own right, is on display in these writings, attended by her coterie, an object of fascination for the ordinary people who are watching her snack and basking in her aura.

With its remove from the rally to the restaurant, "The Camera Eye (26)" implicates "the subjective" in the transition from political engagement to coterie self-regard. Indeed, Dos Passos's arrangement of the "Camera Eye" passages throughout *U.S.A.* can be seen to reinforce that transition. The sections, as Townsend Ludington notes, decrease in frequency from the first installment of the trilogy to the last: "*The 42nd Parallel* has twenty-seven; *Nineteen Nineteen*, fifteen; and *The Big Money*, nine—a reduction of almost half in each successive volume" ("The Ordering of the Camera Eye" 443). Regarding this pattern, Ludington concludes that *U.S.A.* stages a process of integrating the self with society rather than making oneself an aesthetic exception. "What Dos Passos was trying to show with the entire group of Camera Eyes was his gradual assimilation into a world beyond his self-conscious imagination" (444). This process would constitute a reversal of the aesthetic retreat performed by Wilde and high modernism.

Stein and *They*, Hemingway

Townsend's reading of "The Camera Eye" joins mine in revealing the way the subjective style in *U.S.A.* intermingles with representations of political indifference. That the trilogy explicitly links this to modernist authorial self-fashioning is clarified by the way "The Camera Eye (26)" incorporates Dos Passos's modernist contemporaries. The depiction of Goldman at the Breevoort also displays "everybody else that was anybody"—a turn of phrase that echoes Stein[4] and actually anticipates moments in Stein's *The Autobiography* that I examine in Chapter 3 of this book. Stein and Dos Passos both use "everybody" to mean exactly "everybody who was anybody."[5] It may be a stretch to suppose that Dos Passos is specifically using Emma Goldman to allude to Stein, but it may not be a stretch: Goldman, a Jewish woman lionized as the leader of the avant-garde anti-capitalist movement, holds court here among her "myrmidons," much as Stein, a Jewish woman lionized as the leader of the avant-garde artistic movement presides over her modernist salon for two decades.[6] Suitable for a passage about Stein, when the narrator of "The Camera Eye (26)" arrives at the hotel, the scene turns gossipy and so does Dos Passos's prose. The text is now concerned with the wonders of being part of an elite network. The energy of the insurrection has been diminished and turned to platitudes as it enters a more interior, commercialized space.

This scene, in fact, builds on an earlier moment in *U.S.A.*—one from the narrative section focalized through Eleanor Stoddard, a young, middle-class woman from Chicago trying to break into New York's theater world. Stoddard and her friend Eveline Hutchinson are escorted to the Breevoort by an acquaintance named Freddy, who initiates them into his artistic circle:

> Freddy seemed to know so many people and introduced them around to everybody as if he was very proud of them. They were all names she had heard or read of in the book column of *The Daily News*. Everybody seemed very friendly. (217)

In this forerunner to "The Camera Eye (26)," Dos Passos establishes the Breevoort as a counterpart to Stein's 27 rue de Fleurus. It is another location where literary culture turns to gossip, where artistic movements turn fashionable, and where intellectual labor and the discourse of celebrity are visibly linked. It creates a dynamic that, the "Camera Eye" suggests, prioritizes the individual over the public, draining political power from writing.

Thus, in *U.S.A.*, Dos Passos enlists Stein, alongside all the modernists experimenting with a prose that privileges the interior life, to critique the subjectivity that modernist style generates. He does so on the grounds that this particular creation of the individual constitutes a retreat from the public or political realms—an argument not unlike the one that Lukács was making around this time.[7] "The Camera Eye (26)" retains Dos Passos's deployment of modernist style, invokes Stein, and also introduces what will be his particular allusions to the writings of Hemingway—specifically to Hemingway's already iconic, by 1930, first novel, *The Sun Also Rises*. It is a work Dos Passos certainly knew well, having reviewed it upon its 1926 release, not terribly favorably, for the *New Masses*.[8] The "Camera Eye (26)" paragraph set in the Breevoort suggests *The Sun Also Rises* in its repetition of the word "nice," a word Hemingway uses almost compulsively throughout his first novel, including two mentions of a "nice" hotel (94–95).[9] The sense of Hemingway as subtext is heightened by the final moment of the section, which overtly points to Hemingway's novel:

> And we had several drinks and welsh rabbits and paid our bill and went home, and opened the door with a latchkey and put on pajamas and went to bed and it was comfortable in bed.

To the previous list of noticeably modernist tics in the "Camera Eye" sections we might now add this use of Hemingway-esque simple declarative statements linked by coordinating conjunctions, characteristic of both Stein and Hemingway. The Hemingway-esque quality of the prose is heightened by the treatment of adjectives, those old modernist bugaboos. Here, adjectives are kept from modifying nouns and are only used as predicates. Furthermore, paying one's bill, as Hemingway readers know well, is a detail that Hemingway practically owns.[10]

U.S.A. *and Hem*

For further suggestion of Hemingway's presence in the final moments of "The Camera Eye (26)," consider these three passages, each of which concludes a chapter of *The Sun Also Rises*.

> I rang the bell. The door opened and I went up-stairs and went to bed. (71)

> It was a nice hotel, and the people at the desk were very cheerful, and we each had a good small room. (95)

> After supper we went up-stairs and smoked and read in bed to keep warm. Once in the night I woke and heard the wind blowing. It felt good to be warm and in bed. (116)

In the first of these moments, Hemingway's narrator Jake Barnes has retreated from the public spaces of Paris and their attendant anxieties and gone to his room. The second and third moments occur on vacation, during Barnes's fishing trip in Burguete, the idyllic homosocial middle section of the novel. In alluding to these passages, Dos Passos refers not only to characteristic aspects of Hemingway's prose but also to those episodes when characters remove themselves from the public sphere. In other words: what space is more personal than one's private room, or one's bed? The transition from political demonstration to private repose is read as the "Camera Eye" persona's "sense of irony" by critics such as Janet Galligani Casey (148). What readers have left unremarked is that Dos Passos incorporates these specific textual elements to suggest that Hemingway represents a retreat from public engagement. Indeed, Dos Passos seems to have viewed Hemingway's European expatriation as unnecessary if not discreditable; in a 1927 letter, Dos Passos exhorts his friend to "come out of these Parisian swamps, Hem — New York is getting to be just like Paris" (*Fourteenth Chronicle* 368). Though his reasoning, as the letter continues, is based on the arts scene and the easy availability of bootlegged liquor, he is sure to mention the imminent arrival of Max Eastman, radical political figure. In Dos Passos's writings, the ghostly presence of Hemingway, linked to the notion of stylistic idiosyncrasy, conjures the failure to engage with the pressing realm of politics.

Indeed, with his perhaps vulgar ideological critique of modernist style based on Hemingway, Dos Passos reverses the direction represented in *U.S.A.* "The Camera Eye (26)" moves from the political to the personal; Dos Passos's use of Hemingway turns personal matters political, transforming his agon with his friend into a question of the ideological function of fiction. This was one side of a mutual antipathy, of course, and a product of their longtime close relations and the well-chronicled divergence of demeanor in their material lives. Stephen Koch summarizes their differences: "Hemingway's presence in any room would be remembered for a lifetime. People barely noticed Dos [Passos]" (20). One famous photograph distills the antithesis. Against a mountain backdrop, four figures pose on skis: Hemingway, Dos Passos, and friends Frau Lent (far left) and Gerald Murphy (far right). From their poses the photo might as well display Hemingway and three ciphers. Hemingway, second from the left, stands, hands on hips, elbows bent outwards, as if expecting anyone who is anyone to want to link arms with him. He alone directs his gaze toward the camera, smiling as if to indicate the joy of being the modernist exception, soaking up the attention and the space. The others take their cues from this performance, looking aside, standing aside. While the four figures are situated fairly evenly across the shot, Hemingway, by his pose and his position slightly closer to the camera, easily takes up the most room, and gives the impression of requiring even more. His clothes cling to his form. Dos Passos, in contrast, stands farthest back (which disguises the fact that he was quite a tall man) and appears to be looking off-stage. His jacket rumples, and his ill-fitting stocking cap fades away toward the mountains. Hemingway, the image suggests, has style, where Dos Passos has none.

The photograph shows a scene from the ski resort in Shruns, Austria, 1926. It thus captures the initial moments of what later becomes a significant personal rift between the two writers.[11] In *A Moveable Feast* (published posthumously in 1964 from manuscripts written over thirty years earlier), Hemingway lampoons Dos Passos as "the pilot fish" who leads around "the rich."[12] Hemingway's attack on Dos Passos, though it starts with this specious class warfare, is soon made on aesthetic grounds; "the pilot fish" speaks in a manner that demonstrates his irresolution, contrasting with the declarative power that Hemingway values. Hemingway writes, "The pilot fish talks like this. 'Well I don't know. No of course not

FIGURE 6.1. (L-R) Frau Lent, Ernest Hemingway, John Dos Passos, and Gerald Murphy skiing in Shruns, Austria, 1926. Ernest Hemingway Collection/John F. Kennedy Presidential Library and Museum, Boston.

really. But I like them. I like them both. Yes, by God, Hem; I see what you mean but I do like them truly and there's something damned fine about her'" (207). Here Hemingway launches his most insidious attack, via prose style. He depicts Dos Passos as incapable of standing assertively by an opinion, a portrayal that a lengthier study of Hemingway would show to be an accusation of inadequate masculinity.[13]

Furthermore, Hemingway gives Dos Passos speech that echoes the idiom attributed to Robert Cohn, the number one antagonist in *The Sun Also Rises*. Cohn: "There's a certain quality about her, a fineness. She seems to be absolutely fine" (46). The pilot fish: "there's something damned fine about her." Hemingway scorns Dos Passos by giving him Cohn's word, "fine." Walter Benn Michaels writes, "Cohn thinks that Brett [Lady Brett Ashley of *The Sun Also Rises*] has 'a certain quality, a certain fineness'; 'nice' is deployed by Hemingway against descriptions like that" (27). Tit for tat, Hemingway takes the word "fine" from *The Sun Also Rises* and puts it in the mouth of Dos Passos, as Dos Passos takes the word "nice" from the novel to imply Hemingway. Moreover, Hemingway's ventriloquistic linking of Dos Passos with Cohn recalls an instance in his novel that shows the fictional character's intellectual irrelevance: "Cohn made some remark about it being a very good example of something or other, I forget what. It seemed like a nice cathedral, nice and dim, like Spanish churches" (97). According to Michaels, Cohn's "racial inferiority is here reproduced as aesthetic inferiority" (27). The question of race notwithstanding, Hemingway, turning the Dos Passos of *A Moveable Feast* into the second coming of Cohn, attempts to clarify which modernist writer is aesthetically inferior. Depicted as it is in sheer aesthetic terms, Hemingway's rough treatment of Dos Passos turns Hemingway's distaste into a stylistic problem. It thus acts as counterpoint to the way Dos Passos deploys Hemingway's style in *Parallel*, the reference starting with formal traits in order to move to the political.

This rivalry, being played out on the field of prose, revisits the major issues addressed in my study throughout the chapters preceding this epilogue. For example, the two authors' opposition accentuates that Dos Passos's critique of Hemingway, embedded as it is in the "Camera Eye" section, condemns the modernist aesthetic for its similarity with celebrity culture, for the way a distinctive literary style asserts the primacy of the individual by creating the modernist exception. Of course, in American letters, Hemingway is the perfect figure for this critique. By the time Dos Passos published *Parallel*, Hemingway—"certainly the most 'celebrated' classic American author of the modern era" (Glass 26)—already embodied literary fame. Hemingway's renown deserves extensive treatment, and so has received it from Glass, and from Leff, who notes that Hemingway rose to fame in the 1920s partly because he was heralded by journalists and photographers, and partly because of his energetic participation in "the blandishments of a culture of celebrity" (viii). To George Packer, Hemingway by the mid-1930s was not only "an international celebrity" but also, in keeping with the theme of figures who are perceived to lose agency over their lives, "his own chief imitator" (1). Where Dos Passos's brief acclaim incorporates his political progressivism, Hemingway's celebrity remains of the variety more in keeping with the high modernist self-construction as entity apart from the mass. Koch writes, "Hemingway was 'apolitical.' As a modernist, he was seen as the heir to Stein, Pound, and Joyce, admired for the technique of living. . . . Few writers have more effectively turned a sense of how to live—the *technique* of living well—into a credible image of heroism" (20). The creation of the modernist celebrity as the super-individual and the vexed relationship of that individual to its political culture both come under indictment through Dos Passos's manipulations of Hemingway in *U.S.A.*

Now, Hemingway, unlike Joyce or Woolf, is not quite thought of as a writer whose prose experiments discovered new ways of representing character consciousness. But Hemingway perfects the concept of an unmistakable style, not just in his life, as Koch asserts, but more importantly, in his prose. That Dos Passos lays into Hemingway by foregrounding literary technique, and that Hemingway returns the favor, revisits the considerations of modernist style that underwrite my argument in this book, specifically in Chapters 2 and 3. In the modernist aesthetic, the end result is indeed the author: the subject as aloof, textualized object. But Dos Passos shares in this inescapable formulation. His own stylistic play—the avant-gardism on display in *U.S.A.* and his earlier writings (notably *Manhattan Transfer*), and the assertion of his own instantly identifiable voice that made him a critical darling and landed him alongside Joyce at the top of the Soviets' list of decadent writers[14]—can be viewed as his participation in the same dynamic. Certainly, upon opening *U.S.A.* one can see how Dos Passos meets Jameson's parameters of the "high modernist ideology of style—what is as unique and unmistakable as your own fingerprints" (17). Furthermore, Dos Passos's depiction of Hemingway's prose as characteristically Hemingway-esque reinforces the recognizability of that individual style; the reference serves to reinforce Hemingway's own claim to originality, despite its ironic reproduction within the generically modernist style of the "Camera Eye" sections. The Dos Passos/Hemingway exchange of literary barbs across *U.S.A.* and *A Moveable Feast*, both in reference to *The Sun Also Rises*, implicates Dos Passos within Hemingway's celebrity network, burnishing Dos Passos's renown while it simultaneously establishes Hemingway's exceptionalism, much like the dynamic apparent in Stein's writing. Dos Passos, then, emphatically delineates modernism's role as the literature of celebrity, its participation in and revision of the discourse of celebrity, and its new version of the individual, suitable for twentieth-century culture.

The problem with mass culture, Dos Passos suggests, is that it is not "mass" enough at all. Both in its modernism and in its celebrity guises, it is entirely about the individual. Of course, it wasn't long after launching his critique that Dos Passos's thinking, and his writing, took a decided turn to the right, suggesting that his concerns about modernist exceptionalism could lead to real pessimism over whether political progressivism has any place in mass cultural society. We might say that Dos Passos was paving a way for later critiques of celebrity, those in the vein of Boorstin's "known for his well-knownness" formulation, which in the United States formed part of a post–World War II mindset that largely thought of celebrity as a low-cultural phenomenon undeserving of scrutiny. Dos Passos's work situates modernist literature in the same camp as celebrity, making it equally responsible for the elevation of the subject and the resulting implicit disregard for forms of writing that promote mass engagement over individual detachment. To challenge his contemporaries in this fashion indicates that to Dos Passos, modernism, by the 1930s, already looked like a style impossible to separate from celebrity, as it should look to us now.

Notes

Introduction

Author's note: the second epigraph is quoted in Monaco, xi.

1. It has become de rigueur to cite Huyssen as the instigator of the 1990s sea change in the field of modernism. (See for example Latham 7; North, *Reading 1922* 11; Morrisson 5; Dettmar and Watt 1; Jaffe 19, etc.) This constant invocation of his influence, I would argue, signals that the new treatments of modernism are still meeting with resistance within the academic profession—even fifteen years after Kevin Dettmar and Steven J. Watt's anecdote of the senior academic who objects to their *Marketing Modernisms* project on the grounds that it will "belittle Joyce, Woolf, Ford, et al.," by casting them as "junior academics with a way to make" (1).

2. See Jennifer Wicke, *Advertising Fictions* 4. To cite just one example of this strain of criticism: Ellen Berry reads Stein's claim that Stein's use of language resembles the cinema and takes it at face value. Berry proceeds to find that Stein's writings are "drawn with reference to or metaphorically linked with" film (17), but does not go on to consider that the relationship might be more one of shared origins than of appropriation.

3. Tyrus Miller writes, "From writer-critics like Ezra Pound and T. S. Eliot to their latter-day heirs in the academy, critics have defined the movement in large part with figurative and evaluative underpinnings of modernism itself, with the Poundian imperative to Make It New" (5). Miller goes on to give an account of the critical tradition that affirms the high modernists as "rebel experimenters working in emerging modes and forms."

4. The term is from Leo Braudy (588), whose *The Frenzy of Renown* is often cited as the most comprehensive history of fame in western society.

5. Interestingly, Lowenthal's quantitative approach has been employed by scholars who write about the rise of the professional sports star during this period. Warren Susman notes that in 1921 more journalistic words were devoted to Babe Ruth than had ever before been accorded an athlete (145). Statistics, used to gauge competitive achievement, lend themselves to assessing non-traditional celebrity achievement. Numbers are also used to evaluate the fame of the period's ultimate example of a celebrity without intellectual credentials. The racehorse Seabiscuit was the "subject of the most newspaper column inches in 1938" in America (Hillenbrand xi). The horse, one might say, constitutes a variation on my argument that celebrity creates the objectification of the subject.

6. The Frankfurt School writers and associates are particularly effusive on this point. Max Horkheimer and Theodor W. Adorno incorporate celebrity into their attack on "The Culture Industry," writing about the "pseudo individuality" of "the film star whose hair curls over her eye to demonstrate her originality" (154). Walter Benjamin,

similarly, argues, "the cult of the movie star" preserves "the phony spell of the commodity" ("The Work of Art" 231).

7. Chaplin was a British subject whose oeuvre was mostly made in Hollywood. Stein was a famed expatriate who returned to the United States to promote herself. Rhys, less exemplary, was born in Dominica, to which she figuratively returned in her best-known work. Dos Passos was an American heavily influenced by European modernism and his World War I tenure. Joyce never made the Atlantic crossing, but, as I consider in Chapter 2, *Ulysses* did, and that has made all the difference.

Chapter 1

1. "Case Details for Trade Mark 1." Intellectual Property Office. Web.
2. Whether Wilde actually said this is apparently in dispute. Though Frank Harris unflinchingly records it (55), Richard Ellmann remains skeptical (*Oscar Wilde* 152). Of course, we need not quibble; even if apocryphal or invented later and elsewhere, the claim makes the case for Wilde as inventor of this particular brand of celebrity. As the legend has indeed become fact, we print the legend.
3. This is according to L. Lewis and H. J. Smith and their fascinatingly eccentric account of Wilde's journey, *Oscar Wilde Discovers America*, first published in 1936. See pp. 323-324.
4. See Lewis and Smith 74-77. Also see Blake's thorough examination of Whitman's fame.
5. He goes on to say, "Every time my name is mentioned in a paper, I write at once to admit that I am the Messiah." The detail shows Wilde thinking that his fame creates a parallel between himself and Jesus Christ long before writing *De Profundis*, where this idea explodes.
6. See Ellmann 284. As if Yeats needed the exhortation.
7. Such treatment of the tour has recently appeared in no less mainstream a publication than the *New Yorker*. See Gopnik 81.
8. See Ellmann, *Oscar Wilde* 144.
9. See Gagnier 56.
10. Wilde may have had an earlier definition of "genius" in mind, thinking of it as an external, guiding entity.
11. As critics note, Wilde was often called a plagiarist, or some variation of one. See, for example, Ellmann, *Oscar Wilde* 140, 320; Gagnier 84; and Bristow 8. Probably the most thorough exploration of this question is Paul K. Saint-Amour's *The Copywrights: Intellectual Property and the Literary Imagination*, pp. 90-120 particularly, in which Saint-Amour examines Wilde's conception of intellectual property in the contexts of Irish oral tradition and English copyright law.
12. Saint-Amour, for example, manages to include all of Wilde's utterances in his treatment of Wilde's work by arguing, "Wilde is better understood as a self-conscious practitioner of a resuscitated 'orality' than as a writer who happened to talk well and commit the odd plagiarism" (95).

13. See Wilde, *Complete Works* 323. All citations of Wilde's works will be from this edition, with the exception of those from his letters and *The Picture of Dorian Gray*.

14. See Holland, *The Wilde Album* 92. Holland notes that the ensuing lawsuit was a landmark for artistic property: "The case established the legal basis for American copyright law."

15. Sinfield claims that Wilde's trials created this association in the public mind (4).

16. For an exploration of how Wilde transformed dandyism—thought of as a form of self-worship—into a kind of celebrity—being worshipped by others—see Gagnier 51, 83. According to Sinfield, Wilde "was exercising the dandy's ability to transmute gender roles" (73).

17. Quoted by McLees, 4.

18. Beerbohm also takes something, the lily, that is supposed to be a signature of the individual and makes it reproducible, in a gesture quite characteristic of his visual and written works. As a caricaturist, Beerbohm contributed to the cultural fascination with the celebrity body, representing virtually every major male, Edwardian writer in his drawings. In *A Christmas Garland* Beerbohm performs the literary equivalent of caricature, penning stories in imitation of the style of some of his noted contemporaries.

19. This skepticism is further registered when Dorian actually arrives and evinces a rather bland and uninspiring "personality."

20. So, for that matter, is the portrait in Browning's "My Last Duchess" (1842), which also depicts a portrait that has sapped the life from its subject, though the implication is that the onetime Duchess has been gotten rid of by the Duke as a result of his jealousy.

21. Actually, this passage is less elliptical in the novel's initial publication by *Lippincott's*. Naturally, there is speculation that Wilde's handling of Dorian's deeds reflects his wariness about signaling Dorian as a homosexual. See Holland, *The Real Trial of Oscar Wilde* 222-223.

22. Again the novel invites comparison to Poe's "The Oval Portrait," in which the marriage leads to artistic rather than biological reproduction.

23. Robert Ross affixed the title after Wilde's death, according to Small (89).

24. Though it seems obvious to consider to which genre *De Profundis* belongs, Small claims that critics have glossed over the text's generic elusiveness (87).

25. See Ellmann, *Oscar Wilde* 479-481. Also see Small's excellent examination of the textual history of the various manuscripts, which, he claims, might have been meant as multiple texts. Small makes an excellent case that *De Profundis* is uncompleted, a draft (97). His proposal does not contradict my work here.

26. For an account of the blackmail, see Simon Joyce.

27. See Holland, *Real Trial* 262.

28. See Holland's dramatic account of the events leading up to the trials (*Real Trial* xv-xliii).

29. Ellmann writes that Christ appears in the essay as "a type of Wilde in the ancient world" (483).

30. Both of these, in turn, echo Henry's thought that Dorian might be a symbol of a new age (*Dorian* 39). The picture of Dorian Gray, whose bloody hands can be read as resembling stigmata, constitutes another precursor to the treatment of Christ in *De Profundis*.

31. The moment looks ahead to my next chapter. Joyce's Stephen Dedalus echoes this type of language, proclaiming his plan to "forge in the smithy of my soul the uncreated conscience of my race" (*A Portrait of the Artist as a Young Man* 253).

32. Note also Wilde's assertion at his trial that *Dorian* is, after all, "a moral book" (Holland, *Real Trial* 218).

33. See Sinfield 3.

Chapter 2

1. Boscagli and Duffy provide an account of the *Time* article (May 1939) in "Joyce's Face." That Joyce appeared on the cover of *Time* is not as remarkable as it may seem to us, as William Faulkner and Pablo Picasso were featured on the cover the very same year; both Stein and Dos Passos were featured as well in this period. Discussing the scope of Joyce's fame, Robert Scholes stressed to me that details of Joyce's life were not widely available until the 1959 Richard Ellmann biography (at Brown University, March 2001).

2. See Morrisson's account of modernism in the "little magazines," 204-205.

3. Graham Greene seems to have had a bit of a bee in his bonnet about Joyce while working on *The Third Man*. In his novel version, Colonel Calloway, the narrator, refers to himself as "just a man in a mackintosh" at Harry Lime's funeral (24). As every Joyce fan would catch, this is an obvious allusion to the "chap in the macintosh" at Paddy Dignam's funeral in *Ulysses* (90).

4. Stephen Donovan points out that these capitalized phrases are closer in resemblance to a newspaper feature called "crossheads" than they are to headlines (527).

5. Style in *Ulysses* is closely linked to difficulty, which itself would be another, overlapping approach to identifying Joyce's production of the author. Sean Latham writes that *Ulysses* "carves out a place for itself in the complexly structured space of culture by being difficult, trading on a form of cultural capital that will secure Joyce's status as a professional author who differs qualitatively from the middlebrow hack" (120). Jaffe notes that obscurity pays modernist dividends: "It is inaccessibility that gains wider notice" (14). As I have suggested, however, it is also possible to consider the instantly recognizable quality of a writer such as Joyce as instantly accessible, as it does not in fact need to be read for a reader to grasp the code of exceptionalism.

6. Joyce writes to Frank Budgen that Pound wants Bloom "relegated to the background" and "Stephen Telemachus brought forward" (*Letters I* 126).

7. In McCombe's compelling treatment of this debate, Stephen's approach is a form of opposition to "the hegemony of English criticism" (718). Stephen's Anglo-Irish interlocutors, McCombe argues, employ methods drawn from A. C. Bradley, the dominant voice in Shakespeare studies circa 1904 (724-725).

8. McCombe argues that the disavowal is disingenuous, writing that Stephen's

"faith seems unshaken, despite what he claims outwardly to Eglinton" (731n). McCombe contends that Stephen's renunciation "may be connected to the larger discussion of belief that underpins" the episode.

9. See Kenner 31 on the compulsion toward factual accuracy that Joyce began to exhibit as a young man.

10. Joyce provides a colorful articulation of the impulse to use literature as revenge, writing, "Give me for Christ sake a pen and an ink-bottle and some peace of mind and then, by the crucified Jaysus, if I don't sharpen that little pen and dip it into fermented ink and write tiny little sentences about the people who betrayed me" (*Selected Letters* 76).

11. A similar moment arises when Stephen overhears a snippet of conversation: "Our national epic has yet to be written" (158). Certainly, this is Joyce boasting that the novel in readers' hands is, in fact, Ireland's national epic, not yet written back in 1904 when the conversation is supposed to take place.

12. See Ellmann, *James Joyce* 163.

13. For example, McCombe erases much of the distance between Stephen and Joyce in his treatment of Stephen's disclaimer at the end of his *Hamlet* harangue. He writes, "the validity of this critical interpretation seems even more sound when considering that Joyce himself once had a similar ghost theory" (731n).

14. Joyce himself helped define the terms of that argument, telling his favorite, Frank Budgen, "I haven't let this young man off very lightly, have I? Many writers have written about themselves. I wonder if any one of them has been as candid as I have" (Budgen 51). Joyce demonstrates the two typical approaches to Stephen by his own switch between third and first person in reference to Stephen.

15. Here *Ulysses* alludes to a famous example of *Bildungsroman*, Brontë's *Jane Eyre*, which, in a vexed moment, refers to Bertha Rochester as "true daughter of an infamous mother" (261).

16. The word "impalpability" recalls Gabriel Conroy's conception of ghostliness in the final passage of "The Dead." Gabriel thinks, "His own identity was fading out into a grey impalpable world: the solid world itself which these dead had at one time reared and lived in was dissolving and dwindling" (*Dubliners* 203). Joyce's intertextuality itself may be said to heighten the author function of his work.

17. See Gifford 196.

18. The world/word association is, of course, a prominent idea, or wordplay, in *Ulysses*, encapsulated by Martha Clifford's error (orthographical? typographical? volitional?) in her letter to Bloom: "I called you naughty boy because I do not like that other world. Please tell me what is the real meaning of that word?" (63).

19. In "Selling Sex as Art," Wexler writes that *Ulysses* was deemed "too difficult" to be pornographic (93). As Joseph Kelly puts it in his account of the *Ulysses* trial, "Genius requires elite readers, and elitism was crucial to the obscenity exemptions" (117).

20. Both versions of this guide are reprinted in their entirety in Ellmann's *Ulysses on the Liffey*, 188–199.

21. Critics of film and popular celebrity use the word "intertexts" for these objects,

emphasizing how they work intertextually with the films. I am calling Joyce's guide "extra-textual," because it is presented as subordinate to *Ulysses*.

22. See "The Work of Art" 231. Benjamin uses this idea of promotion and personality to cast celebrity as a "phony" substitute for the aura, setting the tone for much of the critical treatment that celebrity has received since.

23. Joyce himself claims that the guides' purpose is to obfuscate (Ellmann, *James Joyce* 519).

24. See Michael Groden's *Ulysses in Progress*, 13–63, for an explanation of how Joyce's conception of the novel changed during its composition.

25. See Kenner 22–23, for an account of Joyce's decisions regarding whether to publish the chapter titles. (One might, at this point, legitimately ask: what *can't* one see Kenner about?)

26. Eliot helps make the Homeric parallels in general central to Joyce criticism, excoriating those who are treating Joyce's use of the *Odyssey* as "an amusing dodge" (175).

27. Consider, also, how critics of *Ulysses* and *Finnegans Wake* are expected to refer to the text by line numbers rather than the *pro forma* page numbers of other scholarship.

28. Not necessarily exact words. Speaker's name not relevant. Trust me.

29. See Jaffe's "Joyce's Afterlives: Why Didn't He Win the Nobel Prize?" for an account of the ongoing reference to Joyce in acceptance speeches.

Chapter 3

1. A variation is the celebrity marriage, particularly those marriages between categorically mismatched pairs such as Marilyn Monroe and Arthur Miller. The celebrity marriage may be seen as a celebrity-culture update of the power couple, pairings arranged to wed social power to social power, a phenomenon that has existed at least since Antony and Cleopatra.

2. See Leick's *Gertrude Stein* for a thorough chronicle of Stein's material fame.

3. *The Hollywood Reporter*, December 1934. See *The Hollywood Reporter: The Golden Years* 234–236.

4. Stein's tour helped establish her as a cultural icon in the eyes of the American public. William Wiser writes of her "enormous personal and professional success" due to the lecture tour (94).

5. She has "succeeded in getting so much publicity," she tells them, "by having a small audience" (283–284). This constitutes an early understanding of Jaffe's notion of the "ideology of scarcity" that underwrites his critical take on celebrity modernisms (*Modernism* 65).

6. See *The Autobiography of Alice B. Toklas* 137. This work will be referred to throughout as *The Autobiography*.

7. Will 135; Dydo 595.

8. Stein's authorship was not announced anywhere in the first edition, though it appeared along with the book's serial publication in the *Atlantic Monthly* (Will 139).

It is important to point out here that Stein's play with *The Autobiography*'s authorship is far from unprecedented; in "Narration: Lecture 3" Stein justifies it through Defoe's authorship of *Robinson Crusoe*, which she undoubtedly thought of as a precursor to *The Autobiography*, writing, "Think of Defoe, he tried to write Robinson Crusoe as if it were exactly what did happen and yet after all he is Robinson Crusoe and Robinson Crusoe is Defoe" (*Writings* 351). Indeed, in the concluding moments of *The Autobiography* Stein tells Toklas that she will write her book for her "as simply as Defoe did the autobiography of Robinson Crusoe" (252).

9. Lacan 153–154; Saussure 115.

10. According to Hemingway's memoir of these events, Pound is purposefully given a chair too small in order to humiliate him (*A Moveable Feast* 28).

11. Particularly acclaimed women (especially writers and artists) are often introduced by both their names. But even Marie Laurencin, whom "everybody called Marie Laurencin" (60), evolves into "Marie" eventually (106).

12. Ellmann, *James Joyce* 626.

13. Regarding Stein's linking of money and literature, Glass writes that to Stein, "Money reduces things and persons to the sheer generality of exchange relations not unlike the categorical abstractions of human thought" (129), and thus writing, specifically the masterpiece, resides in a separate sphere of exchange. Though I am tacitly leaning on Glass here, I believe that his examination of Stein's proclamations does not also apply to her treatment of celebrity names, or to language in general.

14. In fact, in the same essay Stein allows for less certainty regarding the proper name, writing, "Given names of people are more lively than nouns which are the name of anything and I suppose that this is because the name is only given to that person when they are born, there is at least the element of choice even the element of change" (316). Stein's own explanations of her work or of literature in general seem to be willfully contradictory; Ellen Berry writes that her "theoretical essays . . . do not cohere into what might be called a systematic cultural or aesthetic theory" (173).

15. Of course, Toklas is not shown to be quite equal to Stein, as she is placed among the wives' company: "The geniuses came and talked to Gertrude Stein and the wives sat with me" (87).

16. The secret is obliquely revealed earlier when Toklas says, "I thought she was making fun of me and I protested, she says I protest now about my autobiography" (114).

17. Also: "They know they are they because their little dog knows them . . . you are you because your little dog knows you" ("What Are Masterpieces and Why Are There So Few of Them," *Writings* 360).

18. According to Steven Meyer's *Irresistible Dictation: Gertrude Stein and the Correlations of Writing and Science*, these moments demonstrate Stein adapting her teacher William James's "stream of thought" (235). James uses the phrase "I am I that I was yesterday" to demonstrate his own views of a sole consciousness moving through time.

19. See, for example, Steiner's convincing argument that Guillaume Apollinaire's equation of geometry in painting to grammar in poetry spurred much of Stein's por-

traiture technique (136–138). Dydo takes the analogy one step further. Studying Stein's notebooks, she contends, "Stein composes words somewhat as painters, with the tools of their art, model three-dimensional perceptions on canvas" (71).

20. Steiner explains, " 'Ninety-three' and 'Lucretia Borgia' are direct translations of the titles, *Quatre-vingt treize* and *Lucrèce Borgia;* the 'building' is probably a hint at *Notre-Dame de Paris;* the "crime" perhaps refers to *Les Chatiments* or *Lucrèce Borgia*" (113). Steiner goes on to write, "It is obvious that Stein knew that these correspondences would not be available to the reader." Though it is obvious to Steiner that Stein could not have anticipated the depth of research that unearths and decodes such extra-textual references, we must keep open the possibility that Stein, like Joyce, imagined being scrutinized in such a manner, but unlike Joyce, did so privately—especially in light of Stein's use of the extra-textual referentiality of the celebrity name.

21. Stein's successful production of herself as the nexus of a network is reflected in the titles of her biographies: *Charmed Circle: Gertrude Stein and Company* (James R. Mellow), *Favored Strangers: Gertrude Stein and Her Family* (Linda Wagner-Martin), etc. The biographers cannot announce her as a discrete entity.

22. For a compelling examination of the critical habit of turning authors' names into adjectives, see Jaffe, *Modernism* 58–93.

Chapter 4

1. See North, *Machine-Age Comedy* 187.

2. In her astute characterization of the 1930s, Rita Barnard describes *Modern Times* as "encapsulating the period's particular doubleness" in its "presentation of contemporary social ills" set against its "endorsement of consumerism" (22). The doubling of extradiegetic millionaire and diegetic marginal man further illuminates this binary, separating the character who is subjected to social ills from the celebrity who himself constitutes a sort of commodity that is available for the audience's consumption.

3. Maland's is one of the best and most recent of the many accounts of Chaplin's rise to fame. See 3–55 in particular.

4. Fernand Léger picks up on this construction of Chaplin's image, depicting the Tramp as a marionette for the opening sequence of his *Ballet Mécanique* (1924), alongside the words, "Charlot présente le ballet mécanique." Similarly, in "A Look at Chaplin," Walter Benjamin writes that Chaplin's "mask of indifference turns him into a sideshow marionette" (310).

5. To articulate the contrast between Chaplin and other stars, I am simplifying Dyer's and Fowles's arguments. Dyer in particular identifies the ways these approaches to celebrity are made more complex by reference to theoretical debates within film studies regarding the nature of the gaze. Whereas I am highlighting the part of these arguments that relies on an equation of vision and knowledge, seeing and believing, Mary Ann Doane describes why things are not this simple, writing, "moments of slippage between vision and epistemological certitude in the cinema can illuminate something of the complexity of the relations between truth [and] vision" (46).

6. Jean Epstein agrees with Griffiths, arguing, "Possibilities are already appearing for the drama of the microscope, a hystophysiology of the passions.... While we are waiting, we have an initial sketch in the close-up" (11). For more on the importance of the close-up to the origins of film celebrity, see Dyer, *Stars* 14–15; Doane 46–48; Susman 282; and Barthes, "The Face of Garbo," in *Mythologies* 56.

7. The only actual close-up I have found in Chaplin's early films occurs in *A Woman* (1915), which features Chaplin in drag. It depicts Chaplin's face minus the mustache, as if to defamiliarize his recognizability.

8. This move itself is not uncommon, as many of the performers at Keystone took turns at directing.

9. By announcing himself as author, Chaplin participates in a critical discussion concerning whether film should be seen as a product of one mind or many, "the controversy," as Rudolph Arnheim puts it, "between the individuals and the collectivists" (67). Arnheim, in a 1934 article asking the critical question "Who is the Author of a Film?" refers to "a recent conception [which] implies an exaltation of the director.... He alone was said to be the author of a film" (63).

10. Žižek contends that "Chaplin's well-known aversion to sound . . . reveals a far deeper than usual knowledge (or at least presentiment) of the disruptive power of the voice" (2). Though Žižek argues that the voice introduces "a radical split" in the subject, it is possible to consider the resistance to dialogue as a way of maintaining a split between subject and image.

11. Barnard writes that the film is "clearly intended to strip the phrase 'modern times' of its associations with technological boosterism" (22).

12. Miriam Hansen explains that slapstick's emphasis on chance at the expense of physical abilities registers "the emergence of a public sphere that is unpredictable and volatile" (*Theory of Film* xxii). He therefore claims it as a pluralist, in fact anarchic, gesture. Clearly, Chaplin's treatment of his cinematic image revises these pluralistic possibilities. Kracauer's comment underlines how Chaplin's treatment of the celebrity image imposes order rather than anarchy. The tightrope scene gestures toward the particular abilities of the celebrity, rather than the public sphere—hardly an invitation to anarchy.

13. *Modern Times* asks whether it is acceptable to go outside the law in order to pursue the American dream in a time when the system has clearly broken down, and it answers by having the Tramp and the Gamin get caught every time they try. So it sheds a particularly cynical light on the film to think that it proposes that the only solution to poverty is Hollywood stardom.

14. Groucho Marx cops this gag to similar effect for the beginning of *Duck Soup* (1934).

15. See North, *Machine-Age Comedy* 4.

16. Marshall offers a detailed analysis of how celebrities articulate a particular audience in terms of consumption practices throughout his *Celebrity and Power*, particularly 56–76. Whereas Marshall focuses on the particular audience identity, the "audience-subjectivity" generated by each audience, my concern is with the way Chaplin enlists the sheer size of his audience, characterizing his appeal as universal.

17. The factory sequence mimics such iconic 1920s films as *Ballet Mécanique* and Fritz Lang's *Metropolis*. The influence further suggests that these scenes represent a prior historical moment within the narrative.

18. "Smile" was first recorded in 1955 by Nat King Cole, and has led a fascinating life since. It was used as the theme song for Jerry Lewis's television show in 1963 and 1967. A partial list of performers who have recorded it turns up a wealth of rich cultural material: Judy Garland, Michael Jackson, Diana Ross, Lyle Lovett, Ruben Stoddard, Rod Stewart, Barbara Streisand, Nana Mouskouri, Natalie Cole, and Elvis Costello. Perhaps the best-known performance is one of the most recent: Jermaine Jackson's rendition at his brother Michael's internationally televised memorial, July 7, 2009.

19. I unearthed the lyrics on a website named Clown Ministry. The lyrics borrow from Chaplin's speech that concludes *The Great Dictator*, which includes the line, "You'll see the sun come shining through."

20. Maland provides a history of the film and the responses it generated (159–186).

21. See North, *Reading 1922* 164.

22. See the biographical volumes, especially Maland 279–287, and also Milton 483–486, for fuller treatments of these somewhat bizarre events.

Chapter 5

1. "The hats now are very difficult, very difficult. All my clients now say that the hats now are very difficult to wear" (69). Hats for women also emerge as weighty signifiers in Woolf's *Mrs. Dalloway*. The same year Rhys published *Midnight*, Greta Garbo (who had, naturally, starred in the 1928 film version of Michael Arlen's novel *The Green Hat*) was in cinemas playing a Soviet commissar who sees a hat in a Paris window display and asks, "How can such a civilization survive which permits their women to put things like that on their heads?" (And then, shaking her head ruefully, "It won't be long now comrades.") (Lubitsch, *Ninotchka*).

2. See Emery, specifically 144–172, and Britzolakis.

3. This is not Rhys's only echo of Molly Bloom's climax. In *Voyage*, Ana, in the midst of being seduced, thinks "Yes . . . yes . . . yes" (36).

4. See Angier 125.

5. See Angier 294–295, or Rhys's own version of the affair in *Smile Please* (127).

6. The whole of my synopsis of Rhys's life is drawn from Angier unless otherwise noted. Angier's narrative itself is beholden to *Smile Please* and Rhys's fiction, letters, and diaries, as well as to extensive research.

7. In this respect, Rhys's Paris writings such as *The Left Bank and Other Stories*, *Quartet*, *Midnight*, and, partly, *Mackenzie*, function similarly to late modernist texts such as Orwell's *Down and Out in Paris and London* and Miller's *Tropic of Cancer*, which enter into a dialogue with modernism by narrating seedier aspects of Paris's expatriate avant-garde life.

8. See Angier 280.

9. Through her treatment of women in the street, Rhys overlaps with Benjamin

and Buck-Morss again: "Like the flâneur, the whore stands on the brink of extinction in the 20th Century precisely when her characteristics have begun to permeate all of erotic life" (Buck-Morss 124).

10. Here, Rhys's writing, breaking ethnically marked bodies into their component parts—limbs and eyes, etc.—may be said to revert to the casual racism that marks many twentieth-century novels but is most famously exposed as underlying Joseph Conrad's work.

11. Indirectly, *Sargasso*'s allusions to hybridization further suggest how it is a novel primarily concerned with the cultural material of the modernist period. In the 1920s, forms of animal-human hybridization, including xenotransplantation and vivisection, were taken seriously as scientific-medical possibilities, largely spurred by the fame of Serge Voronoff. Voronoff's 1926 book *Studies in Aging and Rejuvenation with Transplants* explains his procedures inserting chimpanzee and baboon glands in humans (Gillyboeuf 44–45). W. B. Yeats is said to have undergone such a procedure in 1934 under the knife of Eugen Steinach. Voronoff's book led to his international notoriety, financial success, and a citation by E. E. Cummings as "the famous doctor who inserts / monkeyglands in millionaires a cute idea n'est-ce pas?" (132). Voronoff also transplanted human ovaries into a chimp named Nora and tried to inseminate her with human sperm; French novelist Félicien Champsaur enlists this episode to create his *Nora, la guenon devenue femme* (*Nora, the Monkey Turned Woman*), a book which also uses as source material the life of super-celebrity Josephine Baker, herself considered "a figure for intermediality" (Ngai 150). This footnote in itself suggests material for a whole other book.

12. The popularity of the "super" prefix during the first decades of celebrity's rise, as explained by Guralnik (105), indicates an equation between celebrity and the comic-book superhero, and thus further suggests a link between this rat and the celebrity-modernism axis.

13. See Angier 606.

14. For another examination of the marketing of the postcolonial, one that alludes to similar ideas to Konzett's but also addresses literary celebrity, see Huggan 209–216.

15. I found the photo as part of the promotional materials for Jan Louter's documentary film of Rhys's life, *They Destroyed All the Roses*, but have not managed to unearth it otherwise or obtain a copy suitable for reproduction. In an email to me, Angier speculates that Jan Van Houts took the photo, but it does not appear in any of the publications that I have seen of Van Houts's interview with Rhys, "Het Gaatje en het Gordijn (The Hole in the Curtain)."

Epilogue

1. George Packer writes, "It's hard now to remember that, several generations ago, the trio of great novelists born around the turn of the century—Hemingway, Fitzgerald, Faulkner—was a quartet, with the fourth chair occupied by Dos Passos. *U.S.A.* . . . has become one of the great neglected achievements of literary modernism" (2).

2. See Gado 23.

3. Westerhoven writes of the sections as representing not "an invented persona" but "the author himself" (341).

4. See the final moments of *The Making of Americans* (1925), for example page 919, which alternates the terms "any one" and "every one." From *The Autobiography*, note page 123: "Everybody brought somebody.... everybody came."

5. They also seem to have been dipping into the same cultural vocabulary on display in the 1932 Mervyn Leroy film *Little Caesar*, in which the title character (Edward G. Robinson) proclaims his intention to "be somebody."

6. Dos Passos's name appears in *The Autobiography* though his person does not; he is excluded from Stein's presence, mentioned only as someone Hemingway knows (217).

7. In "Narrate or Describe" (1936) Lukács divides writers into those whose characters act against a backdrop of their times and those whose characters engage with history and culture. The former, he claims, create a "spurious subjectivity": "Everything in composition becomes arbitrary and incidental.... The levelling [sic] inherent in this descriptive method makes everything episodic" (*Writer and Critic* 134). To Lukács, modernist form represents the movement from social to individual consciousness that correlates, of course, to industrial capitalism.

8. See Carr 224-225. Dos Passos wrote Hemingway two letters vaguely apologizing for the review; in the second he concedes that the novel has merit: "in sections it isn't shitty" (225).

9. "He was a nice boy" (12). "She's a nice girl" (46). "She is very nice.... She was very nice. Very, very nice" (59). "He's nice" (61). "Nice of you" (65). "Nice stuffed dog" (78). "You have a nice friend, Jake.... She's damned nice" (81). "He had very nice manners" (188).

10. "But we had to go back to the hotel to get our bags packed and pay the bill" (*The Sun Also Rises* 97). "We had lunch and paid the bill" (232). "The bill had been paid" (247). And: "That only delayed the presentation of the bill. The bill always came. That was one of the swell things you could count on. I thought I had paid for anything" (152).

11. See Koch 18–19.

12. "The rich" included Gerald Murphy and his wife Sara, who were popular targets for the modernists, also serving as models for the first part of F. Scott Fitzgerald's *Tender is the Night*.

13. Glass writes that Hemingway's attacks on his contemporaries "conflat[e] literary and psychological inadequacy" (156).

14. See Koch 51.

Works Cited

Angier, Carole. *Jean Rhys: Life and Work.* Boston: Little, Brown, and Company, 1990.
Arata, Stephen. "Oscar Wilde and Jesus Christ." Bristow 254-272.
Armstrong, Nancy. *Fiction in the Age of Photography.* Cambridge: Harvard UP, 1999.
———. "Modernism's Iconophobia and What It Did to Gender." *Modernism/Modernity* 5 (1998): 47-75.
Armstrong, Philip. *What Animals Mean in the Fiction of Modernity.* New York: Routledge, 2008.
Armstrong, Tim. "Muting the Klaxon: Poetry, History and Irish Modernism." *Modernism and Ireland: The Poetry of the 1930s.* Ed. Patricia Coughlan and Alex Davies. Cork: Cork University Press, 1995. 43-74.
Arnheim, Rudolph. "Who is the Author of a Film?" 1934. *Film Essays and Criticism.* Trans. Brenda Benthien. Madison: U of Wisconsin P, 1997. 62-69.
Attridge, Derek. "Joyce and the Making of Modernism." *Rethinking Modernism.* Ed. Marianne Thormahlen. New York: Palgrave Macmillan, 2003. 148-161.
Babbitt, Irving. *Rousseau and Romanticism.* 1919. Austin: U of Texas P, 1977.
Barnard, Rita. *The Great Depression and the Culture of Abundance.* Cambridge: Cambridge UP, 1995.
Barthes, Roland. "The Death of the Author." *Image-Music-Text.* Trans. Stephen Heath. New York: Hill and Wang, 1977. 142-148.
———. *Mythologies.* 1957. Trans. Jonathan Cape. New York: Hill and Wang, 1972.
Benjamin, Walter. *The Arcades Project.* Trans. Howard Eiland and Kevin McLaughlin. Cambridge: Belknap Press of Harvard UP, 1999.
———. "A Look at Chaplin." 1929. Trans. John MacKay. *The Yale Journal of Criticism* 9 (1996): 309-314.
———. "The Storyteller." *Illuminations.* Trans. Harry Zohn. New York: Schocken Books, 1968. 83-110.
———. "The Work of Art in the Age of Mechanical Reproduction." *Illuminations.* 217-251.
Benstock, Shari. *Women of the Left Bank.* Austin: U of Texas P, 1986.
Bergson, Henri. *Laughter.* 1911. Trans. Cloudesley Brereton and Fred Rothwell. Copenhagen: Green Integer, 1999.
Berman, Marshall. *All That Is Solid Melts Into Air.* New York: Simon and Schuster, 1982.
Berry, Ellen. "Modernism/Mass Culture/Postmodernism: The Case of Gertrude Stein." Dettmar 167-190.
Blake, David Haven. *Walt Whitman and the Culture of American Celebrity.* New Haven: Yale UP, 2006.
Boorstin, Daniel. *The Image: A Guide to Pseudo-Events in America.* 1961. New York: Atheneum, 1975.
Boscagli, Maurizia, and Enda Duffy. "Joyce's Face." Dettmar and Watt 133-161.

Bourdieu, Pierre. *Distinction*. Trans. Richard Price. Cambridge: Harvard UP, 1984.
Braudy, Leo. *The Frenzy of Renown*. New York: Vintage, 1986.
Bristow, Joseph, ed. *Wilde Writings: Contextual Conditions*. Toronto: U of Toronto P, 2003.
Britzolakis, Christina. "'This Way to the Exhibition': Genealogies of Urban Spectacle in Jean Rhys's Interwar Fiction." *Textual Practice* 21.3 (2007): 457-482.
Brontë, Charlotte. *Jane Eyre*. 1848. New York: Norton Critical Editions, 2001.
Buckley, Jerome H. "Towards Early-Modern Autobiography: The Roles of Oscar Wilde, George Moore, Edmund Gosse, and Henry Adams." *Modernism Reconsidered*. Ed. Robert Kiely. Harvard English Studies 11. Cambridge: Harvard UP, 1983.
Buck-Morss, Susan. "The Flaneur, the Sandwichman and the Whore." *New German Critique* 39 (1986): 99-140.
Budgen, Frank. *James Joyce and the Making of Ulysses*. New York: Harrison Smith and Robert Haas, 1934.
Calinescu, Matei. *Five Faces of Modernity*. Durham: Duke UP, 1987.
Cantwell, Mary. "A Conversation with Jean Rhys." *Critical Perspectives on Jean Rhys*. Ed. Pierette Frickey. New York: Three Continents Press, 1990. 21-27.
Carlyle, Thomas. *On Heroes, Hero-Worship, and the Heroic in History*. 1841. Lincoln: U of Nebraska P, 1966.
Carr, Virginia. *Dos Passos: A Life*. Evanston: Northwestern UP, 2004.
Casey, Janet Galligani. *Dos Passos and the Ideology of the Feminine*. Cambridge: Cambridge UP, 1998.
Chaplin, Charles, dir. *City Lights*. RBC Films, 1931.
———. *The Great Dictator*. United Artists, 1940.
———. *Modern Times*. Perf. Chaplin and Paulette Goddard. United Artists, 1936.
———. *The Rink*. Mutual, 1916.
———. *Shoulder Arms*. First National, 1918.
———. *Sunny Side*. First National, 1919.
———, perf. *Tillie's Punctured Romance*. Dir. Mack Sennett. Keystone, 1914.
———. *The Tramp*. Essanay, 1915.
———. *The Vagabond*. Mutual, 1916.
———. *A Woman*. Essanay, 1915.
Conley, Tim. "Performance Anxieties: On Failing to Read *Finnegans Wake*." *Papers on Language and Literature: A Journal for Scholars and Critics of Language and Literature* 39 (Winter 2003): 71-90.
Cucullu, Lois. "Adolescent *Dorian Gray:* Oscar Wilde's Proto-Picture of Modernist Celebrity." Goldman and Jaffe 36-68. TS.
Cummings, Edward Estlin. *Collected Poems*. New York: Harcourt, Brace and Co., 1966.
Curnutt, Kirk. "Inside and Outside: Gertrude Stein on Identity, Celebrity, and Authenticity." *Journal of Modern Literature* 23 (1999): 291-308.
Dale, Alan. *Comedy Is a Man in Trouble*. St. Paul: U of Minnesota P, 2002.
deCordova, Richard. *Picture Personalities*. Urbana: U of Illinois P, 1990.
Derrida, Jacques. "The Animal That Therefore I Am (More to Follow)." Trans. David Wills. *Critical Inquiry* 28 (Winter 2002): 369-418.

———. *The Post Card*. Trans. Alan Bass. Chicago: U of Chicago P, 1987.
Dettmar, Kevin, ed. *Rereading the New*. Ann Arbor: U of Michigan P, 1992.
Dettmar, Kevin, and Stephen J. Watt, eds. *Marketing Modernisms*. Ann Arbor: U of Michigan P, 1996.
———. Introduction. Dettmar and Watt 1–13.
Dickens, Charles. *David Copperfield*. 1850. London: Penguin, 1996.
Doane, Mary Ann. *Femmes Fatales*. New York: Routledge, 1991.
Donovan, Stephen. "'SHORT BUT TO THE POINT': Newspaper Typography in 'Aeolus.'" *James Joyce Quarterly* 40 (2003): 519–542.
Dos Passos, John. *1919*. 1932. Boston: Mariner Books, 2000.
———. *The 42nd Parallel*. 1930. Boston: Mariner Books, 1991.
———. *The Fourteenth Chronicle: Letters and Diaries of John Dos Passos*. Ed. Townsend Ludington. New York: Gambit, Inc., 1973.
———. *Travel Books and Other Writings 1916–1941*. Ed. Townsend Ludington. U.S.A.: The Library of America, 2003.
———. *U.S.A.* New York: The Modern Library, 1937.
Dydo, Ulla. *Gertrude Stein: The Language that Rises 1923–1934*. Evanston: Northwestern UP, 2003.
Dyer, Richard. *Heavenly Bodies*. New York: St. Martin's Press, 1986.
———. *Stars*. London: BFI, 1998.
Eagleton, Terry. *Against the Grain: Essays 1975–1985*. London: Verso, 1986.
Eckert, Charles. "Shirley Temple and the House of Rockefeller." *American Media and Mass Culture: Left Perspectives*. Ed. Donald Lazere. Berkeley: U of California P, 1987. 164–177.
Eliot, T. S. "Ulysses, Order, and Myth." 1923. *Selected Prose of T. S. Eliot*. Ed. Frank Kermode. New York: Harcourt Brace Jovanovich, 1975. 175–178.
Ellmann, Richard. *James Joyce*. 1959. Oxford: Oxford UP, 1982.
———. *Oscar Wilde*. London: Penguin Books, 1987.
———. *Ulysses on the Liffey*. New York: Oxford UP, 1972.
Emery, Mary Lou. *Jean Rhys at "World's End."* Austin: U of Texas P, 1990.
English, James F., and John Frow. "Literary Authorship and Celebrity Culture." *A Concise Companion to Contemporary British Fiction*. Ed. James F. English. Malden, MA: Blackwell, 2006. 39–57.
Epstein, Jean. "Magnification and Other Writings." Trans. Stuart Liebman. *October* 3 (1977): 9–25.
"Fell Flat." *Daily States*. 17 June 1882.
Felski, Rita. *The Gender of Modernity*. Cambridge: Harvard UP, 1995.
Ford, Sara. *Gertrude Stein and Wallace Stevens*. New York: Routledge, 2002.
Foucault, Michel. "What is An Author?" *Aesthetics, Method, and Epistemology*. Ed. James D. Faubion. New York: New Press, 1998. 205–222.
Fowles, Jib. *Starstruck*. Washington: Smithsonian Institution P, 1992.
Gado, Frank, ed. "An Interview with John Dos Passos." *Idol: The Literary Quarterly of Union College* 45 (1969): 23.
Gagnier, Regenia. *Idylls of the Marketplace*. Stanford: Stanford UP, 1986.

Garbo, Greta, perf. *Ninotchka*. Dir. Ernst Lubitsch. Metro-Goldwyn-Meyer, 1937.
Gay, Peter. *Modernism: The Lure of Heresy*. New York: W. W. Norton and Co., 2008.
Gifford, Don, and Robert J. Seidman. *Ulysses Annotated*. Berkeley: U of California P, 1989.
Gillyboeuf, Thierry. "The Famous Doctor Who Inserts Monkeyglands in Millionaires." *Spring: The Journal of the E. E. Cummings Society* 9 (2000): 44-45.
Glass, Loren. *Authors Inc.: Literary Celebrity in the Modern United States, 1880-1980*. New York: NYUP, 2004.
Gopnik, Adam. "The Invention of Oscar Wilde." *The New Yorker* 18 May 1998: 78-88.
Goux, Jean-Joseph. "Cash, Check, or Charge?" *The New Economic Criticism*. Ed. Martha Woodmansee and Mark Osteen. London: Routledge, 1999. 114-128.
Groden, Michael. *Ulysses in Progress*. Princeton: Princeton UP, 1977.
Guralnik, David B. "Superstar, Supermom, Super Glue, Superdooper, Superman." *Superman at Fifty!: The Persistence of a Legend*. Ed. Gary D. Engle and Dennis Dooley. New York: Collier Books, 1988. 108-115.
Hamilton, Lisa. "The Importance of Recognizing Oscar: The Dandy and the Culture of Celebrity." *The Center and Clark Newsletter* 33 (1999): 3-5.
———. "Oscar Wilde, New Women, and the Rhetoric of Efficiency." Bristow 230-253.
Hammill, Faye. *Women, Celebrity, and Literary Culture Between the Wars*. Austin: U of Texas P, 2007.
Hansen, Miriam. *Babel and Babylon*. Cambridge: Harvard UP, 1991.
———. Introduction. Kracauer vii-xlv.
Harris, Frank. *Oscar Wilde*. 1916. U.S.A.: Dell, 1960.
Haselstein, Ulla. "Gertrude Stein's Portraits of Matisse and Picasso." *New Literary History* 34 (2004): 723-743.
Hemingway, Ernest. *A Moveable Feast*. 1964. New York: Touchstone, 1992.
———. *The Sun Also Rises*. 1926. New York: Charles Scribner and Sons, 1954.
Hillenbrand, Laura. *Seabiscuit*. New York: Random House, 2001.
Holland, Merlin, ed. *The Real Trial of Oscar Wilde*. New York: Fourth Estate, 2003.
———. *The Wilde Album*. New York: Henry Holt and Co., 1998.
Horkheimer, Max, and Theodor W. Adorno. *Dialectic of Enlightenment*. Trans. John Cumming. New York: Continuum, 1993.
Huggan, Graham. *The Postcolonial Exotic: Marketing the Margins*. New York: Routledge, 2001.
Huyssen, Andreas. *After the Great Divide*. Bloomington: Indiana UP, 1986.
Intellectual Property Office. "Case Details for Trade Mark 1." Web. December 4, 2009.
Jaffe, Aaron. "Joyce's Afterlives: Why Didn't He Win the Nobel Prize?" *James Joyce: Visions and Revisions*. Ed. Sean Latham. Dublin: Irish Academic Press, 2009. 189-214.
———. *Modernism and the Culture of Celebrity*. Cambridge: Cambridge UP, 2005.
Jaffe, Aaron and Jonathan Goldman, eds. *Modernist Star Maps: Celebrity, Modernity, Culture*. London: Ashgate Publications, forthcoming 2010. TS.
James, Henry. "The Liar." *Complete Stories of Henry James*. 3 vols. New York: Library of America, 1999.

Jameson, Frederic. *Postmodernism, or The Cultural Logic of Late Capitalism.* Durham: Duke UP, 1991.

Jay, Martin. *Force Fields: Between Intellectual History and Cultural Critique.* New York: Routledge, 1993.

Johnson, Jeri. "Beyond the Veil: *Ulysses,* Feminism, and the Figure of Women." *Joyce, Modernity, and Its Mediation.* Ed. Christine van Boheeman. Amsterdam: Rodopi, 1989. 201–228.

Joyce, James. *Dubliners.* 1914. New York: Vintage International, 1993.

———. *Finnegans Wake.* 1939. New York: Penguin Books, 1976.

———. *Selected Letters of James Joyce.* Ed. Richard Ellmann. New York: Viking, 1975.

———. *Ulysses.* 1922. New York: Vintage, 1986.

Joyce, Simon. "Sexual Politics and the Aesthetics of Crime: Oscar Wilde in the Nineties." *ELH* 69 (2002): 501–523.

Juengel, Scott J. "Face, Figure and Physiognomics: Mary Shelley's *Frankenstein* and the Moving Image." *Novel* 33 (2000): 353–367.

Kafka, Franz. "The Hunger Artist." 1924. *The Metamorphosis and Other Stories.* Trans. Joyce Crick. Oxford: Oxford UP, 2009.

Karnick, Kristine Brunovska, and Henry Jenkins, eds. *Classical Hollywood Comedy.* New York: Routledge, 1995.

Kasson, John F. *Houdini, Tarzan, and the Perfect Man.* New York: Hill and Wang, 2001.

Kelly, Joseph. *Our Joyce.* Austin: U of Texas P, 1998.

Kennedy, J. Gerald. *Imagining Paris: Exile, Writing, and American Identity.* New Haven: Yale UP, 1993.

Kenner, Hugh. *Ulysses.* Baltimore: Johns Hopkins UP, 1987.

Koch, Stephen. *The Breaking Point: Hemingway, Dos Passos, and the Murder of José Robles.* New York: Counterpoint, 2005.

Koestenbaum, Wayne. *Cleavage.* New York: Ballantine Books, 2000.

Konzett, Delia Caparoso. *Ethnic Modernisms.* New York: Palgrave Macmillan, 2002.

Kracauer, Siegfried. *Theory of Film.* 1960. Princeton: Princeton UP, 1997.

———. "Two Chaplin Sketches." 1931. Trans. John McKay. *The Yale Journal of Criticism* 10 (1997): 115–120.

Kreilkamp, Ivan. *Voice and the Victorian Storyteller.* Cambridge: Cambridge UP, 2005.

Kristeva, Julia. *Powers of Horror: An Essay on Abjection.* New York: Columbia UP, 1982.

Lacan, Jacques. *Ecrits: A Selection.* New York: W. W. Norton and Company, 1976.

Latham, Sean. *Am I a Snob? Modernism and the Novel.* Ithaca: Cornell UP, 2003.

Leff, Leonard J. *Hemingway and His Conspirators.* Lanham: Rowman & Littlefield Publishers, Inc., 1997.

Le Gallez, Paula. *The Rhys Woman.* New York: Palgrave Macmillan, 1990.

Léger, Fernand, dir. *Ballet Mécanique.* 1924. Video. Video Yesteryear, 1992.

Leick, Karen. *Gertrude Stein and the Making of an American Celebrity.* New York: Routledge, 2009.

———. "Popular Modernism: Little Magazines and the American Daily Press." *PMLA* 123:1 (2008): 125–139.

Lénárt-Cheng, Helga. "Autobiography As Advertisement: Why Do Gertrude Stein's Sentences Get Under Our Skin?" *New Literary History* 34 (2003): 117–131.

Levin, Jonathan. "'Entering the Modern Composition': Gertrude Stein and the Patterns of Modernism." Dettmar 137–166.

Lewis, L., and H. J. Smith. *Oscar Wilde Discovers America*. 1936. New York: Benjamin Blom, 1967.

Lewis, Wyndham. *Time and Western Man*. 1927. Santa Rosa: Black Sparrow Press, 1993.

Lowenthal, Leo. *Literature, Popular Culture and Society*. Englewood Cliffs: Prentice-Hall, 1961.

Ludington, Townsend. "Explaining Dos Passos's Naturalism." *Studies in American Naturalism* 1:1 & 2 (Summer and Winter 2006): 36–41.

———. "The Ordering of the Camera Eye in *U.S.A.*" *American Literature* 49:3 (1977): 443–446.

Lukács, Georg. *Realism in Our Time*. Trans. John Mander and Necke Mander. World Perspectives 33. New York: Harper and Row, 1964.

———. *"Writer and Critic" and Other Essays*. Trans. Arthur Kahn. New York: Grosset and Dunlap, 1971.

Maland, Charles. *Chaplin and American Culture*. Princeton: Princeton UP, 1989.

Mao, Douglas, and Rebecca Walkowitz. "The New Modernist Studies." *PMLA* 123:3 (2008): 737–748.

Marcuse, Herbert. *Negations*. Boston: Beacon Press, 1968.

Marez, Curtis. "The Other Addict: Reflections on Colonialism and Oscar Wilde's Opium Smoke Screen." *ELH* 64 (1997): 257–287.

Marshall, P. David. *Celebrity and Power*. Minneapolis: U of Minnesota P, 1997.

Marx, Groucho, perf. *Duck Soup*. Dir. Leo McCarey. Paramount, 1933.

Marx, Karl. *Capital*. Trans. Samuel Moore and Edward Aveling. Ed. Frederick Engels. 2 vols. Moscow: Foreign Languages Publishing House, 1961.

Mast, Gerald. *A Short History of the Movies*. Indianapolis: Bobbs-Merrill Educational Publishing, 1976.

Maurel, Sylvie. *Jean Rhys*. New York: St. Martin's Press, 1998.

McCabe, Susan. "'Delight in Dislocation': The Cinematic Modernism of Stein, Chaplin and Man Ray." *Modernism/Modernity* 8 (2001): 429–452.

McCombe, John. "Besteglyster and Bradleyism: Stephen Dedalus's Postcolonial Response to English Criticism." *James Joyce Quarterly* 39 (2002): 717–733.

McLees, Ainslee Armstrong. *Baudelaire's Argot Plastique: Poetic Caricature and Modernism*. Athens: U of Georgia P, 1990.

Meyer, Steven. *Irresistible Dictation: Gertrude Stein and the Correlations of Writing and Science*. Palo Alto: Stanford UP, 2001.

Michaels, Walter Benn. *Our America*. Durham: Duke UP, 1995.

Miller, Tyrus. *Late Modernism*. Berkeley: U of California P, 1999.

Milton, Joyce. *Tramp*. New York: Da Capo P, 1996.

Mobilio, Albert. "The Lost Generator: Gertrude Stein Builds a Better Reader." *Gertrude Stein: A Study of the Short Fiction.* Ed. Linda Watts. New York: Twayne Publishers, 1999. 110–123.

Monaco, James, ed. *Celebrity.* New York: Dell, 1978.

Moran, Joe. *Star Authors: Literary Celebrity in America.* London: Pluto Press, 2000.

Moretti, Franco. *Modern Epic.* Trans. Quintin Hoare. London: Verso, 1996.

———. *Signs Taken for Wonders.* Trans. Susan Fischer, David Forgacs, and David Miller. London: Verso, 1983.

Morrisson, Mark. *The Public Face of Modernism.* Madison: U of Wisconsin P, 2001.

Ngai, Sianne. "Black Venus, *Blonde Venus.*" *Bad Modernisms.* Ed. Douglas Mao and Rebecca L. Walkowitz. Durham: Duke UP, 2006. 145–179.

Nieland, Justus. *Feeling Modern.* Urbana: U of Illinois P, 2008.

Nordau, Max. *Degeneration.* 1892. Lincoln: U of Nebraska P, 1993.

North, Michael. *Machine-Age Comedy.* Oxford: Oxford UP, 2009.

———. "The Picture of Oscar Wilde." *PMLA* 125.1 (2010): 185–191.

———. *Reading 1922.* New York: Oxford UP, 1999.

Orgeron, Devin Anthony, and Marsha Gabrielle Orgeron. "Eating Their Words: Consuming Class a la Chaplin and Keaton." *College Literature* 28 (2001): 84–105.

Packer, George. "The Spanish Prisoner." *The New Yorker.* Web. 31 October 2005.

Pickford, Mary. "The Big Bad Wolf Has Been Muzzled." Wilkerson 234–236.

Plato. "Cratylus." *Plato IV.* Trans. H. N. Fowler. Cambridge: Harvard UP, 1996. 1–192.

Poe, Edgar Allan. "The Oval Portrait." 1849. *The Short Fiction of Edgar Allan Poe.* Ed. Stuart Levine and Susan Levine. Urbana: U of Illinois P, 1990. 65–67.

Ponce de Leon, Charles L. *Self-Exposure.* Chapel Hill: U of North Carolina P, 2002.

Powell, Kerry. "A Verdict of Death: Oscar Wilde, Actresses and Victorian Women." *The Cambridge Companion to Oscar Wilde.* Ed. Peter Raby. Cambridge: Cambridge UP, 1997. 181–194.

Proust, Marcel. *Remembrance of Things Past.* Trans. C. K. Scott Moncrieff. Vol. 1. New York: Random House, 1924.

Rainey, Lawrence. *Institutions of Modernism.* New Haven: Yale UP, 1998.

Reed, Carol, dir. *The Third Man.* 1949. Video. Media Home Entertainment, 1989.

Rhys, Jean. *After Leaving Mr. Mackenzie.* 1930. New York: W. W. Norton and Company, 1997.

———. *The Collected Short Stories.* New York: W. W. Norton and Company, 1987.

———. *Good Morning, Midnight.* 1937. New York: W. W. Norton and Company, 2000.

———. *Letters 1931–1966.* Ed. Francis Wyndham and Diana Melly. London: Penguin Books, 1982.

———. *Quartet.* 1928. New York: W. W. Norton and Company, 1982.

———. *Smile Please.* New York: Harper and Row, 1979.

———. *Voyage in the Dark.* 1934. New York: W. W. Norton and Company, 1982.

———. *Wide Sargasso Sea.* 1966. New York: W. W. Norton and Company, 1999.

Riblet, Douglas. "The Keystone Film Company and the Historiography of Early Slapstick." Karnick 168–189.

Rosenquist, Rod. *Modernism, the Market, and the Institution of the New*. Cambridge: Cambridge UP, 2009.
Saint-Amour, Paul K. *The Copywrights: Intellectual Property and the Literary Imagination*. Ithaca: Cornell UP, 2003.
Saussure, Ferdinand de. *Course in General Linguistics*. Trans. Wade Baskin. Ed. Charles Bally, Albert Sechehaye, and Albert Riedlinger. New York: McGraw-Hill Book Company, 1959.
Savory, Elaine. *Jean Rhys*. Cambridge: Cambridge UP, 1998.
Schickel, Richard. "Fairbanks: His Picture in the Papers." Monaco 121-127.
———. *Intimate Strangers*. New York: Fromm International Publishing Company, 1986.
Schloss, Carol Loeb. "Joyce's Transgressive Genders: A Feminist Perspective." Rev. of *Modernism's Body: Sex, Culture, and Joyce*, by Christine Froula. *Novel* 31 (1997): 115-118.
Schoenbach, Lisi. "Habit, Shock, and Gertrude Stein's Pragmatic Modernism." *Modernism/Modernity* 11.2 (2004): 239-259.
Scholes, Robert. *In Search of James Joyce*. Urbana: U of Illinois P, 1992.
Scott, Bonnie Kime. *The Gender of Modernism: A Critical Anthology*. Bloomington: Indiana UP, 1990.
Seldes, Gilbert. *The Seven Lively Arts*. 1924. New York: A. S. Barnes and Company, Inc., 1957.
Senn, Fritz. "Remodeling Homer." *Light Rays: James Joyce and Modernism*. Ed. Morris Beja and Heyward Erlich. New York: New Horizon P, 1984. 70-92.
Shakespeare, William. *Romeo and Juliet*. In *The Norton Shakespeare*. New York: W. W. Norton & Company, 1997. 865-942.
Silverman, Kaja. "Fragments of a Fashionable Discourse." *Studies in Entertainment*. Ed. Tania Modleski. Bloomington: Indiana UP, 1986. 139-152.
Sinfield, Alan. *The Wilde Century*. New York: Columbia UP, 1994.
Small, Ian. "Love-Letter, Spiritual Autobiography, or Prison Writing? Identity and Value in *De Profundis*." Bristow 86-100.
Stein, Gertrude. "And Now: And so the time comes when I can tell the story of my life." *Vanity Fair* 43.4 (1933): 33, 65.
———. *The Autobiography of Alice B. Toklas*. 1932. New York: Vintage, 1990.
———. *Everybody's Autobiography*. 1937. New York: Vintage, 1973.
———. *The Making of Americans*. 1925. Normal, Il: Dalkey Archive P, 1999.
———. *Paris France*. 1940. New York: Liveright, 1970.
———. *A Stein Reader*. Ed. Ulla Dydo. Evanston: Northwestern UP, 1993.
———. *Writings 1932-1946*. Ed. Catharine R. Stimpson and Harriet Chessman. New York: Literary Classics of America, 1998.
Steiner, Wendy. *Exact Resemblance to Exact Resemblance*. New Haven: Yale UP, 1978.
Stimpson, Catharine. "The Mind, the Body, and Gertrude Stein." *Gertrude Stein*. Ed. Harold Bloom. New York: Chelsea House Publishers, 1986. 131-148.
Susman, Warren I. *Culture as History*. New York: Pantheon Books, 1973.
Turner, John, and Geoffrey Parsons. "Smile." 1954.

Wells, H. G. *The Island of Doctor Moreau*. 1896. London: Penguin Books, 2005.
Westerhoven, John. "Autobiographical Elements in the Camera Eye." *American Literature* 48 (1976): 340–364.
Wexler, Joyce Piell. "Selling Sex as Art." Dettmar and Watt 91–108.
———. *Who Paid for Modernism?* Fayetteville: U of Arkansas P, 1997.
Wicke, Jennifer. *Advertising Fictions*. New York: Columbia UP, 1988.
———. "Enchantment, Disenchantment, Re-enchantment: Joyce and the Cult of the Absolutely Fabulous." *Novel: A Forum on Fiction* 29 (1995): 128–137.
Wilde, Oscar. *Complete Letters of Oscar Wilde*. Ed. Merlin Holland and Rupert Hart-Davis. New York: Henry Holt and Company, 2000.
———. *Complete Works of Oscar Wilde*. Great Britain: HarperCollins, 1966.
———. *The Picture of Dorian Gray*. 1989. New York: Signet Classic, 1995.
Wilder, Billy, dir. *Sunset Boulevard*. Paramount Pictures, 1950.
Wilkerson, Tichi, and Marcia Borie. *The Hollywood Reporter: The Golden Years*. New York: Coward-McCann, 1984.
Will, Barbara. *Gertrude Stein, Modernism, and the Problem of 'Genius'*. Edinburgh: Edinburgh UP, 2000.
Williams, Raymond. *Writing in Society*. London: Verso, 1983.
Wiser, William. *The Twilight Years: Paris in the 1930s*. New York: Carroll & Graf, 2000.
York, Lorraine. *Literary Celebrity in Canada*. Toronto: U of Toronto P, 2007.
Zimring, Rishona. "The Make-Up of Jean Rhys's Fiction." *Novel: A Forum on Fiction* 33:2 (2000): 212–234.
Žižek, Slavoj. *Enjoy Your Symptom! Jacques Lacan in Hollywood and Out*. New York: Routledge, 1992.

Index

Page numbers in *italics* refer to illustrations.

Abin, César, 57, 58
abjection, 133, 135, 140–141, 145. *See also* Rhys, Jean
Adorno, Theodor W., 175n6
aesthetic movement, 23, 25, 26, 29
After Leaving Mr. Mackenzie (Rhys), 136, 146, 149, 185n7
After the Great Divide (Huyssen), 3, 57
"Again the Antilles" (Rhys), 148
Agee, James, 11
Age of Innocence, The (Wharton), 10
Alvarez, A., 157
Anderson, Sherwood, 91
"And Now" (Stein), 104
Angier, Carole, 132, 146, 184nn4–6, 185n8, 185n13, 185n15
Apollinaire, Guillaume, 86, 181–182n19
Arata, Stephen, 49
Arcades Project (Benjamin), 139
Armstrong, Nancy, 9, 53, 107
Armstrong, Philip, 153, 156
Armstrong, Tim, 163
Arnheim, Rudolph, 183n9
Atlantic Monthly, 181n8
Attridge, Derek, 60–61
Authors, Inc.: Literary Celebrity in the United States, 1880–1980 (Glass), 6
Autobiography of Alice B. Toklas, The (Stein), 145, 161, 180n8, 181n15, 186n4; accessible style of, 85, 109; and "aura" of the celebrity name, 88, 90, 145; and authorial genius, 102–104; and destabilization/devaluation of celebrity name, 90–92, 94–97, 101–104; domestication/private vs. public in, 92–94, 97–98, 104, 108; and name-dropping, 14, 84, 85–90, 96–98; Stein and names in home and text, 89–90, 97–98, 109

Babbitt, Irving, 24
Babel and Babylon (Hansen), 9
Baker, Josephine, 11, 185n11
Ballad of Reading Gaol, The (Wilde), 52
Ballet Mécanique (Léger), 182n4
Barnacle, Nora, 74

Barnard, Rita, 182n2
Barnes, Djuna, 146
Barnum, P. T., 22, 30, 136
Barthes, Roland, 1, 13, 22; on Chaplin, 115; on Einstein, 25, 85; "Platonic Idea" of, 57, 133–134; and production of author, 70, 75–76, 80
Bass Ale, 19, 63–64
Beerbohm, Max, 10, 31, 56, 177n18
Being Geniuses Together (Boyle and McAlmon), 145
Benjamin, Walter, 31, 139; on *Bildungsroman*, 73–74; on celebrity, 175–176n6, 180n22; on Charlie Chaplin, 122, 123, 124, 182n4; on film promotion, 77; on relationship between image and temporality, 126–127
Benstock, Shari, 87, 94
Bergson, 117
Berman, Marshall, 3
Bernhardt, Sarah, 9
Berry, Ellen, 175n2, 181n14
Best of Times, The (Dos Passos), 165
Big Money, The (Dos Passos), 167. *See also U.S.A.*
Bildungsroman, 179n15; challenges to, 73–74; example passage from, 69–70; replacement of, with authorial self-fashioning, 13, 69, 142. *See also Jane Eyre*, *David Copperfield*
Blake, David Haven, 6
Book of Kells, The, 63
Boorstin, Daniel, 10, 131, 173
Borgia, Lucretia, 106–107
Boscagli, Maurizia, 59
Bourdieu, Pierre, 26
Bowen, Stella, 145
Bradley, A. C., 178n7
Brandt, Bill, 159
Braque, Georges, 91, 97, 102
Braudy, Leo: on modern celebrity, 8, 56, 163, 175n4; on Wilde, 16
Bristow, Joseph, 21, 22; on Wilde's epigrams, 26
Britzolakis, Christina, 149
Bromley and West Kent Mercury, 146

Brontë, Charlotte, 142, 147, 151, 158, 179n15
Buckley, Jerome H., 29, 48-49
Buck-Morss, Susan, 139
Budgen, Frank, 178n6, 179n14
Byron's Romantic Celebrity (Mole), 6

Calinescu, Matei, 99
Cantwell, Mary, 133
caricature, 28, 31-33, 35, 37-39, 57, 177n18
Carlyle, Thomas, 23-24, 25, 51
Carmen (Bizet), 71
Carte, Richard D'Oyly, 23
Casey, Janet Galligani, 169
celebrity: and audience, 1, 16, 180n22, 183n16; and caricature, 177n18; and comic book hero, 185n12; as commodity, 10, 20, 128, 175-176n6; development of modern, 8-10, 20-21, 56, 66; and diegesis, 87; image of, as sign of history, 127-128; as link between high and low culture, 2-3; and marriage, 180n1; in modernist literature (*see* modernism); in postcolonial literature, 158-159; promotional apparatus of, 77; reaffirmation of individual in, 2, 7, 9, 77, 173; and relationship between subject and object, 2, 7, 117, 118, 160, 175n5. *See also* cinema; *and specific authors*
Champsaur, Félicien, 185n11
Chaplin, Charlie, 2, 82, 84, *112*, *113*, *114*, 136, 176n7; author-production of, via celebrity, 14, 114-115, 119; career of, 116; celebrity of, 9, 111, 117; and close-up, 118, 183n7; critical reception of, 122-123; and dialogue, 119-120, 130, 183n10; and distinction between image and author, 115, 116, 120-123; and historical moment, 14-15, 16, 115, 125-128; as modernist, 111, 114, 115, 127; and music and sound, 128-129; and narrative contradiction, 113-115; and Paris avant-garde, 11; politics and legal troubles of, 130-131; and slapstick, 118-119; technique of, 125-126. See also *Modern Times;* Tramp (character); *and specific films*
cinema, 3; and authorship, 183n9; and close-up, 117-118, 183n6; and production of modern celebrity, 8, 9, 56, 80, 87; promotional apparatus of, 77
Circus, The (Chaplin), 121
City Lights (Chaplin), 124
Clarke, Edward, 46
commodity, 10, 12, 16, 30, 51

"Confidence Men" (Melville), 22
Conley, Tim, 79
Cowper, William, 155
Cucullu, Lois, 33
Cummings, E. E., 185n11
Cunard, Nancy, 95-96, 101
Curnutt, Kirk, 83, 86

David Copperfield (Dickens), 69-70
Day of the Locust, The (West), 10-11
"Days With Celebrities" (Beerbohm), 31
Debs, Eugene, 163-164
deCordova, Richard, 115, 119
Delaney, Paul, 57
De Profundis (Wilde), 135, 177n25; Christ comparison in, 48-50, 176n5, 178n30; circulation of, as private letter vs. public narrative, 45-47; and creation of Wilde as complete subject, 12, 20, 21, 45, 50-51; imagination in, 49, 51, 52; individuality in, 50; and inversion of subject from exterior to interior, 44, 47-54; and text as site of subject, 51-54
Derrida, Jacques, 45, 156
Dettmar, Kevin, 175n1
Dial, 59
Dickens, Charles, 7; and *Bildungsroman*, 69-70, 73; and body as site of originality, 24, 51; imitation of, by Joyce, 62
"Diddling Considered as One of the Exact Sciences" (Poe), 22
Diderot, Denis, 31
diegesis, 13; in film, 114, 119-121; and film music, 61; and Stein, 86-87; and *Ulysses*, 60-61, 67
"Discourse of a Lady Standing a Dinner to a Down-and-Out-Friend" (Rhys), 139
Disraeli, Benjamin, 96
Doane, Mary Ann, 117-118, 182n5
Dos Passos, John, 2, *171*, 176n7; and connection between modernism and celebrity, 165, 172; and critique of modernism's production of the individual, 165-170, 172; and Ernest Hemingway, 168-173, 185n1, 186n6, 186n7; and reconsideration of modernism, 161-165; and use of modernist techniques, 16, 17, 161-162, 165-166, 169; (un)popularity of, 161, 178n1, 185n1
Douglas, Lord Alfred, 45
Down and Out in Paris and London (Orwell), 185n7
"*Dream of Stone, A* (Garval), 6

Dreiser, Theodore, 10
Dressler, Marie, 116
Drumont, Edouard, 31
Dubliners (Joyce), 69, 179n16
Duchamp, Marcel, 97
Duck Soup, 183
Duffy, Enda, 59
du Maurier, George, 28
Dydo, Ulla, 85, 99, 103, 109, 110, 182n19
Dyer, Richard, 9, 77, 117, 182n5

Eastman, Max, 165, 166, 170
Eckert, Charles, 9
Edison, Thomas, 22
Eglinton, John, 65
Einstein, Albert, 25–26
Eliot, George, 7
Eliot, T. S., 2, 86, 87, 146, 175n3; and *Ulysses*, 59, 77, 78, 180n26
Ellmann, Richard, 45, 60, 176n2, 178n1
Emery, Mary Lou, 139, 147, 148
English, James F., 6, 7
Epstein, Jean, 183n6
Everybody's Autobiography (Stein), 82–84, 85, 104, 108–109

Fairbanks, Douglas, 82, 120–121
Faulkner, William, 62, 178n1, 186n1
Federal Bureau of Investigation, 131
Finnegans Wake (Joyce), 63, 180n27
Fitzgerald, F. Scott, 10, 11, 186n1
Flanner, Janet, 11
Flavor Flav, 81
Ford, Ford Madox, 102, 145, 146
Ford, Sara, 101
42nd Parallel, The (Dos Passos), 163–169, 172. See also *U.S.A*
Foucault, Michel, 13; and production of the author, 60, 63, 75–76, 77, 80, 85, 101, 114–115, 119, 123
Fowles, Jib, 117
Frenzy of Renown, The (Braudy), 175n4
Frow, John, 6, 7

Gagnier, Regina, 23, 25, 43, 45
Garbo, Greta, 1
Garval, Michael, 6
Gay, Peter, 53
Geographical History of America (Stein), 104
Gertrude Stein and the Making of an American Celebrity (Leick), 6
Gilbert, Stuart, 79
Glass, Loren, 6, 22, 87, 172, 181n13, 186n13

Goddard, Paulette, 111, *112*, *113*
Goldman, Emma, 165, 166–167
Good Morning, Midnight (Rhys), 15, 134, 146, 151, 185n7; abjection of characters in, 135–137, 154, 156; allusion to Joyce in, 140, 141; characters' failure to reproduce in, 141–142; Wilde in, 157
Goux, Jean-Joseph, 96–97
Great Dictator, The (Chaplin), 129–130
Great Gatsby, The (Fitzgerald), 10
Greene, Belle, 84
Greene, Graham, 178n3
Green Hat, The, 184n1
Griffiths, D. W., 82
Gris, Juan, 19

Hamilton, Lisa, 22, 28
Hamlet, 65, 66, 67, 68, 72
Hammett, Dashiell, 84
Hammill, Faye, 5–6, 164
Hansen, Miriam, 9, 80, 87, 114, 116, 183n12
Harris, Frank, 21, 23, 26, 35, 172n7
Haselstein, Ulla, 105
Hathaway, Anne, 67
Hemingway, Ernest, 11, *171*, 186n13; as celebrity, 172; and John Dos Passos, 16, 161, 168–173, 186n8; and Stein, 86, 91, 106–107, 181n10, 186n6; style of, as trademark, 172–173
"Henry James" (Stein), 104
high modernism, 11, 56, 161, 167, 175n3; ideology of style of, 8, 63; and suspicion of images, 13, 14. See also modernism
Hollywood. See cinema
Hollywood Reporter, The, 82
Homer, 61, 78, 180n26
Hoover, Herbert, 82
Hoover, J. Edgar, 131
Horkheimer, Max, 175n6
Houdini, Harry, 9
Hugo, Victor, 106–107
"Hunger Artist, The" (Kafka), 136–137, 155–156
Huyssen, Andreas, 3, 16, 57, 175n1

Ideal Husband, An (Wilde), 33, 46
"Identity, a Poem" (Stein), 104
Idle Class, The (Chaplin), 121–122
"Illusion" (Rhys), 136
Importance of Being Earnest, The (Wilde), 25
imprimatur (Jaffe), 5, 6, 11, 12, 63, 123
"Insect World, The" (Rhys), 154
Institutions of Modernism (Rainey), 5

"In the Rue de l'Arrivée" (Rhys), 149–150
Island of Doctor Moreau, The (Wells), 153–154

Jaffe, Aaron: on circulation of commodities, 10, 180n5; concept of "imprimatur," 5, 11, 63, 71–72, 123; on Joyce, 59, 64, 178n5
James, Henry, 37, 38, 90
James, Jesse, 22
James, William, 101, 181–182n18
Jameson, Frederic, 63, 173
Jane Eyre (Brontë), 142, 147, 179n15
Jay, Martin, 88
Jean Rhys: Life and Work (Angier), 132
Johnson, Jeri, 73
Joyce, James, 2, 7, 53, 114, 115, 139, 146, 176n7; caricatures of, 57, 58; celebrity and fame of, 14, 55–56, 59–60, 74–75, 141, 146, 178n1; and complete and bounded subjectivity, 57, 76, 77, 78–79, 172; and creation of authorized readership, 60, 76–79; criticism of, 14, 71, 76, 79–80; and disembodiment of himself as author, 74–76; and imitation, 62; on literature as revenge, 179n10; profiled in *Time*, 56, 59, 141, 178n1; relationship of, to high modernism, 56, 59–60, 63, 79, 144; and renunciation of authorial reference, 13; and revision of *Bildungsroman* and *Kunstlerroman* traditions, 69–70, 73, 76, 179n15; in Stein, 91; style of, as trademark, 13, 63–64, 75, 85; technique of, 6; and Wilde, 74–75. *See also* Ulysses
Juengel, Scott J., 118

Kafka, Franz, 136–137, 155–156
Kasson, John F., 8–9
Kelly, Joseph, 179n19
Kennedy, J. Gerald, 108
Kenner, Hugh, 71, 78, 79
Keystone Studios, 116
Kid, The (Chaplin), 124, 125
Kiki, 11
King Lear, 66
Koch, Stephen, 170, 172
Koestenbaum, Wayne, 86, 94, 101
Konzett, Delia Caparoso, 133, 148, 158
Kracauer, Siegfried, 120, 123–124, 183n12
Kreilkamp, Ivan, 24
Kristeva, Julia, 135, 140–141, 145
Kunstlerroman, 64, 69, 73

Lacan, Jacques, 45, 90
Lady Chatterley's Lover (Lawrence), 11

Lady Gregory, 65
Lady Morrell, 96
Larsen, Nella, 146
Latham, Sean, 64, 71, 178n5
Laurencin, Mary, 181n11
Lawrence, D. H., 11, 53
Leff, Leonard J., 172
Left Bank and Other Stories, The (Rhys), 145, 148, 184n7
Le Gallez, Paula, 144
Léger, Fernand, 182n4
Leick, Karen, 6, 85
Lénárt-Chang, Helga, 90
Lent, Frau, *171*
Letters (Rhys), 159
Levin, Jonathan, 100–101
Lewis, Wyndham, 11, 95–96, 101–102
"Liar, The" (James), 37, 38
Lippincott's Magazine of Popular Literature and Science, 40
Lippincott's Monthly Magazine, 40, 177n21
"Literary Authorship and Celebrity Culture" (Frow and English), 6
Literary Celebrity in Canada (York), 6
Little Caesar (Leroy), 186n5
L'Opinion Publique (Chaplin), 123
Lowenthal, Leo, 8, 175n5
Ludington, Townsend, 167
Lukács, Georg, 168, 186n7; on Joyce's technique, 6–7

Madonna, 11
Making of Americans, The (Stein), 99, 186n4
Maland, Charles, 119, 121
Manet, Edouard, 19, 137–138
Manhattan Transfer (Dos Passos), 173
Mao, Douglas, 4
Marcuse, Herbert, 123
Marez, Curtis, 34
Marketing Modernisms, 3, 57–58, 175n1
Marquess of Queensbury, 46, 75
Marshall, P. David, 9, 66, 115, 125, 128, 183n16
Marx, Groucho, 183n14
Marx, Karl, 10, 30
Masses, The, 166
Mast, Gerald, 117
materialist modernism, 3–5, 59
Matisse, Henri, 86, 105
Maurel, Sylvia, 140
McCombe, John P., 65, 178n7, 179–180n8, 179n13
Melville, Herman, 22

200 | *Modernism Is the Literature of Celebrity*

"Metamorphosis, The" (Kafka), 155
Meyer, Steven, 181–182n18
Michaels, Walter Benn, 171
Miller, Tyrus, 161, 175n3
"Mixing Cocktails" (Rhys), 148
modernism, 186n7; allusions in, 87–88; and celebrity, incorporation of the logic of, 2–8, 11–12, 15, 17, 133–134, 160, 161, 173 (*see also* celebrity); consumer culture as means of promotion of, 4–5, 7; and elitism of readers, 59–60; and entrapment of author by self-created object, 16 (*see also* Chaplin, Charlie); and idealized author, 11–12, 15, 21, 53–54, 74, 135, 173; and modernist exception, 7, 16, 57, 79, 81, 133, 144, 160, 162, 170, 172–173; and "modernist latecomers," 161; and photography, 162; and popular culture, rejection of, 3, 8, 10, 57; and style as trademark, 12, 13; stylistic techniques and function of, 6–8, 11–12, 63, 161–162; and suspicion of the body, 53; and temporality, 127, 186n7; and transatlanticism, 13, 176n7; and Wilde as presage of treatment of the subject, 12, 16, 20–21, 53–54. *See also specific authors*
Modernism and the Culture of Celebrity (Jaffe), 5
Modern Times (Chaplin), 15, *112, 113*, 182n2, 183n13; allusions of, to other Chaplin films, 126; celebrity logic in, 113; ending of, 111, 114, 127–129; and invocation of extra-diegetic author, 119–120, 124; use of sound in, 119
Mole, Tom, 6
Monroe, Marilyn, 11
Moran, Joe, 6, 94
Moretti, Franco, 62–63, 164
Morgan, J. Pierpont, 166
Morrisson, Mark, 4
Moveable Feast, A (Hemingway), 170, 172, 173
Mrs. Dalloway (Woolf), 184n1
Murphy, Gerald, *171*, 186n12
"My Last Duchess" (Browning), 177n20

New Criticism, 3, 71
New Masses, 168
New Yorker, 164
Nieland, Justus, 127, 130
Nielson, Brigette, 81
Nineteen Nineteen (Dos Passos), 167. See also *U.S.A.*

Nixon, Richard, 81
Nordau, Max, 28
Normand, Mabel, 118
North, Michael, 3, 19, 120, 122, 126, 128, 129

Odyssey, The, 61, 76. *See also* Homer
Ondajtee, Michael, 158
On Heroes, Hero-Worship, and the Heroic in History (Carlyle), 23–24
"Oval Portrait" (Poe), 37–38, 177n22

Packer, George, 172, 185n1
Paris France (Stein), 107
Parsons, Geoffrey, 128
Pater, Walter, 42
Patience (Gilbert and Sullivan), 23, 24, 28
Philadelphia Press, 22
photography, 8–9, 19, 31, 90, 107
Picasso, Pablo, 19, 178n1; and Stein, 86, 91, 102, 105
Pickford, Mary, 56, *83*; and Stein, 81–84
Picture of Dorian Gray, The (Wilde), 12, 135–136; and *Bildungsroman*, 33, 42, 44; and Dorian as circulating commodity in, 40–42; Dorian's body in, 36–37; Lord Henry and society in, 35–37, 40–41; and marriage trope, 42–44; original publication of, 40, 177n21; portrait in, as caricature, 38–39, 42, 43; portrait in, as having metaphysical connection to subject, 37–39, 178n30; and relationship between image and interior, 34–37, 39–44; relative identity in, 33–34; subjectivity in, 20, 21, 33, 36–37, 40–41, 43; and Wilde's production of celebrity, 33, 36, 39, 42
Plato, 66–67, 98–99
Poe, Edgar Allen, 22, 37–38
Poems (Wilde), 21
"Poetry and Grammar" (Stein), 98
Ponce de Leon, Charles L., 117
"Portrait of Mr. W. H." (Wilde), 50
Portrait of the Artist as a Young Man, A (Joyce), 64, 71, 73
postcolonialism, 158
Pound, Ezra, 64, 175n3, 178n6; and Stein, 91, 181n10
Powell, Kerry, 43
Presley, Elvis, 81
Proust, Marcel, 2, 11
Public Face of Modernism, The (Morrisson), 4
Punch, 28, 31
Purviance, Edna, 124

Quartet (Rhys), 140, 143, 145, 146, 184n7

Rainey, Lawrence, 3, 5, 57
Reed, Carol, 59
Reynold's, 52
Rhys, Jean, 2, 176n7; abjection and obscurity of characters of, 15, 133–141, 143, 184–185n9; anonymity of characters in, 136–139; as anti-celebrity, 132, 133, 145–146; aversion of, to *Bildungsroman* conventions, 142–143; and celebrity, 134, 141; and characters' lack of literary and biological production, 141–142; Ford Madox Ford, relationship with, 145, 146; Franz Kafka, compared with, 155–156; late fame of, 146, 157, 159; as modernist, 133, 139, 141, 145, 146, 148–149, 157, 184n7; obscurity of, 15, 132, 133, 146; parallel between life and work of, 15, 17, 145, 147–148; personal life of, 146–147; and production of unoriginal author, 144; and punctuation, 139; and racism, 185n10; recognizability and identity as based on visual exchange, 135, 136, 151–152, 158–159; rumored death of, 132, 147; and use of vermin to signal abjection, 154–157. See also *After Leaving Mr. Mackenzie*; *Left Bank and Other Stories, The*; *Midnight*; *Quartet*; *Smile, Please*; *Wide Sargasso Sea*; and specific stories
Riblet, Douglas, 116
Richardson, Dorothy, 161
Richardson, Samuel, 74
Rink, The (Chaplin), 118, 126
Robinson Crusoe (Defoe), 181n8
Rocky, 61
Roosevelt, Eleanor, 84
Rosenquist, Rod, 60, 161
Ross, Robbie, 52
Russell, George (A.E.), 65, 69

Saint-Amour, Paul K., 50, 176nn11–12
Sarony, Napoleon, 26, 27
Saturday Night Fever, 61
Saussure, Ferdinand de, 90, 96, 99
Savory, Elaine, 140, 154
Schickel, Richard, 8, 56, 127
Schoenbach, Lisi, 84
Scholes, Robert, 71, 178n1
Scott, Evelyn, 143
Seldes, Gilbert, 119, 125
Senn, Fritz, 56
Sennett, Mack, 116, 117

Shakespeare, William, 65–67, 72–73, 74, 100, 122
"Shirley Temple and the House of Rockefeller" (Eckert), 9
Shoulder Arms (Chaplin), 123
Silverman, Kaja, 29
Simpsons, The, 1, 55
Sinfield, Alan, 28
Sister Carrie (Dreiser), 10
"Sisters, The" (Joyce), 69
slapstick, 14; and Charlie Chaplin, 118–119, 183n12; and luck, 120; and person as object, 116–117
"Sleep It Off, Lady" (Rhys), 134, 154–155
Small, Ian, 51, 177nn24–25
"Smile" (song), 128–129, 184nn18–19
Smile, Please (Rhys), 143, 159
Smith, Soapy, 22
Smith, Tilden, 147. See also Jean Rhys
Sound and the Fury, The (Faulkner), 62
Soupault, Philippe, 122–123
Star Authors: Literary Celebrity in America (Moran), 6
Stieglitz, Alfred, 107
Stein, Gertrude, 2, 11, 93, 114, 136, 146, 176n7, 182n20; on celebrity, 108–109; and celebrity names, 109–100; and creation of elite readership, 85; and devaluation of visuality, 104–108; fame of, 86, 180n4; and William James, 181n18; and money, 181n13; and name-dropping as form of allusion, 87–88; and name-dropping as producer of relative system of celebrity, 14, 16, 84, 85–90, 96–98, 109–110, 173; and Mary Pickford, encounter with, 81–84; portraits of, 105–108, 182n19; and the proper noun, 98–101, 110, 181n14; techniques and trademark of, 14, 84–85, 100–101, 144; and use of time, 98–102; writing of, compared to cinema, 175n2. See also *Autobiography of Alice B. Toklas, The*; *Everybody's Autobiography*
Stein, Leo, 89, 91
Steiner, Wendy, 106, 182nn19–20
Stimpson, Catharine, 93
Strachey, Lytton, 11
Sun Also Rises, The (Hemingway), 145, 168–169, 171, 173
Sunday States, The, 26
Sunny Side (Chaplin), 124–125
Sunset Boulevard (Wilder), 131
Susman, Warren, 111, 113, 175n5
Synge, John Millington, 65

television, 9
Tender Is the Night (Fitzgerald), 186n12
They Destroyed All the Roses (Louter), 185n15
Third Man, The, 59–60, 178n3
Tillie's Punctured Romance, 116, 117, 118
Time, 55, 59, 81–82, 141, 161, 178n1
Toklas, Alice B., 89, 93, 181n15; as narrator in Stein's writing, 88, 102, 103–104, 108, 181n16
trademark, 19. *See also* modernism: and style as trademark; *and specific authors*
Trade Mark Registration Act of 1875, 19
Tramp (character): and audiences, 14–15, 115; and Chaplin's identity, 16–17, 129–130; as Chaplin's trademark, 113, 119, 124–125, 129, 184n16
Tramp, The (Chaplin), 113, *114*
"Trio" (Rhys), 148
Tropic of Cancer (Miller), 185
Turner, John, 128
Twain, Mark, 22, 30

Ulysses, 5; atemporality in, 68, 69, 70, 76; and autobiography, 64–69, 70–73, 75, 78; censorship of, 11, 75, 179n19; compared to Dos Passos's *U.S.A.*, 162, 164; and corporeal patriarchy, 72–73; hypervisuality of text of, 13, 16, 63–64, 136, 178n5; idealization of the author in, 7, 57, 64, 76–77, 178n5; location of subject within text of, 13, 57, 60, 75–76; and merging of Joyce with Stephen character, 67–69, 70, 179n13; and *The Odyssey*, 61, 76, 78, 79, 180n26; production of disembodied author in, 72, 74–76; promotion of, 77; reputation of, 59–60; relationship of style to diegesis in, 60–61; schematics for, 16, 56, 76–79, 180n23; and Shakespeare, 65–67; stylistic changes that reveal presence of author in, 61–63; value of, from difficulty and limited circulation, 59–60, 64, 78–79
Un bar aux Folies Bergére (Manet), 137–138, *138*
United Artists, 82
U.S.A (Dos Passos), 16, 161; and allusion to Hemingway, 168–170; and author's contemporaries, 167–169; and modernist style and authorial individuality, 161–164, 167, 168; narrative styles in, 162; and objectivity, 162; and political engagement, 169–170; prose-poem biographies in, 163–164; reference to Joyce in, 162

Vagabond, The (Chaplin), 118
Valentino, Rudolph, 1, 9, 16, 56
Van Houts, Jan, 185n15
Vanity Fair, 104
vas Dias, Selma, 147
"Verses Supposed to Be Written by Alexander Selkirk, During His Solitary Abode in the Island of Juan Fernandez" (Cowper), 155
Victorian era, 12, 31, 38, 163; celebrity in, 20; gender norms in, 28, 29, 62
Voronoff, Serge, 185n11
Voyage in the Dark (Rhys), 139–140, 141, 142, 146; revised conclusion of, 143–144; setting of, 148

Walkowitz, Rebecca, 4
Walt Whitman and the Culture of American Celebrity (Blake), 6
Waste Land, The (Eliot), 59
Watt, Steven J., 175n1
Waugh, Evelyn, 11
Wells, H. G., 153–154
West, Nathaniel, 10
West, Rebecca, 146
Westerhoven, J. N., 163
Wexler, Joyce, 57, 75, 179n19
Wharton, Edith, 10
Whitehead, Alfred, 102–103
Whitman, Walt, 22
Wicke, Jennifer, 5, 75, 175n2
Wide Sargasso Sea (Rhys), 15, 132, 134, 142; abjection of characters in, 152–153; concern of, with street and individuals' relationship to crowd, 149–152; and hybridization, 185n11; and *The Island of Doctor Moreau*, 153–154; and *Jane Eyre*, 147, 157–158; and postcolonialism, 158; and trope of display and visual exchange, 148, 151–152
Wilde, Oscar, 2, 114, 136, 142; caricatures, illustrations, and photographs of, 21–22, 26, 27, 28, 31–33, *32*; and celebrity as commodity, 12, 20–21, 26–27, 29–30, 33, 47, 53; early fame of, 21–22; and "genius," 20, 23–24, 176n2, 176n10; and originality, 24–25, 28, 29, 50, 56, 163, 176nn11–12; and performance of aestheticism, 22–23, 25, 26, 56; physical description of, 12, 22, 26–27; as presage of modernist treatment of the subject, 12, 16, 20–21, 53–54; and Jean Rhys, 157; self-creation of, 23–24, 29–30, 36, 144;

self-destruction of, 16, 44; and sexual orientation, perception of, 28–29; and trademarking, 19–20, 22, 32–33, 63, 64; trial and imprisonment of, 21, 44, 46–47, 51, 53, 74–75; U.S. tour of, 13, 20, 22–25, 30, 36, 44, 47, 48; wit/epigrams of, 25–27, 52, 85. See also *De Profundis*; *Picture of Dorian Gray, The*
Will, Barbara, 103, 109
Williams, Ella Gwendolyn Rees. *See* Rhys, Jean
Williams, Raymond, 7, 148–149
Wiser, William, 180n4
Wodehouse, P. G., 11

Woman, A (Chaplin), 183n7
Women, Celebrity, and Literary Culture Between the Wars (Hammill), 5–6
Woolf, Virginia, 2, 7, 11, 62, 139, 172, 184n1
Wyndham, Francis, 132

Yeats, W. B., 11, 23, 65, 185n11
York, Lorraine, 6, 158

Zimring, Rishona, 137
Žižek, Slavoj, 121, 124, 183n10
Zorro, 120–121
Zuleika Dobson (Beerbohm), 10, 56

www.ingramcontent.com/pod-product-compliance
Lightning Source LLC
Chambersburg PA
CBHW022100160426
43198CB00008B/293